Introduction to Policing

Introduction to Policing

Michael Rowe

Los Angeles • London • New Delhi • Singapore

First published 2008

 SAGE Publications Ltd
1 Oliver's Yard
55 City Road
London EC1Y 1SP

SAGE Publications Inc.
2455 Teller Road
Thousand Oaks, California 91320

SAGE Publications India Pvt Ltd
B 1/I 1 Mohan Cooperative Industrial Area
Mathura Road
New Delhi 110 044

SAGE Publications Asia-Pacific Pte Ltd
33 Pekin Street #02-01
Far East Square
Singapore 048763

British Library Cataloguing in Publication data

A catalogue record for this book is available from the
British Library

ISBN 978-1-4129-2868-7
ISBN 978-1-4129-2869-4

Library of Congress Control Number: 2007935924

Typeset by C&M Digitals (P) Ltd., Chennai, India
Printed in Great Britain by TJ International, Padstow, Cornwall
Printed on paper from sustainable resources

Contents

Preface

Crime and policing continue to be subjects of intense public scrutiny. Generations of government ministers, politicians and media commentators have variously bemoaned rising crime levels and the inability of the police to enforce the law, and promised renewed crackdowns that will finally restore order. Such debates tend to resemble the film *Groundhog Day*, fated to recur in perpetuity and apparently with no awareness that they repeat previous renditions. This cycle has been apparent for decades, certainly since the development of New Right conservatism under Margaret Thatcher in the 1970s, which itself drew upon themes that emerged in US politics in the 1960s. More recently, law and order has been at the heart of the ideological and political project of 'New Labour' since the mid-1990s. One of the most cited sound-bites of modern times has been former UK PM Tony Blair's credo 'tough on crime and tough on the causes of crime', and the nature of and response to antisocial behaviour have been enduring preoccupations of governments for more than a decade. The apparently endless process of police force modernization and 'reform' that has been driven by central government for a decade or more is discussed at greater length in several of the chapters that follow.

The ubiquity of law and order concerns in many societies is matched by the contradictions and conundrums that surround contemporary policing. While many indicators suggest that crime levels are decreasing, the number of police officers is at record levels, and expenditure on the service has consistently risen, public perceptions and media representations seem to recognize only increasing levels of disorder, fear and incivility. The contradictory evidence about contemporary trends demonstrates that public discourse about crime and policing is shaped by subjective perceptions and relates to wider concerns about the nature and direction of contemporary society. Loader (1997) has noted that centrality of policing, law and order to the cultural landscape of society means that public discourse about these matters has broad metaphorical properties. Similarly, McLaughlin (2007a) argued that pledges to recreate traditional community policing often reflect broader cultural and political attempts to restore a 'golden age' when society was relatively united, cohesive, and ordered. Although the nostalgic reverence for the policing of the 1950s and 1960s bears little resemblance to concerns about crime and policing expressed during that period, it continues to exert a powerful influence on twenty-first-century debates.

The chapters that follow provide a detailed analysis of the themes and issues that underpin much contemporary debate about policing in Britain and beyond. Although political and policy debates are reviewed, the book is not a commentary on current affairs but provides an overview of the broader principles and context of policing, both in terms of the institution of the police and 'policing' as understood in wider terms of social regulation. While the scope of the book is wide in terms of the topics that are covered, inevitably some issues have had to be omitted. Decisions about what to include and exclude have partly reflected changing debates in policing. A recurring theme of the book, for example, relates to the development of plural policing, whereby a broad range of private and public sector agencies are engaged in the delivery of services traditionally associated with the public police. Until relatively recently most books on policing would have paid little attention to such issues, but the changing terrain of policing means that this will be an increasingly salient aspect of discussions of crime, law enforcement and community safety. The technology of policing, and the possibility of developing electronic solutions to crime problems, are also increasingly important and raise significant questions about civil liberties and privacy, as well as the nature of police work itself. Other issues covered in the book are perennially important to a consideration of policing and police work. The legal and institutional powers of the police are reviewed, for example, as are the nature, origin and impact of police occupational cultures, which are much cited in discussion of police malpractice.

The book provides an introduction to policing, by setting the various issues in context, identifying the key controversies and debates, and providing an overview of sources of further information, research findings, and academic debates. While an 'introduction' to policing, it is intended that the book develops a rich understanding of the complexities of policing and provides a framework for further study of the issues discussed. Each chapter outlines clear learning objectives and key terms, and concludes with a series of self-check questions that act as a knowledge check, and broader study questions that provide a basis for further debate. Further academic readings and links to relevant websites are also provided. In this way it is hoped that the book will provide a useful companion for those who are coming to these debates for the first time and a valuable source of further information and avenues of exploration for those already familiar with some of the issues explored in what follows.

acknowledgements

The origins of this book lie in various undergraduate courses taught at different universities over the last few years. Originally, writing up lecture notes seemed like an interesting challenge that would require an extensive and overdue effort to review literature not read for some time. In practice, the preparation of this book quickly became a more significant challenge and, not unusually, one that has taken longer than first anticipated. Many colleagues have contributed to the development of this book and I am happy to acknowledge Neil Chakraborti, Jon Garland and Alison Wakefield with whom I taught undergraduate courses on policing at the University of Leicester. Other colleagues over the years contributed to a valuable academic environment in which the ideas expressed here developed and I am grateful to Adrian Beck, John Benyon, Adam Edwards, Matt Follett, Martin Gill, Mike King, Paddy Rawlinson, Keith Spence, Louise Westmarland, and Andrew Willis. Gordon Hughes has offered much-appreciated encouragement and valuable insight into the changing politics of community safety and policing. Moving from the UK to New Zealand has been one reason why the completion of this book took longer than anticipated. Points of similarity and difference in debates about policing and the police service in Britain and New Zealand have led to reconsideration of some of the central issues, and I appreciate the discussions I have had with colleagues who have viewed these matters from an Australasian perspective, particularly Hamish McArdle, Trevor Bradley, and Charles Sedgwick. John Locker and Michael Webb provided very useful feedback on a couple of draft chapters. Valuable North American insights have been developed through discussion with Bob Vodde and colleagues and students at Fairleigh Dickinson University.

Delays and author prevarication must be part of the daily grind for commissioning editors, but Caroline Porter and Natalie Aguilera at Sage have been encouraging and tolerant in equal measure and I am grateful to them both for the detailed and incisive suggestions offered along the way. I am also grateful to the anonymous reviewers of draft chapters who also contributed greatly to the planning and organization of the book.

As always Anna, Derry, Maggie and Niall have been a great support. Contractually I get 75 per cent of the film rights, and 50 per cent of merchandising. Next time, I'll go for something about a boy wizard.

Guided Tour

---

learning objectives

More than three decades ago, the American sociologist Egon Bittner (1974: 17) observed that the **police service** was one of the 'best known but least understood' of public institutions. The numerous studies and accounts that have emerged in the intervening period might mean that the police service is today even better known, although perhaps still less well understood. Crime and policing, including allegations of malpractice and corruption as well as heroism and selflessness, continue to feature heavily in the press, and the TV schedules and cinema programmes are replete with cop shows. Familiarity, however, should not be confused with understanding, and this chapter aims to do the following:

- to outline different perspectives on what 'policing' is;
- to give an overview of what the police service does;
- to distinguish between the relatively narrow activities associated with the institution of the police service from broader social processes of policing in broader terms.

key terms

bureaucracy; crime control; information work; law enforcement; national identity; police and policing; service role; sovereignty; use of force

introduction

In Britain, perhaps more than most countries, the police service forms part of the historical landscape and the police officer is elevated to the status of national symbol and is a ubiquitous part of the cultural framework (McLaughlin, 2007a). Colls (2002) showed how rhetoric surrounding the law, and its application to all without fear or favour, played an important role in the very development of the British state throughout much of the Middle Ages. Clearly, the law has often not been cast or applied in the interests of the whole population, but mythological accounts can be powerful narratives that shape national identity. Loader (1997: 2) suggested that the police are 'a principal means by which English society tells stories about itself ... an interpretive lens through which people make sense of, and give order to, their world'.

police and policing

Before attempting to answer the question 'What is policing?' a few points of clarification need to be made. Most important is the need to distinguish

WHAT IS POLICING?   3

Learning objectives: Bullet points at the beginning of each chapter outline the material covered and suggest benefits from reading the chapter

---

learning objectives

While Chapter 1 sought to explain policing in terms of the various roles and functions of the service and fundamental principles, the focus of this chapter is to explore the historical development of the police service in England and Wales up to the end of the nineteenth century. Various perspectives that account for these trends are explored in the second part of the chapter. One such, the 'conservative' perspective, suggests that the establishment of the police service in London in 1829 was an innovative – but natural and logical – response to changing social, economic and political circumstances. Alternatively, 'revisionist' accounts explain the establishment of the police in terms of containing threats of political violence and maintaining order among the industrial working class more generally. Although they reach contrasting conclusions, both accounts indicate that the history of the police service needs to be understood against the wider background of the period, just as contemporary police reforms discussed elsewhere in the book are often a reflection of more fundamental social change. The objectives of the chapter are:

- to examine the foundation and development of the police service in Britain;
- to outline the changing social, political and economic context that shaped the establishment of the police service;
- to explore interpretations of these processes.

key terms

attitudes to order; establishment and development of police services; historical interpretation; military; police and policing; political unrest; public involvement in policing; underlying principles; urban crime

introduction

Various countries might claim to have established the first police service, and these competing claims partly reflect the breadth of the various functions that might be defined as 'policing'. As noted in Chapter 1, the word 'policing' developed in relation to general patterns of social regulation, which suggests that it has been continued in one form or another since there have been states or governments. Given the extent of policing history, it might be wondered why so much discussion of the historical development of policing relates to the British experience. Clearly policing traditions in other countries continue

ORIGINS AND DEVELOPMENT OF THE POLICE   23

Key terms: a list of the main topics and concepts covered in the chapter

---

Introduction: an introduction to orient the reader is provided at the start of each chapter

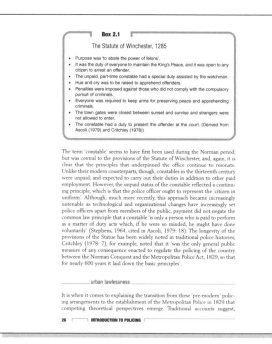

Short summary boxes/boxed examples throughout the chapters: at various stages further details and illustrations of some of the key topics are provided

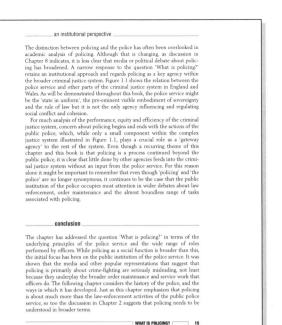

The distinction between policing and the police has often been overlooked in academic analysis of policing. Although that is changing, as discussion in Chapter 8 indicates, it is less clear that media or political debate about policing has broadened. A narrow response to the question 'What is policing?' retains an institutional approach and regards policing as a key agency within the broader criminal justice system. Figure 1.1 shows the relation between the police service and other parts of the criminal justice system in England and Wales. As will be demonstrated throughout this book, the police service might be the 'state in uniform', the pre-eminent visible embodiment of sovereignty and the rule of law but it is not the only agency influencing and regulating social conflict and cohesion.

For much analysis of the performance, equity and efficiency of the criminal justice system, concern about policing begins and ends with the actions of the public police, which, while only a small component within the complex justice system illustrated in Figure 1.1, plays a crucial role as a 'gateway agency' to the rest of the system. Even though a recurring theme of this chapter and this book is that policing is a process continued beyond the public police, it is clear that little done by other agencies feeds into the criminal justice system without an input from the public police. For this reason alone it might be important to remember that even though 'policing' and 'the police' are no longer synonymous, it continues to be the case that the public institution of the police occupies most attention in wider debates about law enforcement, order maintenance and the almost boundless range of tasks associated with policing.

conclusion

The chapter has addressed the question 'What is policing?' in terms of the underlying principles of the police service and the wide range of roles performed by officers. While policing as a social function is more than this, the initial focus has been on the public institution of the police service. It was shown that the media and other popular representations that suggest that policing is primarily about crime-fighting are seriously misleading, not least because they underplay the broader order maintenance and service work that officers do. The following chapter considers the history of the police, and the ways in which it has developed. Just as this chapter emphasizes that policing is about much more than the law-enforcement activities of the public police service, so too the discussion in Chapter 2 suggests that policing needs to be understood in broader terms.

Conclusion: provides a concise final statement of the main themes and their implications

chapter summary

- The police have become a cultural symbol of the British nation. Mythology about the development of the law and policing has been an important element of narratives of national identity.

- Although often treated as synonymous, **police and policing** need to be understood as distinct concepts. Policing relates to broad processes of social regulation that underpin the routines of everyday life; as such, these are performed by a wide range of agencies and institutions. Historically, 'policing' has been understood in these broad terms and not associated with the activities of a particular organization.

- While a broad approach has the advantage of incorporating the wide range of processes that regulate social life, it lacks clarity, since almost anything could be included. A narrower definition, equating policing to the activities of the institution of the police, might lack breadth but it is clearer and a more concise perspective.

- Often policing is understood in terms of law enforcement, and certainly this has been a common perspective in media coverage. Fictional and documentary images of police work tend to centre on crime-fighting, and concentrate on dangerous, action-oriented pursuits and serious crime portraying the police as the 'thin blue line' between social order and chaos.

- The law-enforcement perspective is flawed since police officers use considerable discretion when applying the law, and many laws are rarely enforced by most officers. Moreover, police services perform a wide range of activities that do not relate to law enforcement.

- Other definitions focus upon the police monopoly use of force. Traditionally state sovereignty has been understood in these terms and considering the police as the 'state in uniform' leads to this definition being transferred to the police service. As with the law enforcement perspective, though, the reality of police work suggests that force tends to be under-used and negotiation characterizes police encounters with the public, although the potential for coercive force might shape these interactions.

- Another perspective is gained from studies that consider the nature of the roles that the police perform in practice. Such studies tend to confirm that law enforcement accounts for only a small proportion of police work, and order maintenance and service functions are more significant in terms of the time and resources allocated to them. Bittner (1974) argued that all these functions had in common was that it was not possible to identify another agency that ought to be responsible for them. Fulfilling these public service roles might enhance legitimacy, secure public confidence, and so contribute to crime control and law enforcement.

Chapter summary: an easy-to-reference guide to the content of each chapter

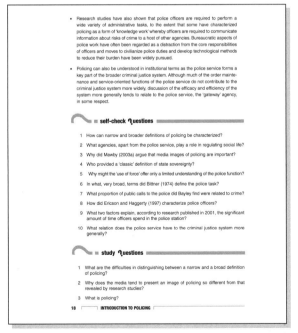

- Research studies have also shown that police officers are required to perform a wide variety of administrative tasks, to the extent that some have characterized policing as a form of 'knowledge work' whereby officers are required to communicate information about risks of crime to a host of other agencies. Bureaucratic aspects of police work have often been regarded as a distraction from the core responsibilities of officers and moves to civilianize police duties and develop technological methods to reduce their burden have been widely pursued.

- Policing can also be understood in institutional terms as the police service forms a key part of the broader criminal justice system. Although much of the order maintenance and service-oriented functions of the police service do not contribute to the criminal justice system more widely, discussion of the efficacy and efficiency of the system more generally tends to relate to the police service, the 'gateway' agency, in some respect.

self-check questions

1 How can narrow and broader definitions of policing be characterized?
2 What agencies, apart from the police service, play a role in regulating social life?
3 Why did Mawby (2003a) argue that media images of policing are important?
4 Who provided a 'classic' definition of state sovereignty?
5 Why might the 'use of force' offer only a limited understanding of the police function?
6 In what, very broad, terms did Bittner (1974) define the police task?
7 What proportion of public calls to the police did Bayley find were related to crime?
8 How did Ericson and Haggerty (1997) characterize police officers?
9 What two factors explain, according to research published in 2001, the significant amount of time officers spend in the police station?
10 What relation does the police service have to the criminal justice system more generally?

study questions

1 What are the difficulties in distinguishing between a narrow and a broad definition of policing?
2 Why does the media tend to present an image of policing so different from that revealed by research studies?
3 What is policing?

Self-check questions (with answers at the back of the book): precise factual questions that provide an opportunity to check understanding

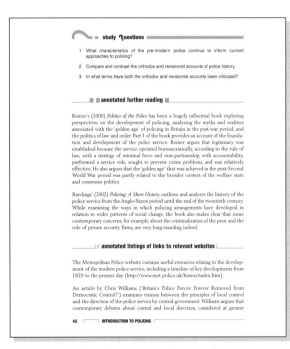

study questions

1 What characteristics of the pre-modern police continue to inform current approaches to policing?
2 Compare and contrast the orthodox and revisionist accounts of police history.
3 In what terms have both the orthodox and revisionist accounts been criticized?

annotated further reading

Reiner's (2000) *Politics of the Police* has been a hugely influential book exploring perspectives on the development of policing, analyzing the myths and realities associated with the 'golden age' of policing in Britain in the post-war period, and the politics of law and order. Part 1 of the book provides an account of the foundation and development of the police service. Reiner argues that legitimacy was established because the service operated bureaucratically, according to the rule of law, with a strategy of minimal force and non-partisanship, with accountability, performed a service role, sought to prevent crime problems, and was relatively effective. He also argues that the 'golden age' that was achieved in the post-Second World War period was partly related to the broader context of the welfare state and consensus politics.

Rawlings' (2002) *Policing: A Short History* outlines and analyzes the history of the police service from the Anglo-Saxon period until the end of the twentieth century. While examining the ways in which policing arrangements have developed in relation to wider patterns of social change, the book also makes clear that some contemporary concerns, for example, about the criminalization of the poor and the role of private security firms, are very long-standing indeed.

annotated listings of links to relevant websites

The Metropolitan Police website contains useful resources relating to the development of the modern police service, including a timeline of key developments from 1829 to the present day (http://www.met.police.uk/history/index.htm).

An article by Chris Williams ('Britain's Police Forces: Forever Removed from Democratic Control?') examines tension between the principles of local control and the direction of the police service by central government. Williams argues that contemporary debates about central and local direction, considered at greater

Study questions: broader questions that provide a starting point for further discussion and debate of key themes

Bittner's (1974) article 'Florence Nightingale in Pursuit of Willy Sutton' is an early account of the complexities and contradictions inherent in the police function that provides a compelling argument against a narrow 'law-enforcement' definition of the role of the police.

The first chapter of Waddington's (1999) *Policing Citizens* contains a useful discussion of the question that has framed this chapter: 'What is policing?'. Waddington explores the force-service dichotomy and similarities and specificities of police work across the world.

Chapters 3 and 4 of McLaughlin's (2007a) *The New Policing* provide an excellent account of the development of 'police studies', focusing on traditional perspectives (including that of Bittner) that emerged in the US in the 1960s and somewhat later in the UK, and 'new perspectives' that consider the changing terrain of policing in post-modern, post-industrial global society.

: // ■ annotated listings of links to relevant websites /

A good starting point for general information on the roles, responsibilities and development of the police in Scotland is available from the homepage of the Scottish Executive, (http://www.scotland.gov.uk/Topics/Justice/Police). Similar information relating to England and Wales can be found at the Home Office website (http://www.homeoffice.gov.uk/police/), and at the Northern Ireland Policing Board at (http://www.nipolicingboard.org.uk/).

The full text of Sir Ian Blair's Dimbleby lecture 'What Kind of Police Service Do We Want?' can be found at http://tinyurl.com/2wg8za.

In response to Blair's call for debate on the purpose of the police service, the Police Foundation – an independent charity that seeks to enhance public and policy debate – held a seminar considering 'What the police are for'. Proceedings of the event and much other useful material can be found at http://tinyurl.com/2kpld5.

Annotated further reading: good sources of further academic and policy-related information

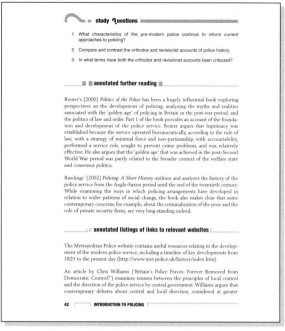

Annotated listings of links to relevant websites: starting points to access more detailed information, statistics and policy documents available on the internet

Glossary

Accountability: relating to the legal and regulatory systems that govern the police service. While the principle of operational independence means that the police service enforces the law without political interference, the priority and general direction of policing in Britain have been overseen by arrangements that combine local and central governance. More specifically, management and auditing procedures seek to hold individual police officers to account by scrutinizing their work in an effort to promote efficiency and effectiveness. Police officers are also held to account by complaints and disciplinary systems. The prospects of accountability in an era when the role of private security and plural policing is increasingly salient are much debated.

Antisocial behaviour: low-level persistent nuisance behaviour, not all of which is criminal, traditionally has not been a high priority for police services, even though it has been a significant problem in many communities. The 1998 Crime and Disorder Act introduced a raft of measures directed at behaviour defined broadly as that which 'caused or was likely to cause harassment, alarm or distress to one or more persons'. Key among these measures have been Anti-Social Behaviour Orders (ASBOs) that seek to regulate future conduct. Police or local authorities can apply for an ASBO in the magistrates' court. Although ASBOs are civil law provisions, breaching them is a criminal offence. Anti-Social Behaviour Contracts (ABCs) are a lower-level intervention that seeks to provide a framework whereby individuals or families are offered support in return for their commitment to improved conduct.

Arrest: there are various common law and statute provisions determining the circumstances in which a person can be arrested. Essentially these fall into two categories: those conducted under the terms of a court warrant and those carried out without warrant. The former category primarily applies to circumstances in which it is necessary to force an individual to be brought to court in connection with a suspected offence that has already been committed. Arrests without warrant can be implemented in a wide variety of circumstances, some of which rely upon specific legal measures that give police officers particular

A glossary of key terms at the end of the text: an easy source of information about commonly used terms, including the key terms listed for each chapter

1

What is policing?

Contents

More than three decades ago, the American sociologist Egon Bittner (1974: 17) observed that the **police service** was one of the 'best known but least understood' of public institutions. The numerous studies and accounts that have emerged in the intervening period might mean that the police service is today even better known, although perhaps still less well understood. Crime and policing, including allegations of malpractice and corruption as well as heroism and selflessness, continue to feature heavily in the press, and the TV schedules and cinema programmes are replete with cop shows. Familiarity, however, should not be confused with understanding, and this chapter aims to do the following:

- to outline different perspectives on what 'policing' is;

- to give an overview of what the police service does;

- to distinguish between the relatively narrow activities associated with the institution of the police service from broader social processes of policing in broader terms.

key terms

bureaucracy; crime control; information work; law enforcement; national identity; police and policing; service role; sovereignty; use of force

introduction

In Britain, perhaps more than most countries, the police service forms part of the historical landscape and the police officer is elevated to the status of national symbol and is a ubiquitous part of the cultural framework (McLaughlin, 2007a). Colls (2002) showed how rhetoric surrounding the law, and its application to all without fear or favour, played an important role in the very development of the British state throughout much of the Middle Ages. Clearly, the law has often not been cast or applied in the interests of the whole population, but mythological accounts can be powerful narratives that shape national identity. Loader (1997: 2) suggested that the police are 'a principal means by which English society tells stories about itself … an interpretive lens through which people make sense of, and give order to, their world'.

police and policing

Before attempting to answer the question 'What is policing?' a few points of clarification need to be made. Most important is the need to distinguish between the narrow set of functions performed by the institution of the police service and the broader processes of social regulation and reproduction that govern everyday lives. The wider account of policing as a social function stresses that many institutions that do not have any formal role in the regulation of social life in practice contribute to the development of social norms and standards of behaviour that underpin the ordinary social interaction of everyday activity. The word 'policing' is etymologically related to 'politics', the governance of the city or state, and was used in broad terms to signify social regulation in the widest sense. Box 1.1 outlines the development of the term. 'Policing' did not come to be associated with the particular activities of a specific institution (*the* police) until relatively recently in many societies. The historical development of the police in Britain is described in the next chapter, which shows that demand for a particular organization to police society emerged in Britain during the eighteenth century.

Box 1.1

The changing meaning of 'policing'

The Greek *politeia* meant all matters affecting the survival and well-being of the state (*polis*). The word and the idea were developed by the Romans (the Latin *politia* can be translated as the state), largely disappeared with their Empire, but were resurrected in the medieval universities to justify the authority of a prince over his territories. By the early eighteenth century in continental Europe *la police* and *die Politzei* were being used in the sense of the internal administration, welfare, protection, and surveillance of a territory. The word 'police' was not popular in England as it smacked of absolutism ... but the word was increasingly used towards the end of the eighteenth century. (Emsley, 1996: 3)

Schools provide a good example of the broader process of social regulation as they play a central role in the socialization of young people by preparing them for adult life. This is not the primary function of the education system, of course, but recent debates about the development of the study of citizenship within schools indicate that preparing young people for their post-school lives is increasingly recognized as an important secondary role. For these reasons it is readily apparent that the education system plays a central role in the policing of society, if that is conceived in terms of the broad process of social regulation. Many other agencies also contribute to this process in ways that are less obvious: religious groups, health providers, and the business sector – to take three examples – contribute in various ways to the organization of social life and so could be regarded as part of the process of policing. Some might argue that the media plays a central role in shaping subjective interpretations of the world and the place of the individual within it and so are important agents of policing in this wider sense. In Chapter 8 the increasing range of institutions engaged in police networks are considered in more detail.

The difficulty in thinking about policing in these broad terms is that it becomes difficult to know where the category can be closed. It might be important to recognize that policing is not just the business of the formal police service and that other institutions play a crucial role in developing, for example, public perceptions of criminal or deviant behaviour, but the same could be said for almost any and every aspect of social life. For this reason, much of this book will focus on the narrow approach to policing and concentrate primarily on the activities of the police service and so this initial discussion of 'What is policing?' is also cast relatively narrow. Other agencies, both in the private and the public sector, play an increasingly important role in the business of polic-ing and, where relevant, these are included in the discussion and analysis in chapters that follow. Since the police service cannot be understood in isolation from broader social developments the wider dynamics of policing are crucial to many of the topics featured throughout the book. For the purposes of understanding 'What is policing?', however, it is to the narrower role of the police service that the analysis now turns.

Even a narrow focus on the institution of the police raises the dilemma of how to answer the question, and two perspectives are taken here. This chapter addresses the question literally by exploring what it is that the police do. Chapter 2 explores the question in historical terms by charting the myriad factors that led to the establishment of the modern police service in the nineteenth century.

what is policing?

Attempts to define policing have focused upon the range of different aspects of the diverse roles that the service performs. Chapter 2 provides an alterna-tive approach by considering the historical development of the police service in Britain. In this section various other perspectives are discussed. First, a tradi-tional 'common-sense' definition of police work – that it is primarily a matter of law enforcement – is considered. Although this approach does not account for the many other aspects of police work that do not, directly or indirectly, relate to crime control and law enforcement, it has the advantage of providing a relatively clear concise definition. Other perspectives that seek to reflect the wider activities performed by the police are then considered. One approach has been to define the police service in terms of its recourse to the **use of force**, and the power of the police service over ordinary citizens. Certainly, the police service exerts a coercive power over citizens not available to many other agencies. However, approaches based on the centrality of force to policing need to account for the recourse that other institutions have to physical force. But these other institutions might still prove coercive in terms of exerting power over the lives of citizens. Moreover, studies suggest that a characteristic of police work is to under-enforce the law and to use persuasion and negotiation rather then physical force, although the potential to do so remains.

Another approach to understanding policing focuses on the routine functions performed by officers. These perspectives tend to note the breadth and diversity of tasks that the police perform, many of which are characterized by a broader public service ethos not related to crime control. In contrast to the law enforcement model, this has the advantage of reflecting the realities of police work, but tends to result in definitions that are so broad that they lack focus. Another approach that tends to suggest that law enforcement is only part of the police role characterizes the bureaucratic and administrative responsibilities of officers. The gathering, interrogation and communication of intelligence relating to crime, disorder and **antisocial behaviour** have, it is argued, become the defining characteristics of police work. A final perspective is an institutional one that relates to the role of the police service in terms of the broader functions of the criminal justice system.

Each of these approaches to understanding policing is explored in greater detail in the discussion below. These are separated into different categories in an effort to illustrate different ways of considering policing. It is not suggested that any one of them ought to be chosen at the expense of the others.

a narrow, law enforcement approach

In November 2005, the **Commissioner** of the Metropolitan Police delivered the annual BBC Dimbleby Lecture, and suggested that increasing social diversity, debates about moral relativism, and social fragmentation meant that policing could no longer be left to the police to decide on their own (Blair, 2005). The time had come, Sir Ian Blair rather portentously argued, for the public to decide what kind of police service that it wanted. Quite how the public – divided and confused as Sir Ian portrayed them – would be able to establish a coherent set of priorities that the police could address was not explained. During a period in which concerns about terrorism, apparent increases in violent gun crime, protests about animal rights and fox hunting, the strict enforcement of speed restrictions on the roads, the safety of police officers, drug use, police racism, debate about the extent of free speech, and many related topics have been at the forefront of popular debate, it might seem appropriate to have a period of considered reflection about the nature of policing and how it might be properly developed in difficult times. As McLaughlin (2007a) noted, however, much of the press response to Sir Ian's bid for dialogue was characterized by two, related, reactions. First, media commentators poured scorn on the Commissioner, claiming that his invitation amounted to a tacit admission that he did not know what the role of the police was. Blair was portrayed as a liberal intellectual – more concerned with political correctness than police work – who was so out of touch that he no longer even knew what the service was for. Second, the newspapers gave a simple and relatively narrow definition of what the police service is for: catching criminals. The *Daily Telegraph* (2005), for example, told Sir Ian in no uncertain terms '"What kind of police service do we want?" The answer is obvious: one that better protects us from crime.'

Clearly political, policy and popular cultural understandings of the police are often centred on their crime-fighting role. Although the following discussion will demonstrate that policing is about much more than crime fighting, it is not surprising that the news media suggest otherwise, given that it is this that features so heavily in all types of media coverage. Both fictional and factual representations of crime and policing tend to focus disproportionately on violent offending and the police response to it. Media coverage of policing is significant since many people get information about crime trends, and the response to them, indirectly through newspapers and television, and because mediated images influence debate about future directions for the police service and the 'state of the nation' more generally (Mawby, 2003a). Clearly generalizing about the media coverage of the police, as though this were a coherent or univocal phenomenon, is unhelp-ful and it should be remembered that ideas about crime and insecurity are communicated in complex and unpredictable ways (Innes, 2004; Lee, 2007). Nonetheless, media coverage of policing often focuses upon the crime-fighting work that officers do. TV shows may give a false impression of the nature and extent of crime for reasons of narrative and drama. These considerations also influence media representations in documentary programmes and 'infotainment' shows that purport to represent the 'reality' of police work, but nonetheless give a selective and partial account. Reiner (2003: 269) noted that the police are subject to occasional negative media coverage and the exposure of police deviance has been a recurring theme. On balance, though, he argued that:

> **The overall picture of crime and control presented in the media, whether fiction or news, is thus highly favourable to the police image. Crime is represented as a serious threat to vulnerable individual victims, but one that the police routinely tackle successfully because of their prowess and heroism. The police accord-ingly appear as the seldom-failing guardians of the public in general, essential bulwarks of the social order. (ibid.)**

Media coverage of the police, clearly, is disproportionately focused on their law enforcement duties. As Mawby (2003a) noted, research suggests that media accounts are the authoritative narrative of policing for large sections of the public. In his Dimbleby Lecture, Sir Ian Blair (2005) wryly remarked that

'Lots of people in this country are actually undertaking a permanent NVQ [National Vocational Qualification] in policing – it's called *The Bill*.'

If these representations are important in terms of public attitudes, it seems equally likely that they have implications for those who work for the police – and for new recruits – who might find themselves working in an environment radically different from that which they had been encouraged by the media to expect. What is also important is that popular cultural representations offer a wholly unrealistic conception of policing. The crime-fighting mandate does provide one answer to the question 'What is policing?'. This might be a somewhat narrow conceptualization of policing, but clearly apprehending offenders and preventing crime are central elements of police activity. Even this narrow perspective of police work, though, raises important questions. The range of acts that contravene the criminal law is huge and diverse. The 1996 Police Act, for example, outlaws the act of 'causing disaffection among police officers'; the Malicious Damages Act of 1861 outlaws the placing of wooden obstacles on railway tracks; the 1985 Companies Act makes 'failing to keep accounting records open to inspection' a criminal offence. Box 1.2 outlines some of the circumstances defined as criminal by the 1351 Treason Act.

Box 1.2

The 1351 Treason Act

[W]hen a man doth compass or imagine the death of our Lord the King, or of our lady his Queen, or of their eldest son and heir; or if a man do violate the King's companion, or the King's eldest daughter unmarried, or the wife of the King's eldest son and heir; or if a man do levy war against our lord the King in his realm, or be adherent to the King's enemies in his realm, giving them aid and comfort in the realm, or elsewhere and thereof be provably attainted of open deed by the people of their condition … and if a man slea the chancellor, treasurer or the King's justices … assigned to hear and determine being in their places doing their offices.

That legal prohibitions on various activities are introduced or repealed over time is one reason why a crime-centred definition of policing needs to be adopted with caution. Furthermore, the breach of certain criminal laws, including most of those examples cited above, may never feature in the work of most police officers. The 'black letter' of the criminal law provides only a very weak indication of what police officers actually do: this is partly because individual officers operate with considerable **discretion** but also a result of the principle of operational independence, which means that **Chief Constables** are able to exercise their discretion in terms of establishing which criminal activities will be prioritized. Not only does the differential enforcement of the law mean that police activity cannot simply be read from statute, it also provides the conceptual space that criminological analysis seeks to fill by exploring the circumstances in which individual officers and the police service collectively enforce certain laws but not others. At various stages in this book the differential enforcement of the law is considered. The significance of officer discretion is discussed in Chapter 5 where the broader topic of police occupational sub-culture and its impact on police work is considered. Chapter 7 explores why hate crimes, such as racist violence, have tended to be under-policed. Chapter 9 considers the extent to which the surveillance and law-enforcement powers of the police have been expanded by CCTV and similar technologies.

In the early 1990s, when the British police service was being reviewed by a Royal Commission on Criminal Justice, the Sheehy Inquiry into Police Responsibilities, and the Home Secretary published a White Paper on **police reform**, an independent committee of inquiry into the role and the responsibilities of the police was established by the Police Foundation and the Policy Studies Institute (Cassels, 1996). The issues that had led to such fervent debate about the police service in the early 1990s continue to dominate twenty-first-century thinking: changing crime problems, expenditure on policing, increasing public insecurity, and the growth of the **private security** industry (ibid.). Before considering these issues in detail, the inquiry considered the role of the police and endorsed the definition of policing contained in the Statement of Common Purpose and Values, namely, that:

> **The purpose of the police service is to uphold the law fairly and firmly; to prevent crime; to pursue and bring to justice those who break the law; to keep the Queen's peace; to protect, help and reassure the community; and to be seen to do this with integrity, common sense and sound judgement.**

This definition of police work is broadly consistent with other influential statements made since modern police services were established in the nineteenth century. The relative unanimity on the role of the police service, though, cannot disguise the enormous complexities and contradictions contained within them. As the Cassels Inquiry noted, agencies other than the police are responsible for achieving some of these goals, and there may be contradictions between some of them, such as enforcing the law and maintaining public order, and priorities need to be established within this broad framework. Definitions of the police role become contradictory once an exclusive focus upon law enforcement is left behind.

the centrality of 'force' to policing

Other efforts to define the police and the policing role more widely have focused upon the police monopoly in the legitimate use of force. If the police embody the state, then Max Weber's classic definition of state sovereignty as the possession of a legitimate use of force over a given territory is clearly an important feature of the police role. Bittner (1974) and Klockars (1985) have argued that it is the ability to use force against their fellow citizens that is the defining characteristic of the police officer. As with definitions that focus upon law enforcement, the emphasis on police use of force reveals important properties of police work but, similarly, are subject to important caveats that muddy the waters. First, research evidence makes it very clear that police officers tend to under-utilize their capacity to use force to resolve conflict. Although there are clearly occasions when the police use of force is properly subject to legal, political and media scrutiny – perhaps the best recent example was the furore surrounding the shooting of Jean Charles de Menezes at Stockwell Park tube station in the aftermath of the July 2005 terrorist attacks in London – negotiation and persuasion characterize most police–public interaction. In part, the doctrine of the use of minimum force has been an important component of securing police legitimacy (Reiner, 2000). Moreover, the police service finds that its monopoly status – never absolute in any case – is increasingly being eroded as other agencies are afforded recourse to the use of force. Other state employees, such as customs officers and environmental health officers, also have legal powers to detain people and impound property. Additionally, quasi-public agencies, such as bailiffs employed by the courts, also have powers to enter property and can use force in a limited way in order to do so.

the practice of policing

Attempts to identify the role of the police reviewed thus far have been based on abstract, normative considerations of what the principles of the police ought to be. Another, more rigorous examination of what the police service does can be gleaned from various research studies that have explored the realities of routine police work and found that service-oriented work and order maintenance – a much more nebulous concept than crime control – characterize much of what officers do. Among the first accounts of police work was Bittner's (1974) review of policing studies, including that of Reiss (1971) and Niederhoffer (1969), in the US that led him to the view that 'when one looks at what policemen actually do, one finds that criminal law enforcement is something that most of them do with the frequency located somewhere between virtually never and very rarely' (Bittner, 1974: 22). Earlier Banton's (1964: 2) study of the British police led him to the view that 'the police are relatively unimportant in the enforcement of law'. More time was spent performing a wide range of public **service roles**, Bittner suggested, that had little in common except that there was no other agency that might be expected to perform the function. Although not greatly helpful to those seeking to understand what policing actually is, Bittner's (1974: 30) observation amply illustrates the breadth of the police task: 'no human problem exists, or is imaginable, about which it could be said with finality that this certainly could not become the proper business of the police'.

The service roles performed by the police are widely noted in studies of routine police work. Much traffic policing, for example, is directed towards keeping roads clear so that vehicles keep moving and public safety is enhanced. This might involve some law enforcement activity but, as with other areas of police work, it has been widely established that officers tend to under-enforce the law and to use other strategies – most obviously negotiation – in order to ensure public co-operation. Bayley's (1994) study of routine police work in Australia, Canada, England and Wales, Japan, and the United States suggested that patrol work accounts for most of what officers spend their time doing, and that most of this is directed – especially in urban areas – by dispatchers who in turn are responding to calls for help from the general public. Bayley (ibid.: 30) estimated that no more than 7–10 per cent of such calls relate to crime, and even that small proportion includes much that is of a non-serious nature. Against this background, much routine policing is about patrol work, such that officers might be understood as 'tour guides in the museum of human frailty' whose role is

> [to] 'sort out' situations by listening patiently to endless stories about fancied slights, old grievances, new insults, mismatched expectations, infidelity, dishonesty and abuse. They hear all about the petty, mundane, tedious, hapless, sordid details of individual lives. Patient listening and gentle counselling are undoubtedly what patrol officers do most of the time. (ibid.: 31–2)

While it might be that officers spend much of their time performing roles that appear to have little or nothing to do with crime fighting, the distinction between law enforcement and **crime control models** of policing is not as clear-cut as it might appear at first. Bittner (1974) presented an imaginary traffic police officer to illustrate the complex priorities that might make the general service role a priority over crime control in some circumstances, as the extract in Box 1.3 demonstrates. Popular representations of police work might present a narrow range of crime fighting activity as typical of policing but the apparently peripheral service work might have broader implications for community relations and law enforcement. A BBC documentary that explored the contemporary nature of British policing was told, by the director of the Police Foundation, of an officer who responded to an elderly lady who requested assistance in opening a tin of cat food (BBC, 2006a). Clearly this illustration is only one remove from the cliché of emergency services rescuing cats from trees, and has as little to do with crime control as can be imagined. Nonetheless, the

Foundation's director pointed to the value of such a service as it provides assurance to the person who receives it, and helps to shore up the legitimacy of the service. It also provides further illustration of the challenge of arriving at a clear and concise definition of the police function.

Box 1.3

The competing priorities facing Bittner's traffic cop

One of the most common experiences of urban life is the sight of a patrolman directing traffic at a busy street intersection. This service is quite expensive and the assignment is generally disliked among policemen. Nevertheless it is provided on a regular basis … Despite its seriousness and presumed necessity, despite the fact that assignments are planned ahead and specifically funded, no assignment to a traffic control post is ever presumed to be absolutely fixed … no matter how important the post might be, it is always possible for something else to come up than can distract the patrolman's attention and cause him to suspend attending to the assigned task … It is virtually certain that any normally competent patrolman would abandon the traffic post to which he was assigned without hesitation and without regard for the state of the traffic he was supposed to monitor, if it came to his attention that a crime was being committed somewhere at a distance not too far for him to reach in time either to arrest the crime in its course, or to arrest its perpetrator … But if the crime that came to the attention of the officer had been something like a conspiracy by a board of directors of a commercial concern to issue stock with the intention of defrauding investors, or a landlord criminally extorting payments from a tenant, or a used-car dealer culpably turning back an odometer on an automobile he was preparing for sale, the patrolman would scarcely lift his gaze, let alone move into action. The real reason why the patrolman moved out was not the fact that what was taking place was a crime in general terms, but because the particular crime was a member of a class of problems *the treatment of which will not abide*. In fact, the patrolman who unhesitatingly left his post to pursue an assailant would have left his post with just as little hesitation to pull a drowning person out of the water, to prevent someone from jumping off the roof of a building, to protect a severely disoriented person from harm, to save people in a burning structure, to disperse a crowd hampering the rescue mission of an ambulance, to take steps to prevent a possible disaster that might result from broken gas lines or water mains, and so on almost endlessly, and entirely without regard to the substantive nature of the problem, as long as it could be said that it involved *something-that-ought-not-to-be-happening-and-about-which-someone-had-better-do-something-now!* (Bittner, 1974; emphasis in original)

There has been considerable oscillation between the twin polices of crime control and service provision in political terms during the past few decades. Some Chief **Constables** have strongly advocated a community policing model predicated upon the co-provision of services with other agencies and with the public more generally (Alderson, 1984) and the development of the police 'Statement of Common Purposes and Values' placed a clear emphasis on the service role (Reiner, 2000: 110–11). However, the mid-1990s saw other proposals and reform, such as the Sheehy Inquiry into officer pay and employment conditions, the Posen Inquiry into core and ancillary tasks, and the 1994 Police and Magistrates Court Act, all of which sought to develop the police service along business lines around the core business of catching criminals (Reiner, 2000: 111; Morgan and Newburn, 1997: 44–73). The tension between service provision and crime fighting – two possible answers to the question 'What is policing?' – turns out to be misplaced if policing is understood in terms of order maintenance; a strategic role that encompasses all of the activities alluded to in the discussion so far. Conceptualizing police work in terms of broader processes of social regulation not only helps understand the sheer breadth of activities that the police actually carry out, it also allows for the complementary contributions made to this process by other agencies.

police as bureaucrats

If policing is to be understood on the basis of the various tasks and functions that officers perform, then a fundamental reassessment of the role is required in the light of the amount of administration that officers do. Although studies of police work often show that officers engage in risky pursuits of offenders and confront danger, these are exceptional events for most officers, although the potential for such encounters might mean that they shape officer perceptions of people and situations (Reiner, 2000). The routines of police work are characterized by administrative and procedural work which might not be understood as 'real' policing by police sub-culture or media representation, but are centrally important in terms of the proportion of time devoted to them. The administrative burden on police officers is often cited as a priority to be tackled by reform programmes and innovative technological solutions that promise to ease the load, and some of these are discussed in Chapter 9. While record-keeping and form-filling are often associated with attempts to micro-manage officer behaviour and hold their managers to account in terms of targets and performance management regimes, the extent of police administration has partly been determined by demands to ensure that powers are discharged fairly, and that legal procedures, for example relating to the security of evidence, are being adhered to. The background to some of these requirements is outlined in Chapter 3, in which police powers are discussed, and in Chapter 7, where considerations relating to diversity issues are reviewed. Efforts to reduce the administrative burden on police officers have sometimes involved **civilianization** of roles previously fulfilled by officers, and the employment of **Police Community Support Officers (PCSOs)** who can perform ancillary functions and allow police to attend to 'frontline' policing tasks. The scope and extent of the pluralization of policing are discussed in Chapter 8.

For whatever reason, though, it is clear that a quantitative answer to the question 'What is policing?' might lead to the conclusion that it is an administrative role. Certainly, Ericson and Haggerty's (1997) study of police work in Canada noted the considerable bureaucratic responsibility that officers faced – they identified, for example, that officers attending the scene of a road traffic accident were required to complete a dozen different forms. The extent of this aspect of police work led Ericson and Haggerty to argue that police officers had become 'knowledge workers' whose primary role was to communicate risk within the police service, the criminal justice system and to a host of other agencies. More recently, a Home Office-funded study of policing in Britain also found that officers were required to spend much of their time on activities that kept them away from patrol work (PA Consulting, 2001). The research, based on analysis of diaries completed by officers, concluded that 43 per cent of officer time was spent inside police stations, most of which was either devoted to the custody process, which took an average of 3.5 hours per prisoner, or was spent completing paperwork. Box 1.4 gives an overview of some of the bureaucratic requirements on officers. Notably the report concluded that computer-based methods could alleviate this position and that this ought to be achievable within three years. There is little evidence that the extent of bureaucratic responsibilities has reduced, and the impact of information work on the nature of policing is discussed at greater length in Chapter 9.

Box 1.4

Routine police work?

But what accounts for the time operational officers spend in the police station? The two main culprits are the time taken to process prisoners and prepare prosecutions, and the other paperwork which the police must produce. Arresting someone – no matter whether they are a petty criminal or a serious offender – keeps officers off the beat for an average of 3.5 hours – often for far longer. At busy times there are bottlenecks in custody and frequent delays in carrying out finger-printing, photographing and criminal record checks. Delays are generally the same for a simple shop-lift as for a much more serious matter. Where a solicitor, appropriate adult or interpreter is required, this can trigger a further wait of on average an hour. If CCTV or an identity parade is involved, further substantial delays can ensue.

Other paperwork includes crime reports, intelligence reports, forms to log recovered property, missing person details, information required for special force initiatives as well as paperwork connected with the shift administration and the officer in question. Often one event (e.g. a crime) can trigger the recording of the same information on multiple separate records. Where forms are available electronically, little officer time is actually saved because the IT system applications are mostly antiquated and do not talk to each other. (PA Consulting Group, 2001: vi)

The distinction between policing and the police has often been overlooked in academic analysis of policing. Although that is changing, as discussion in Chapter 8 indicates, it is less clear that media or political debate about policing has broadened. A narrow response to the question 'What is policing?' retains an institutional approach and regards policing as a key agency within the broader criminal justice system. Figure 1.1 shows the relation between the police service and other parts of the criminal justice system in England and Wales. As will be demonstrated throughout this book, the police service might be the 'state in uniform', the pre-eminent visible embodiment of sovereignty and the rule of law but it is not the only agency influencing and regulating social conflict and cohesion.

For much analysis of the performance, equity and efficiency of the criminal justice system, concern about policing begins and ends with the actions of the public police, which, while only a small component within the complex justice system illustrated in Figure 1.1, plays a crucial role as a 'gateway agency' to the rest of the system. Even though a recurring theme of this chapter and this book is that policing is a process continued beyond the public police, it is clear that little done by other agencies feeds into the criminal justice system without an input from the police service. For this reason alone it might be important to remember that even though 'policing' and 'the police' are no longer synonymous, it continues to be the case that the public institution of the police occupies most attention in wider debates about law enforcement, order maintenance and the almost boundless range of tasks associated with policing.

_____ **conclusion** _____

The chapter has addressed the question 'What is policing?' in terms of the underlying principles of the police service and the wide range of roles performed by officers. While policing as a social function is broader than this, the initial focus has been on the public institution of the police service. It was shown that the media and other popular representations that suggest that policing is primarily about crime-fighting are seriously misleading, not least because they underplay the broader order maintenance and service work that officers do. The following chapter considers the history of the police, and the ways in which it has developed. Just as this chapter emphasizes that policing is about much more than the law-enforcement activities of the public police service, so too the discussion in Chapter 2 suggests that policing needs to be understood in broader terms.

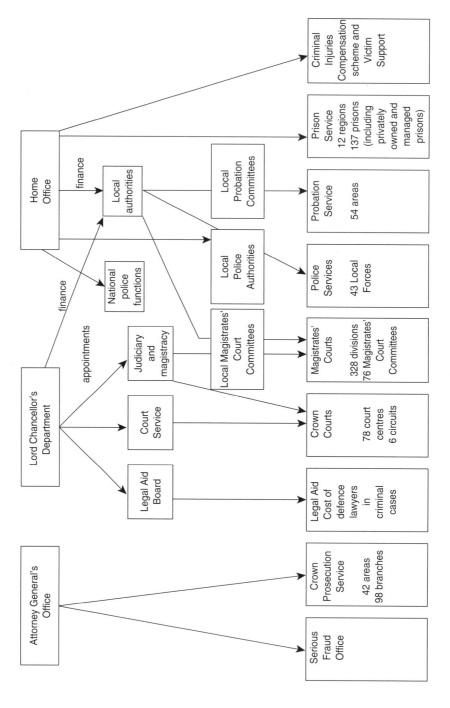

Figure 1.1 The structure of the criminal justice system in England and Wales

Source: Home Office (2000)

- The police have become a cultural symbol of the British nation. Mythology about the development of the law and policing has been an important element of narratives of national identity.

- Although often treated as synonymous, **police and policing** need to be understood as distinct concepts. Policing relates to broad processes of social regulation that underpin the routines of everyday life; as such, these are performed by a wide range of agencies and institutions. Historically, 'policing' has been understood in these broad terms and not associated with the activities of a particular organization.

- While a broad approach has the advantage of incorporating the wide range of processes that regulate social life, it lacks clarity, since almost anything could be included. A narrower definition, equating policing to the activities of the institution of the police, might lack breadth but it is clearer and a more concise perspective.

- Often policing is understood in terms of law enforcement, and certainly this has been a common perspective in media coverage. Fictional and documentary images of police work tend to centre on crime-fighting, and concentrate on dangerous, action-oriented pursuits and serious crime portraying the police as the 'thin blue line' between social order and chaos.

- The law-enforcement perspective is flawed since police officers use considerable discretion when applying the law, and many laws are rarely enforced by most officers. Moreover, police services perform a wide range of activities that do not relate to law enforcement.

- Other definitions focus upon the police monopoly use of force. Traditionally state sovereignty has been understood in these terms and considering the police as the 'state in uniform' leads to this definition being transferred to the police service. As with the law enforcement perspective, though, the reality of police work suggests that force tends to be under-used and negotiation characterizes police encounters with the public, although the potential for coercive force might shape these interactions.

- Another perspective is gained from studies that consider the nature of the roles that the police perform in practice. Such studies tend to confirm that law enforcement accounts for only a small proportion of police work, and order maintenance and service functions are more significant in terms of the time and resources allocated to them. Bittner (1974) argued that all these functions had in common was that it was not possible to identify another agency that ought to be responsible for them. Fulfilling these public service roles might enhance legitimacy, secure public confidence, and so contribute to crime control and law enforcement.

- Research studies have also shown that police officers are required to perform a wide variety of administrative tasks, to the extent that some have characterized policing as a form of 'knowledge work' whereby officers are required to communicate information about risks of crime to a host of other agencies. Bureaucratic aspects of police work have often been regarded as a distraction from the core responsibilities of officers and moves to civilianize police duties and develop technological methods to reduce their burden have been widely pursued.

- Policing can also be understood in institutional terms as the police service forms a key part of the broader criminal justice system. Although much of the order maintenance and service-oriented functions of the police service do not contribute to the criminal justice system more widely, discussion of the efficacy and efficiency of the system more generally tends to relate to the police service, the 'gateway' agency, in some respect.

 ■ **self-check ?uestions**

1 How can narrow and broader definitions of policing be characterized?

2 What agencies, apart from the police service, play a role in regulating social life?

3 Why did Mawby (2003a) argue that media images of policing are important?

4 Who provided a 'classic' definition of state sovereignty?

5 Why might the 'use of force' offer only a limited understanding of the police function?

6 In what, very broad, terms did Bittner (1974) define the police task?

7 What proportion of public calls to the police did Bayley find were related to crime?

8 How did Ericson and Haggerty (1997) characterize police officers?

9 What two factors explain, according to research published in 2001, the significant amount of time officers spend in the police station?

10 What relation does the police service have to the criminal justice system more generally?

 ■ **study ?uestions**

1 What are the difficulties in distinguishing between a narrow and a broad definition of policing?

2 Why does the media tend to present an image of policing so different from that revealed by research studies?

3 What is policing?

Bittner's (1974) article 'Florence Nightingale in Pursuit of Willy Sutton' is an early account of the complexities and contradictions inherent in the police function that provides a compelling argument against a narrow 'law-enforcement' definition of the role of the police.

The first chapter of Waddington's (1999) *Policing Citizens* contains a useful discussion of the question that has framed this chapter: 'What is policing?'. Waddington explores the force–service dichotomy and similarities and specificities of police work across the world.

Chapters 3 and 4 of McLaughlin's (2007a) *The New Policing* provide an excellent account of the development of 'police studies', focusing on traditional perspectives (including that of Bittner) that emerged in the US in the 1960s and somewhat later in the UK, and 'new perspectives' that consider the changing terrain of policing in post-modern, post-industrial global society.

∴ // annotated listings of links to relevant websites /

A good starting point for general information on the roles, responsibilities and development of the police in Scotland is available from the homepage of the Scottish Executive, (http://www.scotland.gov.uk/Topics/Justice/Police). Similar information relating to England and Wales can be found at the Home Office website (http://www.homeoffice.gov.uk/police/), and at the Northern Ireland Policing Board at (http://www.nipolicingboard.org.uk/).

The full text of Sir Ian Blair's Dimbleby lecture 'What Kind of Police Service Do We Want?' can be found at http://tinyurl.com/2wg8za.

In response to Blair's call for debate on the purpose of the police service, the Police Foundation – an independent charity that seeks to enhance public and policy debate – held a seminar considering 'What the police are for'. Proceedings of the event and much other useful material can be found at http://tinyurl.com/2kpld5.

2

Historical origins and development of the police in England and Wales

Contents

While Chapter 1 sought to explain policing in terms of the various roles and functions of the service and fundamental principles, the focus of this chapter is to explore the historical development of the police service in England and Wales up to the end of the nineteenth century. Various perspectives that account for these trends are explored in the second part of the chapter. One such, the 'conservative' perspective, suggests that the establishment of the police service in London in 1829 was an innovative – but natural and logical – response to changing social, economic and political circumstances. Alternatively, 'revisionist' accounts explain the establishment of the police in terms of containing threats of political violence and maintaining order among the industrial working class more generally. Although they reach contrasting conclusions, both accounts indicate that the history of the police service needs to be understood against the wider background of the period, just as contemporary police reforms discussed elsewhere in the book are often a reflection of more fundamental social change. The objectives of the chapter are:

- to examine the foundation and development of the police service in Britain;

- to outline the changing social, political and economic context that shaped the establishment of the police service;

- to explore interpretations of these processes.

| **key terms** |

attitudes to order; establishment and development of police services; historical interpretation; military; police and policing; political unrest; public involvement in policing; underlying principles; urban crime

---

_____ **introduction** _____

Various countries might claim to have established the first police service, and these competing claims partly reflect the breadth of the various functions that might be defined as 'policing'. As noted in Chapter 1, the word 'policing' developed in relation to general patterns of social regulation, which suggests that it has been continued in one form or another since there have been states or governments. Given the extent of policing history, it might be wondered why so much discussion of the historical development of policing relates to the British experience. Clearly policing traditions in other countries continue to be researched and discussed, and comparative accounts note national specificities that reinforce the danger of an ethnocentric perspective that views everything from a limited and partial British vantage point (Mawby, 1999). That the focus of the following discussion is almost exclusively on the development of the police of England and Wales reflects the importance of these arrangements in global terms, as British colonialism exported policing systems – alongside the common law tradition to which it is related – to many countries. This did not mean that a single vision – in terms of principle or practice – of policing prevailed across the British Empire, or that the Metropolitan Police model outlined below was uprooted and transplanted around the imperial system. Clearly, as in other matters, colonial administrators were often able to adapt the institutional arrangements available to them to suit the particular circumstances that they faced. Nonetheless, the principles of policing that evolved in nineteenth-century Britain have provided a framework that has spread and endured in many countries. David Bayley (1985, cited in Mawby, 2003b) argued that modern policing can be distinguished from earlier forms as it is characterized by specialization, professionalism and publicness, organizing principles central to the creation of the Metropolitan Police.

a brief history of the police in England and Wales

While certain dates, events and characters tend to feature in most histories of the police in England and Wales, there is little consensus on how to explain the development of the professional service in the nineteenth century. Facts might be sacred but it is not self-evident which of them are important, relevant, or can safely be disregarded. It is, for example, a fact that the Metropolitan Police (dubbed the 'new police') was established in 1829 following legislation that was steered through Parliament by the Home Secretary, Sir Robert Peel. It is unlikely that there is a history of British policing that does not mention this. There is far less agreement, however, about how significant these facts are in terms of understanding why policing emerged in the ways that it did. Providing an historical overview of the major milestones that have shaped the police in England and Wales while doing justice to the historical controversies about structure and agency, the dangers of teleology, and the importance of locating these developments in their broader context is the challenge addressed in the discussion that follows.

As Emsley (1996: 4) has noted, until relatively recently historical accounts of the development of the British police have only been found in the memoirs of former chief constables, senior politicians and civil servants. These accounts reinforced the established perspective that modern policing systems developed in London in the early decades of the nineteenth century and then, as the wisdom of these arrangements came to be more widely recognized, were slowly expanded across the rest of the country. Orthodox accounts, such as those by Lee (1901) and Reith (1948), regard the establishment of the Metropolitan Police in 1829 as an important stage in the gradual evolution of policing that could be traced back to the Anglo-Saxon era during which a peaceable settled community was directly responsible for its own policing. Lee (1901: ix) introduced his account of the history of the English police in terms that exemplify what Reiner described as the 'palpably conservative' tone of many early histories:

> **Our English police system ... rests on foundations designed with the full approval of the people ... and has been slowly moulded by the careful hand of experience, developing as a rule along the line of least resistance, now in advance of the general intelligence of the country, now lagging far behind, but always in the long run adjusting itself to the popular temper. (cited in Reiner, 2000: 15)**

The consensual view places great emphasis on a strong historical theme of community participation that runs, it is claimed, through English police history from the Anglo-Saxon era to the present. Although many historical accounts tend to regard the establishment of the Metropolitan Police in 1829 as a pivotal point, it is clear that there are many features that have endured from earlier periods. Mawby (1999: 30) noted that policing in England between the 1740s and 1850s was characterized by self-policing, community engagement in street patrols, and that the private sector provided many policing services: all features of twenty-first-century police reform. The grassroots engagement of the public in police activity has been central to much of the discourse and practice of policing in Britain. By the end of the first millennium, the population was organized into groups of ten households, known as 'tythings', which were themselves grouped together into larger 'hundreds' and supervised by a 'hundredman' who was accountable to the 'shire reeve', or sheriff. When a crime occurred, it was the direct duty of all to pursue and apprehend the offender and to present him to the authorities. The subsequent organization of policing and the direct involvement of local people in its operation reflect the early traditions established by the Statute of Winchester in 1285. Ascoli (1979: 16) argued that the Statute was 'one of the most important, and certainly one of the most durable, of all constitutional measures'. Some of the key provisions of the Statute are outlined in Box 2.1; notable among them are the direct involvement of all people in the maintenance of law and order and also that the role of the unpaid part-time constable was to bring offenders before the courts, not to dispense justice summarily. The principle that those accused of offending should be tried by their peers – as encoded in Magna Carta – is one on which the jury system continues to rely.

Box 2.1

The Statute of Winchester, 1285

- Purpose was 'to abate the power of felons'.
- It was the duty of everyone to maintain the King's Peace, and it was open to any citizen to arrest an offender.
- The unpaid, part-time constable had a special duty assisted by the watchman.
- Hue and cry was to be raised to apprehend offenders.
- Penalties were imposed against those who did not comply with the compulsory pursuit of criminals.
- Everyone was required to keep arms for preserving peace and apprehending criminals.
- The town gates were closed between sunset and sunrise and strangers were not allowed to enter.
- The constable had a duty to present the offender at the court. (Derived from Ascoli (1979) and Critchley (1978))

The term 'constable' seems to have first been used during the Norman period, but was central to the provisions of the Statute of Winchester, and, again, it is clear that the principles that underpinned the office continue to resonate. Unlike their modern counterparts, though, constables in the thirteenth century were unpaid, and expected to carry out their duties in addition to other paid employment. However, the unpaid status of the constable reflected a continuing principle, which is that the police officer ought to represent the 'citizen in uniform'. Although, much more recently, this approach became increasingly untenable as technological and organizational changes have increasingly set police officers apart from members of the public, payment did not negate the common law principle that a constable 'is only a person who is paid to perform as a matter of duty acts which, if he were so minded, he might have done voluntarily' (Stephens, 1964, cited in Ascoli, 1979: 18). The longevity of the provisions of the Statue has been widely noted in traditional police histories; Critchley (1978: 7), for example, noted that it 'was the only general public measure of any consequence enacted to regulate the policing of the country between the Norman Conquest and the Metropolitan Police Act, 1829, so that for nearly 600 years it laid down the basic principles'.

urban lawlessness

It is when it comes to explaining the transition from these 'pre-modern' policing arrangements to the establishment of the Metropolitan Police in 1829 that competing theoretical perspectives emerge. Traditional accounts suggest, implicitly or otherwise, that the process by which a professional institution came to be invested with responsibility for law enforcement and order maintenance was a rational response to changing social circumstances. The twin processes of industrialization and urbanization, it is held, accelerated the crime problem while at the same time rendered prevailing provisions ever less effective. Certainly those directly responsible for establishing the 'new police' in 1829 couched their arguments in terms of the need to stem the rising tide of street crime. Home Secretary Peel argued in Parliament that the Metropolitan Police ought to be established because crime levels were accelerating even faster than the urban population was growing (Bailey, 1981: 13; Emsley, 1996: 25). Not only did the growth of urban areas foster problems such as public drunkenness, street disorder, prostitution and the like, it also eroded the informal social controls that had existed in pre-industrial society (Hay, 1975). There had been a number of attempts to modernize policing arrangements from the mid-eighteenth century onwards, and often these were advocated in terms of the need to develop new arrangements to meet the particular challenges of new times. Sir John Fielding oversaw the work of the Bow Street Runners from the 1740s onwards and was a committed advocate of reform of the policing system, although not along the lines eventually followed (Emsley, 1996: 248). He associated the crime problems of the period with illegal drinking establishments, and painted a picture familiar to those who have followed more recent debates about 'binge drinking':

> **At the ale-house the idle meet to game and quarrel; here the gamblers form their strategems; here the pick-pockets hide themselves till dusk, and gangs of thieves form their plots and routs; here conspirators contrive their hellish devices; and here the combinations of journeymen are made to execute their silly schemes. (in Sharpe, 1984: 104)**

Reith (1948) also noted the role that alcohol played in rising street crime and disorder and noted that the policing authorities of the time were implicated in this as many deputy constables were also retailers of cheap gin. Reith also suggested that 'the poverty and destitution of many of the slum-warren and cellar dwellers was such that they were compelled to live by theft and other forms of crime' (ibid.: 6).

political unrest and the limits of the military

Not only was crime growing as a general social problem but political unrest was also posing renewed challenges to the authorities. The 'hunger riots' of the mid-eighteenth century and the political unrest that occasionally accompanied campaigns for democratic reform in the nineteenth century both demonstrated that the military were unable to secure public order in ways that were both effective and publicly acceptable. The limitations of the military's capacity to maintain order were brought into sharp focus at the Chartist rally held at St. Peter's Field in Manchester in 1819. Thousands of people gathered to hear Henry Hunt press the demands for universal suffrage, annual Parliaments and free elections in what has been described as the 'most numerous meeting that ever took place in Great Britain' (Marlow, 1971). As the authorities sought to **arrest** Hunt and other leading figures appearing at the rally, the crowd panicked and many were trampled underfoot by the yeomanry who, under the guidance of local magistrates, were responsible for upholding order. The actions of the military, which resulted in the deaths of 15 people and injury to hundreds, were quickly condemned in the local and the national press, who quickly coined the phrase 'Peterloo Massacre'. While public outrage at such events, and others such as the Gordon Riots of 1780, highlighted the ineffectiveness of the military when it came to the maintenance of law and order in such circumstances, it would be simplistic to suggest that the disproportionality of the response to these challenges was the main spur for seeking other means by which crowd control could be exercised. Emsley (1996: 60) pointed out that one reason why the loss of life and injuries inflicted at Peterloo caused such an outcry was because they were so rare, and that those responsible for deploying the army were well aware of the dangers of overreaction and the public vilification that might ensue. The continued use of the military also became untenable for practical as well as political reasons since their physical isolation in barracks away from urban areas meant that they could not be quickly mobilized in response to disorder (Reith, 1948). Furthermore, the use of the police service as a legitimate and effective alternative to the deployment of troops against 'the mob' was not wholly successful as concerns about the policing of public disorder continued throughout the nineteenth and into the twentieth century. Fielding (2005) noted that concerns about the inability of the military to respond to the Gordon Riots in the 1780s recurred a century later in respect to the policing of political protests in Trafalgar Square.

the 'demand for order'

Whether in terms of general urban lawlessness or emerging challenges of political and industrial disorders, the above perspectives suggest that policing developed in response to changing social and political conditions. Another perspective suggests that the development of policing reflected wider demands for a more regulated and orderly society. Thompson (1968) has argued that disorder was often regarded as a relatively legitimate means by which political and economic grievances could be advanced in pre-democratic and pre-industrial British society, but that this discourse shifted as society became urbanized and industrialized. Similarly, Silver (1967) demonstrated that perceptions of crime and lawlessness chimed with more fundamental insecurities about threats to social order in more general terms, often relating to the moral depravity of immigrants and the 'dangerous classes'.

The breadth of the activities ascribed to the mid-nineteenth-century police reflected their role as 'domestic missionaries', charged with tackling behaviour regarded as an affront to the moral and ethical sensibilities of the middle classes. The police service, authors such as Storch (1976, see Box 2.2) argued, developed in tandem with efforts at social reform intended to improve the standing of the urban masses, such as the Temperance Movement that sought to tackle alcoholism. Similarly, Dunning et al. (1987) noted the important role of the police service in the regulation of the leisure pursuits of working-class communities in the early years of the twentieth century, through, for example, suppressing informal street gambling.

Box 2.2

The policeman as domestic missionary

The initiatives of the police authorities in these areas of course cannot be viewed apart from the attitudes, prejudices, and momentary reformist enthusiasms of the municipalities, magistrates, and local elites who employed them. This was especially the case outside of London where the police were much less independent of local control than in the metropolis. For this reason police actions must be considered as forming the cutting edge of a wider and larger effort in northern industrial towns to impose new standards of urban discipline. It was the boroughs, after all, who charged the police with the monitoring and suppression of popular activities and recreations considered conductive to immorality, disorder, or crime; it was the police who had to discharge that mandate as best they could or at least convince those to who they were responsible that they were doing so … In February 1836, the Leeds council requested the mayor to direct the police to give information 'as shall lead to the conviction of all … persons as shall continue to prophane the Lord's day', to pay particular attention to drinking places on Saturday nights, to strictly enforce proper closing times, and to 'observe those who resort to the public house or use sports in time of divine service'. (Storch, 1976: 483)

---

establishing the metropolitan police

It was against this background of changing threats of crime and disorder that the Metropolitan Police was established in 1829. By June 1830, the Metropolitan Police comprised two Commissioners, 17 Superintendents – one for each division – 68 Inspectors, 323 Sergeants, and 2906 Constables

(Lee, 1901: 236). The legislation that initiated the force left the detail of these arrangements to the first Commissioners, Charles Rowan and Richard Mayne, who devised the recruitment and training methods, the style of the uniform, pay and conditions, and other provisions. Many of the decisions made by Rowan and Mayne appear to have been intended to overcome the widespread opposition to the establishment of the Metropolitan Police. The initial instructions given to police officers by the Commissioners stressed the importance of civility and caution when it came to interaction with the public; while this emphasis seems to have been designed to assuage public opinion, it was also understood to bring practical benefits, since a 'quiet and determined manner' would cause an officer to 'excite the well-disposed of the bystanders to assist him, if he requires them' (Critchley, 1978: 53). In addition to shaping officers' demeanour in an effort to overcome suspicion of and hostility to the new police, other practical details were attended to. The symbolic value of the police uniform in signalling the presence of the police on the streets, for example, was recognized by the Commissioners, who were also mindful that suspicion of officers acting as undercover agents would be overcome by the wearing of uniforms (Reynolds, 1998: 151). In practice, the wearing of uniform by most officers did not preclude surveillance activity, which was conducted against Chartists and particularly developed by the establishment of the Special Branch in the wake of Fenian bombing campaigns in the 1860s and 1880s (Emsley, 2003: 75). For general public relations, though, it was considered important that uniforms were blue in colour and so distinct from the red tunics used by the military. The desire to avoid the trappings of militarism also partly explains the relatively unarmed nature of the new police, who were equipped only with wooden truncheons, although cutlasses and pistols were available for emergencies (Emsley, 1996: 26). In other respects, though, perceived benefits of militarism were incorporated into the new policing arrangements, as the centrality of drill in police training and the billeting of officers in section houses to help maintain discipline testify (Reith, 1948: 32). In operational terms, the focus of the new police was firmly on establishing a symbolic presence on the streets, reflecting a fundamental belief in the preventative value of patrol work. That two-thirds of officers were deployed on night-time patrols suggests that the Metropolitan Police were continuing the long-established role of watch and ward. Reith's description of the specifications intended to guide officers on patrol suggests that this long-established role was subject to bureaucratic regulation under the new policing arrangements:

> **The men were not permitted to sit down or to lean against anything or to have any kind of rest. They were expected to patrol their beats, steadily and constantly, for nine consecutive hours, at the steady rate of two and a half miles per hour. (ibid.: 32)**

Public opposition to the new policing arrangements did not abate once the Metropolitan Police force had been established. Some local authorities were concerned that the new police were more expensive and less effective than previous arrangements and complained that the local watch committees had been deprived of their role in the governance of the police, a function that had been taken over by the Home Office, and yet were required to continue funding the new institution and that the cost of doing so had greatly increased (Emsley, 1996; Palmer, 1988; Reynolds, 1998). Early criticism of the new police also related to the inability of the Metropolitan Police to meet public demands for **visible patrols**, which suggests that the perceived lack of 'bobbies on the beat' has been a concern as long as there have been bobbies. In the early 1830s, a parish official from Southwark reported to the Home Secretary that local inhabitants were dissatisfied with the new arrangements as they never saw an officer on patrol and in 1830 a public meeting in Shoreditch resolved:

> **That an experience of nine months under the system of the New Police has fully proved that its operations are inimical to the interests of the parish containing up to 60,000 inhabitants for so far from being better protected, one half of the parish is never visited by the New Police. (Reynolds, 1988: 158)**

The apparently poor quality of police recruits might have meant that their presence on the streets did little to improve public perceptions. Bailey (1981: 48) argued that an early feature of the force was 'inefficiency, indiscipline (notably drunkenness) and a massive turnover of constables' that was so great that within four years of the establishment of the Metropolitan Police only one-sixth of the 3000 original recruits were still in post (Critchley, 1978: 54; Reiner, 2000: 20). Opposition is also evident from the list of negative epithets used to describe the new police – Reiner (2000: 48) lists vivid terms such as 'Crushers', 'Peel's Bloody Gang', 'Blue Locusts', 'Jenny Darbies', and 'Raw Lobsters' – and from the real threat of physical violence that officers routinely faced. Ascoli (1979: 95) argued that officers faced a 'baptism of fire' and that physical assault was 'commonplace', which suggests that officers were not over-reacting when they adopted the habit of carrying their wooden rattles in the chest pocket of their uniforms in order to protect the heart in the event of being stabbed (Reith, 1948: 41). Such makeshift forms of protection were not enough to prevent the first murder of a police officer, as PC Long was fatally stabbed in August 1830 (Ascoli, 1979: 95). In 1833, a police charge on a protest meeting at Cold Bath Fields in Clerkenwell, London, organized by the National Political Union led to disorders in which 'the police were stoned, baton charges ensued, and three policemen were stabbed, one of whom was killed outright' (Critchley, 1978: 55). It is a mark of the public mood about the actions of the new police that the subsequent coroner's inquest into the officer's (PC Culley) death returned a verdict of justifiable homicide, although this was subsequently overturned following an appeal by the government.

Public concern about the Metropolitan Police emanated, Reith (1948: 45) argued, from wide swathes of society. While it might be easily imagined that criminals were against more organized policing, the range of groups Reith found to be opposed to the new police is so broad that it might be wondered if there were any sections of society not against the new arrangements. For different reasons Reith suggested that hostility was shared among the labouring classes, artisans and small shopkeepers, affluent shopkeepers, merchants and industrialists, titled, aristocratic landowners and that even King George IV made public comments against the Metropolitan Police.

Given this breadth and depth of criticism, it is remarkable how quickly public opposition to the new police appears to have subsided. As Reiner (2000) noted, orthodox accounts of police history suggest that the deaths of officers such as Long and Culley helped to turn public opinion in favour of the police. Critchley (1978: 55–6) certainly took the view that securing public **consent** could be attributed to 'the way in which 3,000 unarmed policemen, cautiously feeling their way against a hostile public, brought peace and security to London, in place of the turmoil and lawlessness of centuries'.

Although, as Reiner (2000: 29) noted, Storch (1975), Cohen (1979) and Brogden (1982) have argued that opposition to the police has continued among many sections of society and that anti-police riots have been a recurrent feature of police history, it does seem that the ferocity of anti-police feeling decreased during the 1830s. Palmer (1988: 313) suggested that 'the unthinkable was slowly becoming the acceptable' by the mid-1830s, which might have been due in part to a decrease in violent protest as political reform progressed during this period. No doubt the government's agreement, in 1833, to contribute to the financing of the police, which effectively reduced the local police rates, helped overcome the opposition from parish authorities (ibid.: 313). In addition, it seems that the police came to be regarded as efficient in terms of dealing with the problem of crime. Reith (1948: 53) suggested that the Metropolitan Police were credited with decreasing burglary and street disorder and that this success led to demands from adjacent areas that the new policing arrangements be extended to them. Those arguing for new policing to be developed outside of the capital often suggested that the success of the Metropolitan Police had led to criminal activity being displaced into areas not previously troubled by significant problems.

expansion and consolidation

The process by which police forces came to be established across the country as a whole began as a matter of enablement whereby county and borough authorities were given the opportunity to establish police forces should they so wish. While the Municipal Corporations Act of 1835 required that Watch Committees be established, their remit was to oversee police organizations deemed suitable to local requirements, which sometimes meant that little changed in terms of the routine arrangements of nightwatchmen and other officials (Emsley, 2003: 70; Wall, 1998: 27). Further legislation extended this opportunity to county authorities in 1839 and 1840, but control over Chief Constables in rural areas remained in the hands of local magistrates, rather than elected Watch Committees, and in that context chief officers enjoyed greater autonomy and a higher social status than their counterparts in urban areas (Wall, 1998). Although many accounts of the historical development of the police in mid-nineteenth-century Britain tend to present an unfolding process whereby the metropolitan model was rolled out across the country at the same time that constabularies were being established, steps were also taken in the opposite direction that sought to improve the efficiency of 'pre-modern' policing arrangements (Wall, 1998: 25). That established policing patterns existed in conjunction with the new police for some time demonstrates that different local authorities embraced the new arrangements more eagerly than others (Bailey, 1981: 12; Reynolds, 1998: 4). Critchley (1978: 90) noted the patchwork of arrangements in the following terms:

> **Outside London two different systems of policing existed for some years side by side. In some rural areas, as in a few large boroughs, the new professional police were well entrenched, but tens of thousands of acres of rural England continued to rely on the old system of parish constables, augmented here and there by a paid watchman or two, employed under the Lighting and Watching Act, or local improvement powers.**

It was not until the 1850s that arrangements were put in place that established a uniform policing system across England and Wales. The 1856 County and Borough Police Act required that each county establish a police force under the direction of the magistracy. The Act also provided central funding for one quarter of the cost of pay and clothing providing that **Her Majesty's Inspectorate of Constabulary (HMIC)** were satisfied that the force was being run efficiently. To this end the inspectors were required to report annually to Parliament (Emsley, 2003: 71). Bailey (1981: 15) suggested that HMIC faced an 'uphill struggle' in their early efforts to promote consistency in the practices of the 200 or so forces that existed after the 1856 legislation but that the system of inspection helped to secure the consent of the middle classes by imposing a raft of service roles on the police, including the inspection of weights and measures, the inspection of lodging houses, and the enforcement of the licensing and vagrancy laws. The 1856 Act established a framework that provided the basis for policing in England and Wales that persisted until the 1960s and introduced a mixture of local and central control in terms of the management and financing of the new police. Wall (1998: 42–3) identified three salient features in the emergence of the Metropolitan, borough and county forces during the middle decades of the nineteenth century. First, that there was no coherent concept of police professionalism or of the tasks and duties that officers should perform. Second, local factors determined the management structures of forces and the nature of officers recruited to senior positions. Third, that the priorities of each force were determined, to a large degree, by the particular concerns and priorities of local power elites. While initial opposition, as has been outlined, was entrenched and broadly cast, the latter half of the nineteenth century saw the police elevated to a 'sacred status' in British political, social and cultural life as they adopted the role of 'an all purpose emergency service upon which the local townsfolk relied when in trouble' (ibid.: 45). While serious resistance to the police service continued to be a feature among many communities and incidents of anti-police violence recurred on a regular basis, by the mid-nineteenth century police forces were established as a central feature of the landscape of the state.

perspectives on the development of the police

Reiner (2000) distinguished between orthodox and revisionist accounts of the history of the British police, and this section begins by outlining these perspectives, exploring the assumptions behind them, and suggesting that – despite the differences between them – there are important similarities in these approaches. The discussion then moves on to consider other perspectives on and interpretations of the development of policing in England and Wales. Emsley (1996: xi) offered a cautionary reminder to those seeking to explain the historical development of institutions, namely of the need to avoid the problem that 'the text can finish as a celebration of a steady progress to the present' – a warning echoed in the discussion that follows that stresses that the police service did not unfold along pre-ordained lines solely according to a plan conceived by Home Secretary Peel or by Commissioners Rowan and Mayne.

orthodox and revisionist accounts

Early accounts of the historical development of the police are primarily found in the memoirs of politicians or senior officers who were in various ways responsible for establishing policy and practice for the emerging institutions. As Emsley (1996) and Rawlings (2002) have noted, police historians such as Lee (1901), Reith (1948), Critchley (1978) and Ascoli (1979) implicitly or explicitly regard the Metropolitan Police as a beneficent legacy of far-sighted reformers such as Peel, Rowan and Mayne. The establishment of the new police is explained in terms of the inefficient system of parish constables and watchmen that was unable to respond to increasing problems of crime, especially street crime. In this respect, orthodox police histories broadly accept the rationale for the new policing arrangements that were advanced by those campaigning for reform in the first decades of the nineteenth century. As was noted earlier, the Metropolitan Police Bill was presented to Parliament as the most effective way to deal with a burgeoning crime problem. Orthodox accounts suggest that those who opposed the introduction of the Metropolitan Police, many and varied though they were, were motivated either by romantic loyalty to a system that had served well but was increasingly anachronistic or by misplaced fear that the new arrangements would drastically curtail civil liberties. As the reality of the new policing arrangements began to emerge, and their successes in reducing crime became apparent, orthodox histories suggest that critics were silenced. Reiner (2000: 19) noted that 'in the ortho-dox view, opposition to the police might have been nasty and brutish, but it was blessedly short'.

Rising crime and the apparent decreasing ability of the authorities to respond to it were attributed, by both police reformers and orthodox police historians, to the social dislocation wrought by the combined forces of indus-trialization and urbanization. The Metropolitan Police are often presented as the epitome of English pragmatic genius, whereby new constitutional arrange-ments were introduced in a way that continued principles and traditions whose pedigree was all but lost in the mists of time. Reiner (ibid.: 16) noted the tendency for orthodox accounts to read as 'jingoistic eulogies' for the police service and the introductory remarks provided by Lee (1901) and Reith (1948) ably demonstrate this, as the former noted that 'our English police system … rests on foundations designed with the full approval of the people … and has been slowly moulded by the careful hand of experience' (Lee, 1901: ix) and the latter struck a modest tone in his Preface (Reith, 1948):

> **someone suggested that I should write a brief account of the story of the police which could be made easily available to the general public and provide for foreigners answers to the innumerable, eager questions which they customarily ask, following their first experiences of the methods and behaviour of our police.**

In addition to the problems posed by street crime, orthodox histories of the police explain the establishment of the new police in terms of the need to respond to the incipient threat posed by public disorder. The impact of the 1819 'Peterloo Massacre' on public and political opinion has already been mentioned, but this was only one of a number of disturbances that suggested that the military could not provide an appropriate response. Reith (ibid.: 10) argued that urbanization meant that, from the mid-1700s onwards, it became increasingly easy for citizens to raise a mob (with an indication of the 'prospect of loot') in pursuit of their private grievances. Clearly, though, the threat of public disorder was not entirely a manifestation of lawlessness and 'mob rule' since unrest relating to a range of social and political grievances was a frequent occurrence during this period. Rawlings (2002: 110–12) argued that the practical difficulties of using the military to suppress disorders was a compounded by fears that soldiers might side with protestors and 'the mob' rather than the authorities. The use of police officers, orthodox accounts suggest, offered the prospect of a more disciplined and timely response to disorders and, as with crime more generally, the possibility of effectively preventing disturbances in the first place.

Conventional accounts suggest that the Metropolitan Police Service overcame the life-threatening public opposition that beset it during its infancy and came to be recognized, in adulthood, as an imitable model to be extended country-wide so that the constable came to embody the national character. Subsequent revisionist interpretations of police history have emphasized the enduring opposition to the police among sections of the population that have been the focus of intrusive coercion. Reiner (2000: 29) noted that police historians such as Storch (1975), Cohen (1979) and Brogden (1982) explored the lineage of opposition that endured from the early days of the Metropolitan Police, as was described in the previous section, throughout the nineteenth and the twentieth centuries. Dunning et al. (1987) showed that opposition to the police among working-class communities in the first half of the twentieth century was centred as much on efforts by constables to regulate everyday social activities – such as gambling and drinking in public places – as it was on the control or suppression of mass political activity. Underlying perspectives that draw attention to the enduring uneasy relationship between the police and marginalized communities is an explanation of the origins of the police service that also starkly diverges from orthodox accounts.

Although conventional accounts acknowledge that the role of the new police was, at least in part, to respond to heightened challenges to public order, revisionist accounts explain this in terms of the establishment's need to suppress nascent working-class activism. Much of this related to the Chartist movement in the early period of the new police, although the actual threats to public order were exacerbated by anticipation that the revolutionary fervour alive in many European countries during the 1840s and 1850s would spread to Britain (Rawlings, 2002: 162–4). Revisionist explanations of the suppression of political unrest mirror a general account that explains the development of the new police in terms of the changing demands of industrial capitalism. It was not only the police role in responding to public disorder that can be explained in terms of changing class relations but also the broader role in maintaining discipline and order among the working class more generally. From this perspective, as was suggested in Box 2.2, Storch described the police role as a 'domestic missionary' that ought to be understood in the context of other efforts to regulate the behaviour of the masses:

> **In northern industrial towns of England these police functions must be viewed as a direct complement to the attempts of urban middle-class elites – by means of Sabbath, educational, temperance, and recreational reform – to mould a labouring class amenable to new disciplines of both work and leisure. The other side of the coin of middle-class voluntaristic moral and social reform ... was the policeman's truncheon. (1976: 481)**

limits to orthodox and revisionist perspectives

The orthodox and revisionist accounts clearly have distinct theoretical foundations. Whereas the former presents the establishment of the new police as a rational and enlightened response to a growing problem of crime and lawlessness, the latter directs attention to the capacity that the police offered the state when it came to the suppression of political disorder and the regulation of the dangerous classes. Despite the clear divergence in terms of the analysis offered by orthodox and revisionist interpretations, they share a framework in that they are, as Styles (1987) described them, 'problem-response' models that see the police service as a reaction to changing social circumstances. One difficulty with historical narratives of the police service is the tendency towards a teleological account that presents each development as though it were a step towards some pre-determined final position. In practice, the police services established in the mid-nineteenth century did not always mirror the intentions of those politicians and policy-makers who legislated for them. Not only did the process of getting the various pieces of legislation through Parliament lead to negotiation and compromise over the exact role and structure of the new police forces but financial constraints meant that, in practice, the activities of the police were sometimes curtailed (Emsley, 1996). The need to recognize the multiplicity of causes is further demonstrated by Reynolds' (1998: 4) argument that local and national leaders had different reasons for extending the new policing arrangements across the country. As well as considering the complexity of the historical development of the police, this tends to be underplayed by orthodox and revisionist perspectives so it is important to consider other contributions to the process that do not relate easily to either account. Bailey (1981) provided several examples of such factors, including the transition from imposing the death sentence for many offences to the use of transportation. Since this meant that the severity of punishment for many offences decreased, it was considered important to maintain deterrence by increasing the prospect of being caught, and the new police offered greater institutional capacity to apprehend offenders. Additionally, Bailey has argued that the development of the modern police must be understood in the context of the expansion and bureaucratization of the state regulation, which meant that:

> No longer was the enforcement of the criminal law made to rely upon the private initiative of thief-takers, voluntary associations for self-protection and contractor-gaolers. Instead, the responsibility was progressively delegated to the agents of a professional police and prison system. In the realm of criminal justice, laissez-faire retreated before the imposition of a widespread apparatus of law and order. (ibid.: 11)

old wine in new bottles?

Another perspective on the historical development of the modern police service is that which stresses the continuities and similarities between the old and new arrangements. Zedner (2006) warned that while the identification of historical epochs provides a useful way of distinguishing different features of particular periods, it can be misleading since the focus tends to be on points of difference rather than continuities. A number of authors (Styles, 1987; Emsley, 1996; Reynolds, 1998) have argued that the establishment of the Metropolitan Police in 1829 represented less of a break with old policing styles than has often been assumed in both orthodox and revisionist accounts. Reynolds (1998: 162) argued that many of the working practices of the Metropolitan Police, such as the crime prevention focus, the employment of full-time officers and the bureaucratic organization – all of which are celebrated in historical accounts – actually pre-date the establishment of the 'new police'. Emsley (2003: 68) noted that the first instructions issued to police constables in 1829 detailed some of the duties that had been inherited from the old watchmen, such as powers to apprehend those suspected of criminal activity, as well as vagrants and prostitutes, and the power to demand the names of people so that they could be summoned to appear before the magistrates in connection with offences relating to the licensing laws, for example. Not only had some tasks transferred from old to new police, there was also clear continuity in personnel, since many of the officers first employed by the Metropolitan Police previously had been night watchmen or constables employed by the parishes. Moreover, Reiner (2000: 41) emphasized that the social background of officers was similar to that of those employed under the earlier arrangements. More generally, Styles (1987) explored many of the features held to distinguish the Metropolitan Police from the preceding arrangements and suggested that many of these were apparent long before the supposed watershed of 1829. That the Metropolitan Police were salaried, professional, organized, state-appointed, preventative, and uniformed did not, Styles noted, actually distinguish them from the police arrangements of the preceding decades. For example, watchmen in the eighteenth century were salaried and while they might not have been professional in terms of their training or career structure, the same could be said of the Metropolitan Police for most of its early decades. One aspect of the Metropolitan Police that literally distinguished it from its forebears was that officers were uniformed. Styles argued that it is highly significant since the distinguishing feature of the new police was that it was presented and perceived as innovative. Coupled with the efforts of the first commissioners to secure popular support by promoting the service-orientation of the new police, it seems that concerns with public opinion, legitimacy and the benefits of high visibility policing have a longer history than contemporary commentators on the police might realize.

conclusion

Whether radical or traditional, perspectives on the history of policing in Britain tend to relate the development of the Metropolitan Police Service in 1829 – a model of professional specialism that has been influential in many societies – to the changing political, economic, and social context of the period. Other perspectives suggest that concentrating on the circumstances in which the 'new police' were established detracts attention from considerable continuities in terms of personnel and activities. Moreover, many features of policing in the period before the establishment of the Metropolitan Police mirror contemporary patterns, trends and controversies. Public engagement in police work and the diverse range of agencies engaged in policing were core characteristics of the 'old' policing and, as later chapters indicate, are enduring concerns in the twenty-first century.

chapter summary

- The history of policing in England and Wales is significant since the model developed in London in the nineteenth century has influenced public policing in many parts of the world. Colonial policing systems adapted to local circumstances and so varied between themselves; nonetheless, modern public policing systems characterized by specialization and professionalism can be traced back to the establishment of the 'new police' in the form of the Metropolitan Police, created in 1829.

- Traditional histories of policing tended to be written by retired senior officers, politicians and civil servants, which partly accounts for a conservative tone that explains the development of the modern police service in terms of a natural evolution of arrangements long established in British history.

- Policing in Anglo-Saxon times was characterized by the direct involvement of ordinary people in the pursuit of offenders and the maintenance of order. The

Statute of Winchester, of 1285, provided a framework for policing that endured into the eighteenth century.

- Pre-modern policing systems became ineffective as urbanization and industrialization developed. From the mid-1700s, problems of urban lawlessness and political unrest exposed the inadequacy of established informal and non-professional policing arrangements and the use of the military to quell public disorder.

- Additionally, the cultural and political demand for order increased during this period and the role of the new police can be understood in terms of wider efforts at social reform intended to regulate what was perceived as the problematic behaviour of the lower 'dangerous' classes in the nineteenth and early twentieth centuries.

- In 1829, the Metropolitan Police was established with two Commissioners, 17 Superintendents, 69 Inspectors, 323 Sergeants and 2906 Constables. The Commissioners stressed that their officers ought to approach the public cautiously and with civility. Along with efforts to avoid the trappings of militarism, by having a blue uniform, unlike the red of the military, and a predominantly unarmed service, the service-orientation of the new police was intended to overcome public suspicion and to cultivate co-operation.

- Public opposition to the police was not abated by these measures, however. The financial burden on local Watch Committees, the inability of the police to meet new demands for public patrols, and the perceived poor quality of officers led to sustained antipathy to the Metropolitan Police. Public opprobrium was evident in the proliferation of negative epithets applied to the new police and continuing concerns about physical assaults on officers.

- Although opposition to the police has continued among significant sections of the population, from the middle of the eighteenth century anti-police feeling was overcome. As central government contributed a greater share of resources and it was perceived that the Metropolitan Police were becoming more effective in tackling crime and lawlessness, the model of the 'new police' came to be regarded as relatively successful.

- Authorities in other urban areas cited the benefits experienced in London in efforts to establish police services in other parts of England and Wales. Central government legislation and local demand meant that the 'new policing' model expanded during the mid-nineteenth century and was increasingly subject to central scrutiny, such as that provided by Her Majesty's Inspectorate of Constabulary, established in 1856.

- Orthodox accounts outline the development of policing in the nineteenth century in terms of a natural, if inspired, response to changing problems of crime and disorder and a growing realization that established arrangements were ill-suited to the emerging urban and industrial landscape. The 'genius' of the new arrangements, orthodox histories suggest, was that they incorporated long-standing traditions of local policing that reflected the demands of the public.

- Revisionist perspectives explain the development of the 'new police' as an attempt to control increasing working-class activism that emerged alongside urbanization and industrialization. The challenge that Chartism, for example, posed to established order, and concurrent concerns about the growth of revolutionary movements elsewhere in Europe, led the authorities to develop more effective means of control and suppression.

- Although reflecting different perspectives, both orthodox and revisionist accounts interpret the development of the police in terms of response to changing social conditions. Others have argued that policing developed in the nineteenth century in a piecemeal fashion and cannot be understood as the coherent or consistent expression of a particular programme.

- Another perspective notes that the tradition between traditional 'old police' and the 'new police' of the nineteenth century is less marked than many accounts have suggested. In organizational and personnel terms, and in relation to the general roles that the police were expected to fulfil, considerable continuities can be identified.

 ■ self-check questions ▬▬▬▬▬▬▬▬▬▬▬▬▬▬▬▬▬▬▬▬

1   What features characterized policing in England between the 1740s and 1850s?

2   Name the constitutional arrangement that enshrined the key features of policing from the thirteenth century until the establishment of the 'new police' in the nineteenth century.

3   To what did Sir John Fielding attribute the crime problems of the 1740s?

4   Who addressed the Chartist rally at St Peter's Field, Manchester, in 1819 that fuelled concern about using the military to control crowds?

5   How did Storch characterize the role of the police in the mid-nineteenth century?

6   What measures were introduced in an effort to overcome public suspicion of the 'new police' in the early nineteenth century?

7   What proportion of the 3000 officers recruited to the Metropolitan Police when it was established in 1829 is it estimated were still in post four years later?

8   What legislation required counties to establish a police force?

9   How do orthodox perspectives explain dissatisfaction with the use of the military to respond to political and social unrest?

10 How do revisionist accounts tend to explain the development of the 'new police'?

■ study Questions

1　What characteristics of the pre-modern police continue to inform current approaches to policing?

2　Compare and contrast the orthodox and revisionist accounts of police history.

3　In what terms have both the orthodox and revisionist accounts been criticized?

■ ■ annotated further reading ■

Reiner's (2000) *Politics of the Police* has been a hugely influential book exploring perspectives on the development of policing, analyzing the myths and realities associated with the 'golden age' of policing in Britain in the post-war period, and the politics of law and order. Part 1 of the book provides an account of the foundation and development of the police service. Reiner argues that legitimacy was established because the service operated bureaucratically, according to the rule of law, with a strategy of minimal force and non-partisanship, with accountability, performed a service role, sought to prevent crime problems, and was relatively effective. He also argues that the 'golden age' that was achieved in the post-Second World War period was partly related to the broader context of the welfare state and consensus politics.

Rawlings' (2002) *Policing: A Short History* outlines and analyzes the history of the police service from the Anglo-Saxon period until the end of the twentieth century. While examining the ways in which policing arrangements have developed in relation to wider patterns of social change, the book also makes clear that some contemporary concerns, for example, about the criminalization of the poor and the role of private security firms, are very long-standing indeed.

; // annotated listings of links to relevant websites /

The Metropolitan Police website contains useful resources relating to the development of the modern police service, including a timeline of key developments from 1829 to the present day (http://www.met.police.uk/history/index.htm).

An article by Chris Williams ('Britain's Police Forces: Forever Removed from Democratic Control?') examines tension between the principles of local control and the direction of the police service by central government. Williams argues that contemporary debates about central and local direction, considered at greater length in Chapter 6, can be traced back to the nineteenth century. His article is available at the History and Policy website (http://tinyurl.com/29frbm).

James Sharpe examines the history of crime in the centuries before the establishment of the 'new police' and the apparent decreasing effectiveness of the 'old police' to respond to emerging challenges. His paper, 'The History of Crime in England, 1550–1914', can be found at http://tinyurl.com/2ys5hy.

3

Police powers:
The legal framework

Contents

A common response to real or imagined threats from criminals, terrorists or those committing antisocial behaviour is that the police, courts, and criminal justice system in general need to be given new powers in order to provide an effective response to novel and emerging challenges. In November 2005, during an unsuccessful attempt to extend to 90 days the period that terrorist suspects could be held by the police without charge, the Prime Minister defended his efforts by arguing that his responsibility was to listen to the views of senior police officers and then to grant them the powers that they claimed necessary to fulfil their role. Prime Minister Blair told the House of Commons:

> We are not living in a police state, but we are living in a country that faces a real and serious threat of terrorism – terrorism that wants to destroy our way of life, terrorism that wants to inflict casualties on us without limit – and when those charged with protecting our country provide, as they have, a compelling case for action, I know what my duty is: my duty is to support them, and so is the duty, in my view, of every Member. (Hansard, 2005)

Similarly, the introduction of antisocial behaviour orders in the 1998 Crime and Disorder Act, which provided the police with the capacity to use civil orders in response to incivilities, was justified on the grounds that the police and the criminal justice system needed enhanced powers to respond to new challenges. Although the suggestion that the police can more effectively fulfil their role if they have improved legal powers seems no more than common sense and might have some appeal to the police service and to politicians eager to establish their law and order credentials, the link between the two is far from straightforward. With this in mind, this chapter aims to do the following:

- to examine the development and consolidation of police powers into the 1984 Police and Criminal Evidence Act;

- to outline police powers in respect of stop and search; entry, search and seizure; arrest; detention; questioning and treatment; documentary evidence in criminal proceedings; complaints and discipline, and other matters;

- to demonstrate that police powers derive from much more than the legal frameworks that stipulate what officers can, and cannot, do. The institutional and political power of the service also shapes the role of the police.

key terms

arrests; citizens' arrest; Criminal Justice and Public Order Act 1994; institutional and symbolic power of police; the Judges' Rules; Police and Criminal Evidence Act 1984; police custody; rights of suspects; stop and search; Terrorism Act 2000; warrants

Parliamentary interest in the powers of the police is a relatively recent phenom-enon; for most of their history the powers of British police officers have remained ill-defined in legal terms. In part, this seems to have been a reflection of the wider tendency to conceptualize the police constable as nothing more than the 'citizen in uniform' that has been integral to the process of legitimating the police service. Since the officer was of equal standing to the ordinary citizen, it was not considered necessary to grant the police extraordinary legal powers that would differentiate constables from the rest of the community. Leigh noted that the tradition had been that the 'constable's duties were wide, but his powers were limited' (1985: 5), while Commissioner of the Metropolitan Police from 1972 to 1977, Sir Robert Mark had suggested that the only power the police had over the ordinary citizen was the power to inconvenience them (Judge, 1986: 175). The 1929 Royal Commission on Police Powers and Procedure explained the relative silence of Britain's unwritten constitution on the topic of police power in the following terms:

> **The police of this country have never been recognized, either by the law or by tradition, as a force distinct from the general body of citizens. Despite the imposition of many extraneous duties on the police by legislation or adminis-trative action, the principle remains that the policeman, in the view of the common law, is only a person paid to perform, as a matter of duty, acts which if he were so minded he might have done voluntarily ... Indeed a policeman possesses few powers not enjoyed by the ordinary citizen, and public opinion, expressed in Parliament and elsewhere, has shown great jealousy of any attempts to give increased authority to the police. (Robillard and McEwan, 1986: 2)**

This chapter explores the ways in which the powers of the British police service have been developed and increasingly codified since the last decades of the twentieth century. In particular, some of the provisions of the 1984 Police and Criminal Evidence Act (PACE), which continues to provide the frame-work from which many police powers are derived, are outlined. Following on from this review of some key police powers, the chapter moves on to consider the broader context of debates about the legal powers of the police. It is suggested that there are various reasons why the 'black letter of the law' provides only a weak explanation of what the police service actually does and, furthermore, that much of the real power of the police derives not from the statute books but from the institutional and political framework in which the service operates. In this sense the concept of police 'power' needs to be consid-ered in more complex and nuanced terms.

In keeping with the conception of the constable as a 'citizen in uniform', police powers have remained uncodified and developed only in a piecemeal fashion on the basis of case law. Prior to the 1984 Police and Criminal Evidence Act (PACE), police powers were derived from individual pieces of legislation, Home Office directives, case law, and the 'Judges' Rules' – introduced in 1912 to govern the treatment of those held in police custody. In legal terms, police constables are independent officers of the Crown – rather than employees – with personal discretion in terms of when, where and how they enforce the law. Although accountable to senior officers and the local police authority, constables cannot be given direct orders in relation to the application of the law. Since officers are not technically employees, they cannot be dismissed, unless they are in breach of specific disciplinary rules, and are subject to various legal obligations that extend into their private lives in ways that do not apply to conventional employees. On this basis, the police regulations issued by the Home Office in 1952 stipulated that 'every constable must devote his whole time to the police service' and required that chief officers' permission be granted if a constable resided at premises where a business was conducted by family members. More recently the requirement that officers refrain from activity 'likely to interfere with the impartial discharge of his duties or which is likely to give rise to the impression amongst members of the public that it may so interfere', as the regulations put it, has been used to prohibit officers joining extremist political parties such as the British National Party (ACPO, 2003).

The powers that police officers have, over and above those available to the ordinary citizen, were, until the 1980s, derived from individual pieces of legislation. One implication of this was that the powers available to officers were neither clearly defined nor consistent across the country. For example, the 1824 Vagrancy Act, which predated the establishment of the Metropolitan Police, gave constables in London powers to stop and search people in the streets but these did not extend to all officers in other parts of the country. However, officers in some other cities had similar powers, as granted, for example, by the 1921 Liverpool Corporation Act or the 1944 Manchester Police Act. Although legislation such as the 1968 Firearms Act and the 1971 Misuse of Drugs Act gave powers to search people in particular circumstances, there was no general law that gave the police power to search for offensive weapons or stolen goods. It was in response to a series of public scandals that the 1984 Police and Criminal Evidence Act was introduced, replacing the Judges' Rules (Box 3.1) that had guided police behaviour for decades.

Box 3.1

The Judges' Rules

For many years it had been apparent that stipulations in the Judges' Rules, for example to provide legal advice to people in custody, were often regarded by officers as advisory rather than binding. Zander (2003) argued that this disregard for the Judges' Rules might have stemmed from the arbitrary and isolated manner in which they were developed, a process from which the police had been excluded. Additionally, Judge (1986) noted that the non-statutory nature of the Rules also undermined their status among police officers who sometimes felt they were inimical to the investigation process. The particular circumstances by which the Judges' Rules were replaced stemmed from the wrongful imprisonment of three boys who had falsely confessed to the 1972 murder of Maxwell Confait. An inquiry into the episode found that the youths had been denied the right to legal advice, improperly questioned, and that there had been improprieties in the charging process (Reiner, 2000: 65). The report also found that officers had been unaware of what was required of them under the Judges' Rules and recommended that a Royal Commission be established to consider further reforms (ibid. 65). The subsequent Royal Commission on Criminal Procedure was established in 1978 with a brief to strike the appropriate balance between promoting the interests of the public by prosecuting offenders and protecting the rights of those suspected or accused of an offence.

police power vs the rights of the suspect

Although there was a case for creating a single statutory basis for police powers as an exercise in good legal and administrative housekeeping, the proposals contained in the Police and Criminal Evidence Bill 1982 generated huge controversy. The passage of the Bill was delayed by a general election but was eventually enacted as the 1984 Police and Criminal Evidence Act. Described by Reiner (2000: 176) as 'the single most significant landmark in the modern development of police powers', most of the provisions of the Act took effect from 1986. Opposition to the Act came from two distinct camps. Essentially a 'law and order' lobby welcomed the extension of police powers contained within the Act, but argued that establishing a statutory framework of rights for those in custody would erode the power of the police and weigh the scales of justice too far in the interests of suspects. Former Metropolitan Police Commissioner Sir David McNee, for example, claimed that the new regulations concerning the interviewing of suspects in custody 'gives virtually no assistance to police and every assistance to a suspect wishing to hide his guilt' (Koffman, 1985: 12). The Chief Constable of Merseyside, Kenneth Oxford, represented ACPO during **consultations** over the Bill, and argued that it was a widely misunderstood piece of legislation and that those aspects of PACE that extended police powers effectively did little more than codify prevailing police practices into law. However, Oxford argued that those parts of the Act relating to police treatment of suspects in custody were cause for concern and that 'I and my fellow chief constables feel the balance has been tipped too far in favour of the wrongdoers against the interests of the law-abiding citizen and an effective police service' (1986: 68).

In the other camp were those who opposed the extensions of police power contained in the Bill and doubted that the accompanying procedural safeguards would be meaningful in practice. Opposition was raised to the extension of police powers in terms of stopping and searching individuals, taking fingerprints and other 'non-intimate' samples, and searching premises. Often these critics argued that the provisions were a pernicious step on a path towards the paramilitarization of the police service. Lea and Young (1993: 254) argued that the measures amounted to 'a draconian increase in police powers, in precisely those areas of activity which feature heavily in military policing'. Baxter and Koffman (1985) noted that the type of defence mounted by Oxford, as described above, was worrying since the implication that PACE simply encoded existing practices was a tacit admission that the police had been acting beyond the law in the first instance. They suggested that PACE heralded a fundamental shift in the paradigm of policing:

> **The Police and Criminal Evidence Act 1984 has now officially provided a substantial increase in intrusive, confrontation-oriented powers and it is an indication of how our society is to be policed in the future. The new mode of policing is by coercion, and not by public consent. (ibid.:1)**

PACE in practice

From a vantage point more than twenty years after the Act took effect, neither set of objections appears to have been borne out by experience. Although various concerns have emerged about the extent to which the Act has proved effective, there is little evidence that the Act has hampered the ability of the police to go about their duties; indeed, some of the provisions required by the Act, for example to tape-record interviews with suspects, have come to be valued by officers who find it in their interests to have an objective record of their interrogation. While concerns continue to be expressed about the impact that police stop-and-search procedures have had upon some sections of the community, these tend to relate to the manner in which officers interact with the public, rather than the legal powers at their disposal (Stone and Pettigrew, 2000). Morgan and Newburn (1997: 51–2) argued that 'there is absolutely no doubt that the legislation has, in a number of vital respects, had a significant impact on the behaviour of the police and on the culture of policing'.

PACE has had an impact in a number of ways. First, the Act itself provides a clear framework for police powers in relation to individual citizens in respect of the following key areas, each of which form separate sections of the Act:

- stop and search;
- entry, search and seizure;
- arrest;
- detention;
- questioning and treatment;
- documentary evidence in criminal proceedings;
- complaints and discipline;
- other miscellaneous matters.

The following paragraphs detail some of the key police powers defined by PACE. By no means do they amount to an exhaustive, or legally definitive, account of police powers. Such a task is very effectively performed by Zander's (2005) analysis of the legal nuances relating to powers granted to the police by PACE. In more general terms, recent texts by English and Card (2006) and by Jason-Lloyd (2005) provide excellent reviews of police powers, including but not limited to those established by PACE. Instead, general principles relating to police powers regarding stop and search, entry, search and seizure, arrest, and the treatment of those in custody are outlined.

PACE powers to stop and search

Section 1 of PACE authorizes the stop and search of a person or a vehicle for stolen or prohibited articles if a constable has 'reasonable suspicion' for suspecting that such items will be found. These powers apply in any public place, which is defined as a place to which the public has access rather than in terms of strict legal ownership of land. The Code of Practice (see Box 3.2) that provides more detailed advice stipulates what constitutes 'reasonable' in this context and makes it clear that there must be some objective basis for the stop and search. Information or a description received from a witness to a crime or a person being seen to act covertly or warily might be grounds for reasonable suspicion but this can never be justified purely on the grounds of personal appearance. While the Code stipulates that age, ethnicity, or hairstyle do not provide reasonable grounds for a stop and search, this might be ambiguous in practice as the Code also states that an individual dressed in a style associated with a gang that is known to be involved in criminal activity might be reasonably stopped on that basis.

Box 3.2

Extract from PACE Code A

Principles Governing Stop and Search

1.1 Powers to stop and search must be used fairly, responsibly, with respect for people being searched and without unlawful discrimination. The Race Relations (Amendment) Act 2000 makes it unlawful for police officers to discriminate on the grounds of race, colour, ethnic origin, nationality or national origins when using their powers.

1.2 The intrusion on the liberty of the person stopped or searched must be brief and detention for the purposes of a search must take place at or near the location of the stop.

1.3 If these fundamental principles are not observed the use of powers to stop and search may be drawn into question. Failure to use the powers in the proper manner reduces

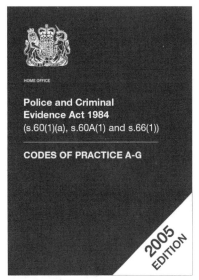

HOME OFFICE

Police and Criminal Evidence Act 1984
(s.60(1)(a), s.60A(1) and s.66(1))

CODES OF PRACTICE A-G

2005 EDITION

their effectiveness. Stop and search can play an important role in the detection and prevention of crime, and using the powers fairly makes them more effective.

1.4 The primary purpose of stop and search powers is to enable officers to allay or confirm suspicions about individuals without exercising their power of **arrest**. Officers may be required to justify the use or authorisation of such powers, in relation both to individual searches and the overall pattern of their activity in this regard, to their supervisory officers or in court. Any misuse of the powers is likely to be harmful to policing and lead to mistrust of the police. Officers must also be able to explain their actions to the member of the public searched. The misuse of these powers can lead to disciplinary action.

1.5 An officer must not search a person, even with his or her **consent**, where no power to search is applicable. Even where a person is prepared to submit to a search voluntarily, the person must not be searched unless the necessary legal power exists, and the search must be in accordance with the relevant power and the provisions of this Code. The only exception, where an officer does not require a specific power, applies to searches of persons entering sports grounds or other premises carried out with their **consent** given as a condition of entry.

The powers extend to any vehicle, including aircraft, and to any items contained within the vehicle. Stolen or prohibited articles are defined in particular terms in the Codes of Practice. Stolen items include those being handled by the person stopped, even if they were not actually stolen by that person. Prohibited articles fall into two main categories: those that are offensive weapons of some kind, and those that might be used for the commission of a criminal act. Offensive weapons fall into three categories. First, those items that are specifically designed for this purpose, such as a flick knife or a cosh. Second are articles that might not be designed to be offensive weapons but that have been adapted in some way for that purpose such as, for example, a screwdriver that has been sharpened. Third is the potentially very wide category of any item that is intended to be used as an offensive weapon, which could, of course, include everyday items that could, if so intended, be used in a violent manner.

Section 1 of the Act outlines that these powers are available to officers:

> **(a) In any place to which at the time when he proposes to exercise the power the public or any section of the public has access, on payment or otherwise, as of right or by virtue of express or implies permission, or**
>
> **(b) in any other place to which people have ready access at the time when he proposes to exercise the power but which is not a dwelling.**

In these terms, public space is defined broadly in relation to the nature and extent of public access, rather than in terms of property ownership. A football ground, for example, maybe privately owned but, since the public have access to it, even though they are required to pay for the privilege, it constitutes a public place under the terms of the Act. By referring to public places as those to which people have 'ready access', it is not necessary that people have a legal right to be present, merely that the place is readily accessible, which means that those trespassing on private land are liable to be stopped and searched. While the Act expressly limits the powers to spaces that are not dwellings, it stipulates that those whom the officer believes are not residents of the property and do not have permission, even if only implicit, to be on the property are susceptible to being stopped and searched. The Act does not give the police power to stop and search people on their own private land.

It should be noted that the tendency to talk about 'stop and search' in unitary terms is somewhat misleading, since there is a distinction between the two in the Act and associated Codes of Practice. While an officer needs reasonable suspicion to stop an individual in order to conduct a search, they must not do so until the person stopped has been questioned and given an opportunity to explain their behaviour or presence in the area. The response to these questions might confirm the officer's suspicion or reveal grounds to believe that the person is in possession of other types of prohibitive items. In either case the person stopped can then be searched. Alternatively, though, the explanation might be credible and the person eliminated from the investigation. If the officer decides that a search is necessary, then this must be carried out at or nearby the place where the person was stopped. While consent ought to be sought for the search, force can be used if this is not given or if the person resists. The search should be restricted, the Code of Practice stipulates, to a 'superficial examination of outerclothing' and a constable is only permitted to require the removal of outer garments, jackets and gloves. It is permissible for an officer to search inside pockets, feel inside collars or cuffs, socks and shoes but any more intimate search many only be conducted away from the public space in a police van or at a police station. More intimate searches must only be conducted by officers of the same sex as the person stopped and no-one of the opposite sex is allowed in the vicinity unless specifically requested by the member of the public.

PACE required from its inception that officers make a record of all stops and searches at the time that they were made unless it were 'wholly impracticable' to do so. In such circumstances the officer must make a record as soon as is possible afterwards. More recently, in 2003, the Code of Practice was amended such that the person stopped ought to be provided with a copy of this record, in order to promote public confidence in the integrity and transparency of the stop and search powers of the police. The record ought to contain the name, address and date of birth of the person being stopped – although there is no obligation that the individual stopped disclose these to the officer – the person's self-defined ethnic origin, the details of any vehicle involved, the date, time and place of the stop, the purpose of the stop, the grounds for making it, and the identity of the officer involved. As Zander (2003: 19–20) noted, proposals contained in the Macpherson Inquiry Report into the death of Stephen Lawrence led the Home Office to consider extending the require-ment for officers to issue records of PACE stop and searches to all stops under legislative provisions, including those of a voluntary nature. Concerns were expressed that such a requirement would disproportionately increase bureau-cracy and would discourage routine informal interactions between police and public. Following a period during which the proposed requirements were piloted in seven forces, the Codes of Practice were amended so that officers do not have to provide a record of 'general conversations' with members of the public, even if these are connected with gathering background information to criminal offences. However, in other situations, even if not as formal as a PACE stop and search, where officers require an individual to account for themselves, a record must be provided.

additional powers to stop and search

While PACE was intended to consolidate earlier legislation relating to stop and search, there have been subsequent pieces of legislation that have given additional powers. Among the most high profile of these have been the Criminal Justice and Public Order Act (CJPOA) of 1994 and the Terrorism

Act 2000 (TA). Section 60 of the CJPOA permits senior officers to authorize officers to search anyone present in a designated place where it is reasonably anticipated that incidents involving serious violence may take place. The Act explicitly states that this means that an officer can stop any person or vehicle within the area whether or not there is reasonable suspicion that they are carrying a prohibited weapon or might be intent on violent activity. The removal of the requirement for reasonable suspicion is a significant break with the PACE framework and was originally introduced to deal with public order situations where, it was argued, this had been a major impediment to the police (Jason-Lloyd, 2005: 47). Although these powers are only available to officers under certain circumstances, since they must be authorized by an Inspector, and subsequently ratified by a Superintendent, and can only apply for a period of 24 hours, subject to one extension of a further 24 hours, they do appear to offer officers very broad grounds to conduct stop and searches outwith the framework of checks and balances introduced by PACE. While it might be that these provisions prove useful in the context of public order events, such as a football match at which there is intelligence to suggest a known gang of hooligans intends to provoke violence, concerns have been expressed that these powers have become part of the routine policing of town and city centres and that increasing numbers of people are being subject to stop and search procedure where the test of 'reasonable' suspicion has not been met (Rowe, 2004: 95–6).

Similarly Sections 44, 45, and 46 of the Terrorism Act 2000 allows for stop and search of people and vehicles to be authorized by an officer above the rank of Assistant Chief Constable in a given area for a limited period. These stops must be conducted for the purposes of uncovering items connected with a terrorist attack and the authorization can only be given if there is specific intelligence or information to suggest that a terrorist attack is planned in the area concerned. The Home Secretary must be informed that such authority has been given and can decrease the time period for which the authority is granted. The code of practice governing the Act stipulates that care should be taken not to unnecessarily target these powers against those of a specific ethnic background, although this warning becomes somewhat ambiguous as the code also points out that certain terrorist activity is associated with particular ethnic groups and so there might be circumstances in which ethnic profiling is an appropriate basis to stop and search under the Act (English and Card, 2005: 45).

PACE powers of entry, search and seizure

The police powers to search outlined above apply only to public places. The powers to enter private property are outlined in Sections 8, 17, 18 and 32 of

PACE. Police enter private property either with a warrant issued by a magistrate or, under specified circumstances, without a warrant. Other legislation also allows the police to enter premises: the 1971 Misuse of Drugs Act, for example, grants officers power to enter the business premises of someone who produces or supplies controlled drugs to examine records and stocks; the 1988 Road Traffic Act affords officers the power to enter premises to take a breath test following an accident that has led to personal injury (Jason-Lloyd, 2005: 95). The PACE provisions stipulate that a magistrate can issue a warrant granting an officer the power to enter premises if it is not possible to gain entry with consent. A warrant is issued to enable officers to look for material relating to a serious arrestable offence which is likely to be of substantial value to the investigation and be relevant evidence. Certain items are identified as legally privileged and so cannot be included in such searches, for example communication between a client and professional legal advisor. Further items, including journalistic documents, medical records, items held in confidence for business purposes, are treated as either 'excluded material' or 'special procedure material' and cannot be searched under the a general warrant, although other authorization can be sought to search these. In addition to identifying materials not included by search warrants, PACE introduced other safeguards in terms of the steps that officers must take when making an application to the magistrate. It is required that the police identify the nature of the evidence that they expect to find, and the crime(s) to which it may relate. If the premises are multi-occupancy, then only those parts relating to the individual identified in the warrant may be searched. The code of practice issued under the terms of PACE makes detailed stipulation about the conduct of searches, for example that questions asked during the process must relate to the conduct of the search itself and must not become an interview about the alleged offence (Zander, 2003: 67). While force may be used to gain entry, this must only be done when and to the extent necessary.

_____ other powers of entry _____

Additionally, the police continue to have a wide range of powers of entry that do not require a warrant. Section 17 of PACE covers powers of entry for the purposes of executing a warrant for arrest, arresting someone for committing an arrestable offence, arresting a youth or child remanded to local authority care, recapturing someone who is unlawfully at large, or to 'save life or limb' or prevent serious damage to property. In addition, police officers have common law powers to enter property to prevent or respond to a breach of the peace. Officers must give an explanation of why they are entering a property, unless it would be 'impossible, impractical or undersirable' to do so (English and Card, 2005: 76). Officers must have reasonable grounds to believe that the person they are seeking is at the property and, if the property is multi-occupancy then the officer(s) can only enter those parts where the person may be.

Section 18 of PACE grants powers to enter premises of any person arrested for an arrestable offence if it is believed that a search of the premises would reveal material related to that offence, or one similar to it. Searching the home of someone arrested for burglary in order to find stolen goods or proceeds from burglaries, for example, is permitted but a search for drugs (unrelated to the burglary) would not be (ibid.: 77). These searches must be authorized by an Inspector and the basis for the search must be explained to the occupier of the property. The same conditions apply to the searches of multiple occupancy premises as outlined in relation to Section 17 searches. Further powers of entry and search are provided by Section 32 of PACE, which stipulates that officers might, after making an arrest, enter and search the premises where the person was immediately before or when they were arrested. Such action can only be taken if it is reasonably believed that evidence of the offence for which the arrest was made will be found. As with all of the provisions described here, the term 'premises' has been interpreted very widely by the courts (Zander, 2003).

_____ police powers of arrest _____

Again, a legal distinction is made between arrests carried out as a result of a warrant and those made without warrant. Section 24 of PACE outlines officers powers of arrest for 'arrestable offences', of which there are three categories, as outlined in Box 3.3.

Box 3.3

Police powers of arrest

Police officers can arrest without a warrant in circumstances relating to:

- offences for which the punishment is fixed by law; currently only the offence of murder falls into this category;
- offences for which a convicted person over the age of 18, who has no previous convictions, would be liable for a sentence greater than five years' imprisonment – this category includes a large number of offences, such as theft, burglary, assault, robbery, indecent assault and common law offences such as kidnapping and attempting to pervert the course of justice (Zander, 2003: 95);
- a miscellaneous list of offences that, although not punished with a sentence greater than five years, are considered serious in some aspect, including acts criminalised by the Wireless Telegraphy Act of 1949, the 1981 Wildlife and Countryside Act, the Football (Offences) Act 1991, and the Sexual Offences Act 2003 (Jason-Lloyd, 2005: 64–8).

An arrest can be legally made by any person, police officer or otherwise, who reasonably believes that an offence in one of these three categories is in the process of being committed. The key to the legality of an arrest in such circumstances is the reasonable belief that an offence is being committed, even if it turns out not to be the case. In circumstances where an arrestable offence has already been committed, any person can make a lawful arrest of the guilty offender. However, unlike a situation in which a crime is in progress, in these circumstances if a person is subsequently acquitted of the alleged offence then the arrest itself is rendered illegal if carried out by a member of the public other than a police officer. As English and Card (2005: 60) point out, it is reasonable for the law to allow a private citizen to intervene and arrest an offender in the act of committing a crime – even if only on the basis of reasonable belief that the person is committing an offence, but a 'citizen's arrest' under other circumstances is hazardous as compensation for wrongful arrest might be claimed. While PACE only gives police officers, not ordinary citizens, power to arrest to prevent an arrestable offence from being committed, other legislation, namely the 1967 Criminal Law Act, gives anyone the right to intervene using reasonable force to prevent crime or lawfully arrest an offender (Jason-Lloyd, 2005: 70–1).

The police do not have direct power of arrest for offences not classified as 'arrestable'; instead these – usually more minor – offences ought to be dealt with by reporting them and summoning the suspected person to court. However, Section 25 of PACE outlines some general conditions of arrest that mean that, if an officer is unable to obtain a reliable name and address of the person suspected of committing such an offence, an arrest might be made. The same section of the Act also allows for a person to be arrested in order to prevent them causing harm to themselves or to prevent damage to property.

Only a minority of arrests are made under the terms of a warrant issued by a magistrate and these are issued in only limited circumstances, such as when the identity of an offender is known but the person cannot be located or when an individual has failed to attend court in response to a summons (ibid.: 85). Once a warrant has been issued, it remains in force until it is executed, which can be done by any police officer and by civilian enforcement officers. Since 2004, arrest warrants issued in certain other EU countries can be enforced in the United Kingdom (English and Card, 2005: 22).

For an arrest to be legal, certain procedures must be followed by the police. Prime among these is the need to inform the person of the grounds for their arrest immediately or as soon as is practicably possible. Section 28 of PACE outlines these requirements, which are a long-standing feature of common law. Handcuffs or other means of restraint must only be used if there is reason to believe that the person arrested is likely to use violence or to escape. The person must be issued with a caution, although minor deviation from it does not render the arrest illegal (see Box 3.4).

Box 3.4

The police caution

You do not have to say anything. But it may harm your defence if you do not mention when questioned something which you later rely on in court. Anything you do say may be given in evidence.

Following arrest, a person must be taken to a 'designated police station', essentially one that has the necessary facilities to keep people in custody, immediately. In areas where there is not a designated police station in the immediate vicinity, then the person can be held for up to six hours before being taken to such a station. In the following section the powers of the police during the detention process are outlined.

police powers of detention

Concern about police abuse of the Judges' Rules that had lightly regulated police behaviour in relation to those held in custody was a central factor in the development of the provisions enacted by PACE. The safeguards introduced from 1986, when PACE came into force, were often cited as demonstration that the abuses of police power revealed by miscarriage of justice cases uncovered in the 1980s were historical remnants of police malpractice impossible in the contemporary period, a claim that does not entirely bear scrutiny (Reiner, 2000: 66–7).

One of the main innovations introduced by PACE is the role of custody officer, who has legal responsibility for keeping people in custody, ensuring that their rights are safeguarded, and for the eventual release of the person, whether they are remanded in custody, or released on bail or unconditionally. Formally, the custody officer has to decide if there is sufficient evidence to justify a charge against a person who has been arrested and brought to a police station, although the **Crown Prosecution Service** is ultimately responsible for prosecuting cases. In practice, individuals are seldom charged immediately upon arrival at the police station and it is more usual for the custody officer to book an individual into custody so that they can be subject to further interview (Zander, 2003: 123–4). Although PACE stipulates that the detention of a person is only legal if it is necessary to allow further enquiries to be made, for example to prevent that person from destroying evidence or interfering with witnesses, in practice it seems likely that custody officers authorize detention at a lower threshold in circumstances where it makes the process of investigation more straightforward (ibid.: 124). As part of this booking-in process the custody officer is required to advise the person of their right to legal advice and to make a phone call to allow someone to be informed of their arrest. The custody officer records and takes charge of the personal property of a person when they are booked into custody. If the person is under 16, or has special needs of some kind, then it is up to the custody officer to see that an 'appropriate adult' is brought in to represent the interests of that person. Additionally, the custody officer completes a risk assessment of each person, asking them questions about any problems that they have with drugs or alcohol, and assessing if they are likely to harm themselves. The custody officer is responsible for ensuring that a detailed record is kept of decisions applying to each person detained, including those relating to the periodic review of the basis of their detention that should be completed every six to nine hours.

Although the Judges' Rules had stipulated that private legal advice should be made available to anyone taken into custody, it was widely accepted that this principle was neither well known nor frequently practised. PACE stipulates that free legal advice be made available to anyone in custody at any time, and that such advice ought to be communicated in private. A duty solicitor scheme operates such that advice is available, perhaps via telephone, at all times, although the quality of legal advice provided in this way has been cause for concern (ibid.: 187). Delaying the person's access to legal advice is only permitted in relation to serious crimes and with the authorization of a Superintendent if there are reasonable grounds for believing that informing a solicitor that the person is in custody would serve to alert others who might be implicated in the crime, would harm relevant evidence, or would allow the disposal of proceeds arising from the offence. Other changes introduced by PACE include the tape, or more recently video, recording of police interviews, and the stipulation of the ways in which interviews must be conducted. PACE also requires that those in custody are given proper periods of rest, and are provided with regular meals. Clearly many of these provisions have been introduced to ensure that police powers are not disproportionate to individuals' rights and the broader interests of justice. As was noted earlier, many objections to PACE suggested that these requirements would tip the balance too far in the interests of the suspect and would hamper the police fight against crime.

A cartoon published in *Police* magazine in March 1984 showed two harassed officers trying to complete a mountain of paperwork while overlooked by a collection of stereotypes, including a bowler-hatted bureaucrat, a doctor, and a social worker. In the corner a waiter is laying a table opposite a comfortable sofa and slippers, in anticipation of the arrival of the prisoner. Overlooking the whole scene, from a balcony, are ten lay visitors, one of whom is equipped with binoculars! Such nightmares of a politically correct future have not been borne out, and it is notable that, as Morgan and Newburn (1997) and Dixon (1997) have stated, some of the provisions that were greeted with suspicion have come to be accepted as routine practice. The value of recording interviews has come to be recognized by many in the police service since it has reduced arguments in court about what was said by whom and in what way (Reiner, 2000: 180). Interestingly, when proposals were introduced in 2005, following recommendations of a review of PACE, to civilianize the role of the custody sergeant, many of those in the police service argued that this post was of central importance to the effectiveness and credibility of the service and could only be performed by experienced officers. The 2006 Serious and Organised Crime Act over-rode these objections and allowed civilians to perform this role. It is interesting that many voices within the police service opposed the ways in which PACE changed the role of the custody sergeant and then, twenty years later, defended the office as central to the whole business of policing and this illustrates that the experience of PACE has been more complex than was imagined by those involved in the vociferous debates that greeted its introduction.

police power: the wider context

The previous paragraphs have reviewed various police powers in relatively narrow legal terms. There are several reasons for believing, however, that these provide only a weak indication of what the police service actually does. Not only is this because the majority of police work is not related to law enforcement, as Chapter 1 made clear, or because police officers do not abide by these legal requirements, although sometimes that is the case, as Reiner's (2000: 173) 'law of inevitable increment – whatever powers the police have, they will exceed by a given margin' attests. In addition, the statute books only reveal a partial picture of police powers. As the following discussion demonstrates, the notion of 'police powers' needs to be considered in more nuanced terms because power is derived from many sources other than the law and many of the legal powers given to the police have come to encompass other agencies.

That policing is about more than the activities of the police service was firmly established in Chapter 1, and a recurring theme of this book is to explore the range of agencies, public and private sector, that contribute in various ways to policing in this broad sense. Related processes of social transformation and political reform have meant that policing is now a fragmented activity, provided for by different actors at different levels and in different places. The diversity or plurality of policing, as Johnston (2000) has argued, is inextricably linked to changing practices and processes of governance, whereby central government rules 'at a distance' via complex networks and coalitions of state, private and civil partnerships. Against this background the policing 'family' has been extended in Britain (for more details see Chapter 8) and some of the powers detailed in the previous section have been granted, in full or part, to civilians within the police service or to other agencies altogether. Not only have some police powers, for example those relating to detention, been partially extended to civilians within the police service, such as Police Community Support Officers and civilian investigating officers, but also to other agencies altogether. Social landlords, for example, many of whom exist within civil society, have been given certain powers to issue Fixed Penalty Notices. The granting of formal powers more widely across a network of agencies complements structural transformations in the nature of space which have meant that the powers of the public police have become relatively marginal to the practices of policing because the private sector explicitly has assumed a more central place in process of social regulation. Although, as was seen in much of the earlier discussion, PACE provisions mean that the legal powers of the police service tend to apply to places defined as public in terms of access rather than ownership, increasingly, private security regimes are acting as gatekeepers and regulators of large swathes of land in urban areas and so assume greater significance in the routine organization of social life that bears little relation to the specific individual powers of police officers (Wakefield, 2004; Coleman et al., 2005).

Not only does consideration of police power need to address the implications of extending legal provisions to a wide range of agencies, it must also be noted that only a proportion of what the public police service does is related to their formal statutory powers. Chapter 1 noted David Bayley's comparative analysis which led him to the estimate that only between 7 and 10 per cent of routine police work is related to crime, which suggests that formal legal powers of the type described in previous paragraphs are only even notionally significant a small proportion of the time (Bayley, 1994). A focus on the legal framework of police powers reflects a jurisprudential approach to policing that fails to address the cultural and sociological determinants of police practice. Central to a proper understanding of policing are the informal skills associated with the negotiation of complexities and contradictions of human relations. Although it might not be immediately apparent that the persuasive skills of a police officer, for example, to convince a member of the public to behave in a certain manner is related to the specific power granted by the law to that officer, the more that power is understood in broad and complex terms, the more it becomes clear that it infuses all policework. The legal and constitutional position afforded to the police officer is but a very narrow element of that officer's power. As a plethora of social theorists have argued, power must be conceived as a relatively elusive and multi-faceted construct. While legal frameworks such as that laid down by PACE might mean that the police ought to operate on the basis of consent and only invoke more formal legal powers where to do so is unavoidable, it is clear that even the most consensual of interactions between police officer and citizen unfolds against a background of power dynamics. One reason why it is important to preserve the legitimacy of the police service is that this helps to invest the individual officer with the authority that makes it easier to perform routine duties. Such authority becomes a resource that officers can use in the 'production of intended effects', which is how Bertrand Russell defined power (Barry 1981: 80). On a micro-level, officers have other related resources at their disposal that provide additional opportunities to exercise power. The organizational and logistical possibilities provided by the communication systems and resources at their disposal also amount to another source of power, since these enhance the coercive potential of the individual officer and the police service as an organization. The constable politely requesting that a street corner beggar 'moves on' does so in the knowledge that both parties are aware that this may be an offer that cannot be refused!

These informal and non-statutory powers available to individual police officers reflect other forms of power that accrue to the police service institutionally. As theorists such as Foucault (1981), Lukes (1974) and Bourdieu (1991) have argued, power is also constituted by the ability to shape knowledge and discourse and so influence subjective readings of the world. Much of the power of the police service institutionally stems from their status and ability to provide authoritative narratives on a wide range of social issues, most particularly those relating to crime, disorder and social conflict but, inter alia, family structure, personal morality, sexuality, and 'deviance' in many forms. Prime Minister Blair's claim, as outlined at the beginning of this chapter, that his obligation was to respond to the self-identified needs of the police service, suggests that the service holds considerable power among social and political elites. Loader and Mulcahy (2001a, 2001b) have detailed the changing ways in which senior police officers have exercised their collective 'power of legitimate naming', whereby they have been able to do the following:

> **authorize, categorize, evoke, represent, reinforce and undermine elements of the wider culture, whose presence as interpreters of social institutions, conflicts and hierarchies presupposes something significant about the ownership and framing of relevant issues, and whose individual and collective utterances circulate meanings that contribute in potentially telling ways to the formation of opinion and belief. (Loader and Mulcahy, 2001a: 42)**

Although chief police officers, especially those in rural parts of England and Wales (Wall, 1998), have always been part of elite networks with powers of influence, Loader and Mulcahy traced how this broad form of police power extended since the 1970s as senior police officers have developed an increasing corporate voice under the auspices of the **Association of Chief Police Officers**. Significantly, however, the broader the definition of police powers, the more nebulous and contestable they become. Case law and revisions to instruments such as the PACE Codes of Practice always provide for re-interpretation of police powers as defined in relatively narrow legal terms but, these develop-ments aside, the 'law in books' is relatively fixed and stark: either an officer has the legal power do to something or not. For the reasons outlined in these final paragraphs, this provides only a weak guide to police power in practice, since other factors such as institutional power and the authority of the police in general terms, are also crucial determinants of what the police do. These powers, though, must be endlessly reproduced and vary according to context to an extent that they cannot be taken for granted. The power of the police cannot be understood without reference to the statute book but, equally, cannot be understood apart from the broader social context in which policing is practised.

conclusion

Political debate about policing often centres around whether officers have sufficient legal powers to confront the ever-changing problems of crime and disorder apparently confronting society. The chapter has explored reasons why police powers became increasingly codified in Britain and reviewed the arguments that surrounded the 1984 Police and Criminal Evidence Act. A 'pro-law and order' lobby argued that the new law would tie the hands of the police and put too much emphasis on protecting the rights of suspects. Others argued that PACE would damage civil liberties by giving extensive new powers to the police. Most of the research evidence now tends to suggest that the PACE framework, once hugely controversial, has come to be widely accepted. Just as the previous chapter argued that the concept of policing needs to be understood in broad terms, this chapter has shown that police powers also need to be considered widely. Although the law is a necessary part of much policing, it does not provide an adequate explanation of the routine activities of police officers. The cultural, political and organizational powers of the police service are considerable.

chapter summary

- Historically the police powers have been loosely defined in law. The principle that police officers are 'citizens in uniform' has meant that the legal powers afforded to them have been broadly those available to ordinary members of public. The 1984 Police and Criminal Evidence Act codified many of the powers that police officers have over citizens, in terms of stop and search; entry, search and seizure; arrest; detention; questioning and treatment; documentary evidence in criminal proceed-ings; complaints and discipline, and other matters.

- Police officers differ from many other employees in that they are independent officers of the Crown. Although accountable to senior officers and the range of bodies that govern the police service, officers exercise their discretion independently. Historically, legal powers afforded to officers were derived from individual pieces of legislation and were not codified in a single piece of legislation.

- The contradictory and confusing legal foundations of police powers and concern that officers were exceeding their powers and disregarding the rules designed to govern the treatment of people in custody led to the development of the Police and Criminal Evidence Bill in the early 1980s. The Bill was hugely controversial: a law and order lobby welcomed the extension of powers available to the police but was concerned that concomitant provision of rights to those in custody would 'tie the hands' of the police. Those concerned with civil liberties doubted that the 'safeguards' on police power would prove effective in practice.

- PACE gives police officers power to stop and search a member of the public where they have 'reasonable suspicion'. The Codes of Practice that reinforce PACE stipulate that 'reasonable suspicion' cannot be related to the age, ethnicity or appearance of the individual, although if the person is dressed in a style associated with a criminal gang that might constitute grounds to stop and search them. These powers apply in public spaces, although that is defined broadly in terms of localities to which the public routinely have access.

- Persons stopped, whether searched or not, should be provided with a record of the encounter that includes information about the circumstances that informed the officer's decision, the identity of the officer, and the means by which they might complain about their experience.

- Section 60 of the Criminal Justice and Public Order Act (1994) and the Terrorism Act (2000) permit the stop and searching of members of the public for much more general reasons. 'Section 60' enables officers to stop and search any individual present in places where it is anticipated that incidents of serious violence might take place. These have come to be applied relatively frequently as a routine resource in the policing of town centres on Friday and Saturday nights. Similarly, the Terrorism Act 2000 enables officers to stop and search individuals at times and places where it is anticipated there might be terrorist activity.

- PACE stipulates that officers can enter private premises, without being invited, if in possession of a warrant. Magistrates provide warrants so that officers can search for substantial evidence relating to a serious arrestable offence. Officers can enter premises without a warrant in order to effect an arrest, to recapture someone unlawfully at large, or to save life and limb. As with stop and search powers, they must have 'reasonable grounds' to support their decision.

- Officers can arrest a person without a warrant if they are suspected of committing an 'arrestable' offence, which is murder, any offence that carries a sentence longer than five years, or a range of other offences, subject to lower tariffs but still considered serious in other respects. If any person, police officer or civilian, believes such a crime is in the process of being committed, they can legally arrest the suspected perpetrator.

- Custody officers are legally responsible for deciding if there is sufficient evidence to hold an individual once they have been arrested and for ensuring that the rights of those in custody are observed. Free legal advice must be made available to those held in custody. PACE regulates the conduct of police interviews, requiring them to be tape- or video-recorded.

- Discussion of the formal legal powers of police officers needs to be broadened, partly to recognize that a range of other agencies – policing in more general terms – share some of these provisions, and because police power also derives from institutional framework and resources, and from the symbolic authority of the service. Additionally, the police service is powerful in that it can shape public and political discourse about contemporary issues.

 ■ self-check Questions ■

1 How did Sir Robert Mark characterize the power of the police over the citizen?

2 What was introduced in 1912 to govern the treatment of those held in custody?

3 What is the general condition for the police powers to stop and search an individual under Section 1 of PACE?

4 How does PACE define a 'public place'?

5 Why did the Home Office reject the Macpherson Report recommendation that police officers be required to issue a record for all stops involving members of the public?

6 What documents cannot be searched under the terms of a general search warrant?

7 Under what circumstances can magistrates issue a warrant for arrest?

8 What conditions does PACE stipulate justify detaining an individual in custody prior to their being charged with an offence?

9 Why does a concentration on the legal powers granted to the police provide only a partial understanding of police work?

10 How did Loader and Mulcahy characterize the power of senior police officers to identify and define crime problems?

1 What are the main principles underlying police powers defined in the Police and Criminal Evidence Act 1984?

2 For what reasons is the 'law in books' (Dixon, 1997) an imperfect guide to police activity?

3 Apart from the law, what are the other bases of police powers?

■ ■ annotated further reading ■

English and Card's (2005) *Police Law* reviews the general principles under-pinning the police as well as specific nature of police legal powers in relation to the treatment of suspects, traffic, drinking and a drug-taking, public order and a myriad other criminal matters.

Many of the particular powers reviewed in this chapter are subject to extended discussion in Jason-Lloyd's (2005) *An Introduction to Policing and Police Powers*. Zander's (2005) *Police and Criminal Evidence Act 1984* is in its fifth edition and provides an authoritative account of the application of PACE.

Loader and Mulcahy (2001a, 2001b) argue that police power needs to be understood in broader terms, deriving not only from the law but also the institutional, political, social and cultural position of the service in general and senior officers in particular. The development of the Association of Chief Police Officers as a corporate voice for the police service, they argue, has greatly extended the power of senior officers to define crime problems and identify the most appropriate solutions to them.

∴ // annotated listings of links to relevant websites /

The codes of practice that provide detailed guidance on police powers can be found at http://tinyurl.com/2ax523.

Ten years after the introduction of the Police and Criminal Evidence Act, the Home Office instigated a review of the impact of the legislation on police practice. A summary of the results of the review can be found at http://tinyurl.com/2drtzt.

The Home Office has launched a review of PACE, and background information and documents relating to the process of public consultation can be found at http://tinyurl.com/yq26tm.

4

Community policing

Contents

Community policing is a nebulous concept used to describe a range of programmes and initiatives from those that closely involve members of the public in the routines of the police service to those that seem to represent little more than a public relations exercise intended to secure legitimacy. In many respects it might be tempting to reject the phrase entirely on the grounds either that it is tautologous (what else, apart from 'the community' in some shape or form, could be policed?) or that it is applied to such a wide spectrum of policing styles and practices that it is virtually meaningless. However, the ubiquity and resilience of promises to deliver community policing mean that this temptation has been resisted. This chapter does the following:

- explores the multiple ways in which community policing has been defined and practised;

- considers links between community policing, law enforcement and public legitimacy;

- outlines some of the key challenges facing efforts to develop community policing.

| **key terms** |

consent; consultation; co-production; legitimacy; Neighbourhood Policing

_____ **introduction** _____

Even though the principle of community policing is problematic, it remains a vital starting point in how we think about the relationship between the police and the public. As indicated in Chapter 1, the idea that the public confer consent on the police that hold power over them is an important organizing principle for the police in many societies. Difficult though it may be to implement – and many of the obstacles are outlined later in the chapter – community policing in some form remains the only viable way for the police to retain public support and a vital prerequisite for attempts to reduce crime. Alongside moral and ethical arguments for embracing the principles of community policing lies a pragmatic case based upon the need to cultivate public support so that problems of crime and disorder can be addressed.

The chapter begins by considering the wide range of approaches to the concept of community policing, and the implications that these variously have for the development and delivery of policing programmes. The discussion continues by exploring the various efforts to develop community policing that have been made in Britain, the USA, South Africa and elsewhere in recent decades, and considers the social and political context against which such programmes have been introduced. In the penultimate section, the chapter considers some of the generic problems that have hampered the effective delivery of community policing. The conclusion argues that although the principles of community policing might never be wholly realized in practice, they continue to provide an important philosophy around which policing ought to be organized.

defining 'community policing'

As will be seen below, definitions of community policing often seem vague, and more than a little aspirational. Even so, there are core themes common to many outlines of the principles and practices of community policing. Some of these focus on the ways in which policing is produced – the processes through which the activities of the police are co-ordinated and delivered. The following section describes these in some detail, in the context of Britain and the United States. Following that, another perspective is outlined, which focuses instead on understanding community policing in terms of the different outcomes that are produced compared to other models of policing.

process-led approaches

As has been noted, the ubiquity of community policing and the ease with which it is endorsed by police services with fundamentally different histories and characteristics might lead one to conclude that the concept contains little concrete meaning. Indeed, some advocates of community policing have argued that the term ought to remain somewhat vague since it ought to provide a general framework rather than a detailed programme of activity (Moore, 1992; Eck and Rosenbaum, 1994/2000). Skogan (2006) acknowledged that community policing has been widely endorsed by the police services in the United States and that a very diverse range of activities have been developed under this rubric. He suggested that community policing is a process rather than a product and embraces three key elements: citizen involvement, problem-solving, and decentralization (ibid.: 28). The first of these was emphasized in the influential work in the United States by Trojanowicz and Bucqueroux (1990, cited in Tilley, 2003: 314) who outlined the principles of community policing in the following terms: 'Community policing is both a philosophy and organisation strategy to allow community residents and police to work together in new ways to solve problems of crime, fear of crime, physical and social disorder and neighbourhood decay.'

Clearly this approach is broadly similar to that later described by Skogan (2006), although it is interesting that the quote above makes no reference to decentralization. The notion that policing ought to be jointly directed and produced by the public and the police service emerges, however, as a core similarity between these two definitions, and is one found in most accounts of community policing. Another perspective from the United States is offered by Thurman et al. (2001: 8) who offer a fourfold definition, summarized in Box 4.1.

Box 4.1

A four-fold definition of community policing

First, 'community-oriented police departments value citizen input, define their mission more broadly than just law enforcement, and believe that policing must be tailored to the needs of the community'.

Second, 'the strategic dimension has to do with translating the philosophical side into practice through planning. Here the department thinks through how best to reorient its operations, geographic focus, and emphasis on crime prevention'.

Third, 'community-oriented police departments will stand out from more traditionally focused departments in that the former emphasize positive citizen interactions, police–community partnerships, and problem-solving activities'.

Fourth, 'concerns the structure of the department and its personnel … community policing favours a work environment where employee input is highly valued, mentoring is encouraged, and systematic evaluation methods are in place'.

Again it is clear that this typology has much in common with those already outlined; however, it is notable that the definition of community policing has been broadened somewhat to refer to the internal organization and culture of the police service. It might also be significant that while the first element emphasizes the value of public input into policing, the following three aspects all foreground the police department itself, suggesting that they continue to be 'first among equals' in relation to the public. The primacy of the police service among multi-agency partnerships and the power that this affords to them in terms of defining agendas in terms of crime and antisocial behaviour have been noted in the British context and will be explored in more detail later in the chapter when a range of obstacles to the effective development of community policing are outlined.

Although they do not always explicitly acknowledge it, the definitions of community policing described above all relate to the experience of the United States, from where Brogden (1999) has argued the dominant discourse for police reform across much of the rest of the world has emerged. He suggested that the apparent failures of community policing in many contexts has partly been due to poor implementation but is also explained by the 'alien legal, cultural and organizational history' that pertains outside of the United States (ibid.: 167). Definitionally, if not operationally, though, it seems that British perspectives on community policing are broadly similar to those developed in the USA. Weatheritt (1987) argued that the term 'community policing' in the British context had been used to describe a wide range of programmes and that it tended to be used to denote projects of which authors approved. Some of the core characteristics of community policing initiatives in Britain are similar to those identified in the USA. Smith (1987), for example, argued that community policing, in common with other efforts to develop a community orientation for social policy, had three central features: decentralization, partnership, and the incorporation of the informal and voluntary sectors.

outcome-led approaches

While the definitions outlined in the previous section focus on the structures and systems by which policing is delivered, other commentators have instead emphasized that community policing encompasses a broader set of policing outcomes that go beyond a focus of crime control and law enforcement. Along these lines, Friedman's (1994) study led to the view that what defined the broad range of activities brought together under the umbrella of community policing was that they 'aimed at achieving more effective and efficient crime control, reduced fear of crime, improved quality of life, improved police services and police legitimacy'. An early proponent of community policing in Britain was John Alderson, who, when Chief Constable of Devon and Cornwall police, promoted objectives for the police service, as outlined in Box 4.2, many of which go far beyond the traditional definitions of policing that were outlined in Chapter 1.

Box 4.2

Alderson's model of community policing

- To contribute to liberty, equality and fraternity.
- To help reconcile freedom with security and to uphold the law.
- To uphold and protect human rights and thus help achieve human dignity.
- To dispel criminogenic social conditions, through cooperative social action.
- To help create trust in communities.
- To strengthen security and feelings of security.
- To investigate, detect and activate the prosecution of crimes.
- To facilitate free movement along public thoroughfares.
- To curb public disorder.
- To deal with crises and help those in distress involving other agencies where needed.

(Alderson, 1979, cited in Tilley, 2003: 314)

Clearly, any list of this kind raises further questions. It might be wondered, for example, what are the 'criminogenic social conditions' that the police ought to be seeking to dispel. Whatever difficulties might arise with this definition of the police role, however, it is clear that a highly ambitious and wide-ranging scope for the police service was envisioned, and that this has often been at odds with political rhetoric, from all quarters, during the intervening quarter of a century that has stressed the need for the police to vigorously pursue a more narrow goal of 'cracking down' on crime.

community policing as a means to recover public consent

Waddington (1999: 207) argued that Alderson's advocacy of community policing can only be properly understood as a rejection of the technocratic professionalism of policing that took place in England and Wales during the late 1960s. In the interests of economy, efficiency and modernization, policing had been transformed in that period into Unit Beat Policing, a key feature of which was that officers were deployed in cars and so were able to cover larger geographical areas. While it had been thought that this would lead to improved relations with the public, it is widely argued that this is more or less the 'polar opposite' of what actually happened (Newburn, 2003: 85). Along with other developments, such as the closure of many 'police houses' and the replacement of police telephone boxes with two-way radios, the drive to promote a more efficient system of policing had the unintended consequence of separating police officers from the public. While traditional police patrol work came to be regarded as inefficient in terms of tackling crime, it had secured a relatively high public profile for the police. They became a regular presence in the community, which provided some symbolic reassurance for the wider society. Police efforts to become more professional in the 1960s meant that officers became increasingly separated from the people they were supposed to serve. Constables were not able to develop personal relations with the public when they drove past them in cars rather than walking around on the beat.

It was against this background of decreasing routine contact between the police and the public that advocates such as Alderson were introducing measures that sought to reintroduce the police into community life. That such aims underpin the contemporary drive toward **Neighbourhood Policing** in England and Wales suggests that earlier demands for community policing remained unrealized to some extent. The nature of the Neighbourhood Policing plan and some of the key challenges for efforts to reinvigorate community policing in the twenty-first century are considered later in this chapter.

Efforts to define community policing remain problematic. Some have argued that the term is subject to such a range of uses, and abuses, that it ought to be dispensed with altogether. Tilley (2003: 315) noted that his review of the literature on community policing led him to the view that '"community policing" is widely endorsed, though at the same time widely seen to be close to meaninglessness'. Perhaps the most reliable way of conceptualizing community policing is provided by Brogden and Nijhar's (2005: 2) approach, which is to define the concept in terms of *what it is not*:

> **It is not military-style policing with a central bureaucracy obedient to directive legislation which minimises discretion. It is not policing that is autonomous of public consent and accountability. It is not policing that is committed primarily to reactive crime-fighting strategies. It is not policing that is measured by output in terms of professional efficiency. Rather it is policing which is determined by strategies, tactics and outcomes based on community consent. (ibid.)**

practising community policing

Just as the principles of community policing are wide-ranging, so too are the practices introduced in its name. In the mid-1980s, before the multi-agency working and community engagement became the predominant motif of crime and policing initiatives, Ekblom (1986) noted the following range of initiatives in England and Wales:

- Community constables
- Specialist community liaison officers
- Crime analysis

- Police facilities for young people
- Schools liaison

- Police shops
- Community surveys
- Inter-agency initiatives such as Victim Support
- Joint training with other agencies
- Local consultative committees

Many of these kind of activities have been further promoted by New Labour as multi-agency partnership approaches to crime prevention and community safety, advocated since the early 1990s (Home Office, 1991). Programmes such as reassurance policing and, subsequently, Neighbourhood Policing have placed considerable emphasis on the co-production of policing and on responding to the priorities of local communities (Innes, 2004). The establishment of the role of Police Community Support Officer (PCSO) represents an expansion, albeit with some variation in that they do not have the full powers of a police officer, in the role of the community constable, and community surveys have become a key part of auditing police performance.

A survey conducted in the United States in 2002 identified the following 16 most common community policing activities (Roberg et al., 2005: 93–4):

- Citizens attend police–community meetings

- Citizens participate in Neighbourhood Watch

- Citizens help police identify and resolve problems

- Citizens serve as volunteers with the police agency

- Citizens attend citizen–police academies

- Police hold regular meetings with community groups

- Agencies give special recognition for good community policing work by employees

- Agencies classify and prioritize calls

- Police have inter-agency involvement in problem-solving

- Police have youth programmes

- Police have victim assistance programmes

- Police use regulatory codes in problem-solving

- Police work with building-code enforcement

- Agencies use specific assignments to specific beats or areas

- Agencies do geographically based crime analysis

- Agencies use permanent neighbourhood-based offices or stations

Although the nature of initiatives designed to deliver community policing is extremely diverse, they can be considered as falling into two broad categories: those initiatives designed to increase consultation between the police and the public; and those designed to enhance collaboration (Bennett, 1990). Those schemes designed to increase consultation may involve the police questioning the public to find out how well (or badly) they are doing their job, a process that may not, necessarily, effect subsequent operational decisions. It can mean more than this, and involve officers consulting with the community in order to discover what their priorities are and what types of crime they wish to see the police concentrate upon. Alternatively it may mean that the police develop means to make themselves formally accountable to the local community by ensuring that they explain and justify their actions to local people. The 1998 Crime and Disorder Act requires that the police, working in conjunction with other agencies in Crime and Disorder Reduction Partnerships, conduct periodic audits of problems relating to crime and disorder. Although these audits tend to make use of recorded crime data, statistics gathered by the probation service, incidents recorded by local authorities and other statutory sources, often they also entail surveys of local communities to gauge public perceptions of these problems (Phillips et al., 2000).

A key formal method whereby the police consult local communities has been via community meetings. Section 106 of the 1984 **Police and Criminal Evidence Act (PACE)** required that the police establish consultative groups as a means of consulting the public and establishing what their priorities for policing were. Since 1984, the police have had a legal duty to consult the public. Often police services established a number of these committees, commonly one for each division of the force. Research has suggested that these committees do not, for a number of reasons, tend to fulfil their role effectively, as is discussed further in Chapter 6. Partly this seems to be due to the police themselves: the meetings tend to be held on police premises and very much under the direction of the force itself with few resources committed to them. Without support from the force in general, it is difficult for these meetings to influence policing across the whole constabulary, and there is a perception that the meetings become little more than 'talking shops', providing the chance for grievances and concerns to be aired but little more. Keith's (1988) study of the Section 106 provisions as they operated in London led him to note that the arrangements often failed to match expectations because the officers engaged in them, however well intentioned, were often simply unable to deliver change in policing provisions across the board. Issues and concerns raised at meetings were not subsequently reflected in policing as experienced in practice. More fundamentally, Keith argued, the PACE provisions confused consultation with **accountability**; and suggested that the creation of opportunities for the former would make the police accountable to the local community. Keith's argument that the two processes are fundamentally different and that unequal power relations between the parties will be unaffected by processes of consultation applies to current proposals in England and Wales to develop Neighbourhood Policing, and is discussed in more detail later in this chapter. Another, more general, problem is that the members of the public who attend do not appear to be representative of the population as a whole; they tend to be white, middle-class, middle-aged males. Those 'hard to reach groups' who are actually more likely to come into conflict with the police are unlikely to attend (Jones and Newburn, 2001). As McLaughlin (1991: 116) has argued, these efforts to identify issues of concern to local communities are unlikely to incorporate those for whom 'the police were the problem'. Generally, police community consultative committees proved to be relatively powerless and appear to offer little more than an opportunity for the police to be seen to be taking community relations seriously without always doing very much about it in concrete terms. This does not mean that such channels for community input into policing priorities are wholly without merit. Despite his criticisms, Keith (1988) suggested that there were occasions in London during the 1980s when the dialogue maintained by the consultative groups diffused tensions and seems likely to have averted damaging conflicts.

There are, however, other methods whereby the police can liaise with the public. Often this occurs more informally and through individual officers whose role it is to work with minority groups, in schools and youth projects, among the elderly, and with other groups in the community. Formal methods of consultation also exist as the police work with other public agencies including local government, business, educational, and charitable groups. As these opportunities are often informal and usually based on personal contacts and interactions, it is very difficult to ascertain how effective they are. Since the 1998 Crime and Disorder Act gave, for the first time, local authorities statutory responsibility to tackle problems that had previously been the domain of the police service, the already developing trend towards multi-agency partnerships has accelerated further. Such networks often seem to have been undermined by institutional and organizational problems relating to agencies having competing agendas, being relatively unequal in terms of power and commitment to projects, and being dominated by a small cohort of agencies. Edwards (2002) has stressed that the nature and quality of partnerships vary from place to place and are often contingent on local factors that are difficult to predict or to generalize about. He noted that 'partnerships can provide opportunities for building stable, long-term, exchange relationships built on trust and co-operation, yet they can also create opportunities for destabilising, short-term, self-interested competitive behaviour' (ibid.: 146). Fraught and unpredictable though such mechanisms might be on occasion, they do offer at least the prospect of the police service liaising with and consulting other agencies and contribute to a process whereby the police are not isolated and atomized from other institutions but become engaged and integrated with them. In the 1980s, Lea and Young (1993) argued that community policing would only be fully realized when the community itself decided on its priorities and then enlisted the police service in order to tackle them. More recently Johnston and Shearing (2003) have argued that disadvantaged communities, unable to compete in the market place to purchase additional security services made available from diverse providers, ought to be provided with public funds to be allocated via policing boards that will contract services from that range of agencies deemed most suitable to meet their particular needs. While developments of the past two decades might not have seen such a radical re-calibration of police–community relations, there have been important changes that have opened up the police service, relatively speaking, to the influence of other agencies and community groups.

police–community collaboration

Police–community collaboration refers to developments designed to directly involve local people in the policing of their own neighbourhoods. These approaches rely upon the idea that the incorporation of the community directly into policing will help to prevent crime in the first place and to increase chances of arresting criminals. Initiatives such as Neighbourhood Watch, discussed more fully below, where residents provide informal surveillance of their localities so that their mutual security is increased, have been introduced with this end in mind. Neighbourhood Watch schemes were introduced in Britain in the mid-1980s and quickly flourished. By the mid-1990s it was estimated that there were 115,000 schemes across England and Wales, and in 2006 it was estimated that some 10 million people lived in areas covered by Neighbourhood Watch. The rapid expansion of Neighbourhood Watch has led to the establishment of similar schemes designed to promote effective communication as a method of crime prevention in a range of niche areas. For example, Business Watch, Office Watch, Vehicle Watch, Boat Watch, Shop Watch, Farm Watch, Pub Watch, School Watch, Golf Watch, Post Office Watch, Church Watch, Bed and Breakfast Watch, Child Watch, and Horse Watch have been among the programmes introduced to extend community policing beyond residential neighbourhoods. Box 4.3 provides some background on Neighbourhood Watch and the key elements of its approach.

Box 4.3

Neighbourhood Watch in Britain

Neighbourhood Watch is the largest community safety organisation in the country with an estimated 10 million members. Neighbourhood Watch works by developing close liaison between households in a neighbourhood and the local police. It aims to help people protect themselves and their properties and to reduce the fear of crime by means of improved home security, greater vigilance, accurate reporting of suspicious incidents to the police and by fostering a community spirit.

Neighbourhood Watch schemes and associations across the country are always coming up with new ideas and initiatives to extend the effectiveness of this valuable community safety organisation. You can search the database of good practice on this website using the search engine on the right of this page.

If you would like to be part of a Neighbourhood Watch scheme in your area, contact the Crime Prevention Co-ordinator at your nearest police station, who will give you further information or will put you in contact with the Neighbourhood Watch Co-ordinator of the established scheme.

If there is no scheme in existence the crime prevention officer will be able to advise you and assist you how to establish a scheme. Obviously, as the title suggests, Neighbourhood Watch relies on participation of the neighbours who live in area, whether this is a close, a road or a block flats.

(Continued)

Objectives of Neighbourhood Watch

- To prevent crime by improving security, increasing vigilance, creating and maintaining a caring community and reducing opportunities for crime by increasing crime prevention awareness.
- To assist the police in detecting crime by promoting effective communication and the prompt reporting of suspicious and criminal activity.
- To reduce undue fear of crime by providing accurate information about risks and by promoting a sense of security and community spirit, particularly amongst the more vulnerable members of the community.
- To improve police/community liaison by providing effective communications through systems such as the Neighbourhood Watch Ringmaster system, which warns Co-ordinators of local crime trends which they can disseminate to their scheme members, and by members informing the police of incidents when they occur.

  (http://www.crimereduction.gov.uk/neighbourhoodwatch/nwatch09.htm)

While Neighbourhood Watch has undoubtedly been a success in terms of the number of schemes established and has become a ubiquitous feature of the urban landscape, it is difficult to discern the impact it has had on levels of crime. To some extent this lack of clarity reflects the huge diversity of activities encompassed under the umbrella of Neighbourhood Watch and the fact that many schemes become dormant after an initial burst of energy. Furthermore, the range of neighbourhoods in which schemes have been established is considerable and it is difficult to develop robust evaluation methodologies that can attribute changing crime patterns to the introduction of a scheme. Comparing the performance of Neighbourhood Watch in these circumstances is very problematic. Most of the evidence from the UK experience is that Neighbourhood Watch schemes seem to have some initial impact in reducing offending when introduced into areas that had previously experienced high volumes of crime. Bennett (1990, cited in Fleming, 2005) found that crime levels actually rose in some areas where Neighbourhood Watch had been introduced; a trend he attributed to schemes established in middle-class areas with relatively low crime rates that encouraged local residents to report incidents to the police that would not previously have been recorded. Since Neighbourhood Watch claims that crime prevention and detection are among its key objectives, it is reasonable, if difficult, to seek to establish the extent to which these goals are being met. However, as Fleming (2005) has argued, it seems likely that schemes can also play an important role in developing communication between police and public and providing enhanced reassurance.

Given the increasing recognition that the fear of crime is as important as the reality of crime levels in terms of the deleterious effect that it can have on people's quality of life, it is clear that any benefits Neighbourhood Watch can bring in this regard are likely to mean that it continues to be a feature of community policing. However, while the co-production of policing aims to promote reassurance, it might be argued that risk and danger are communicated when community police officers, for example, inform local residents about crime problems in their area, and that the posters, window-stickers and street signs that constitute the paraphernalia of Neighbourhood Watch schemes might reinforce, rather than assuage, public fear of crime (Lee, 2007). The impact of surveillance technology and communication relating to risks of crime is considered further in Chapter 9.

community policing and reassurance

That the police need to focus on providing reassurance to the public is the central principle underlying recent government commitment to establishing neighbourhood policing. At the heart of these developments is the conundrum that public concern and fear about crime have risen despite a sustained reduction in crime levels. Recorded crime levels in Britain have fallen consistently since the mid-1990s, a trend also noted by the British Crime Survey (BCS), which found between 1995 and 2005–06 domestic burglary fell by 59 per cent, vehicle theft by 50 per cent, and violent crime by 43 per cent (Walker et al., 2006). The BCS also found that public perception of crime trends did not appear to recognize this decrease, as 63 per cent stated that they thought crime had risen during the previous two years (ibid.). One implication of this 'reassurance gap' is that fear of crime is relatively autonomous of actual patterns of offending. Additionally, it suggests that fear of crime has wider implications for community cohesion and ought to be addressed by the police, criminal justice system, and other agencies. Innes (2004: 156) argued that the divergent trends in crime rates and fear of crime contributed to the development of 'reassurance policing' that is predicated on renewing connections between policing and communities:

> as was being made evident, public perceptions of security/insecurity are not and never have been, solely dependent upon the police's efficacy in preventing and detecting crime. Nor are they determined by the recorded crime rate ... In the academy, this situation stimulated careful and detailed investigation of the fear of crime concept and the instruments that had been used to measure it. These investigations identified a number of problems with both the concept and the survey measures in which the concept had become grounded ... In policy-making circles, attention began to focus upon the 'reassurance gap'. In essence, the

notion of a reassurance gap sought to diagnose why people did not believe that they were becoming safer in terms of the declining objective risk of being a victim of crime. The resulting diagnosis suggested that fear was only ever partially a function of objective victimization risk, and that in fact expressions of fear involve complex, situated, adaptive and subjective appraisals of risk.

The reassurance policing programme developed in England and Wales was based upon a threefold strategy comprising of 'high visibility patrols performed by officers who are known to the local public; the targeting of "signal crimes" and "signal disorders"; and informal social control performed by communities' (ibid.: 151). Like other aspects of community policing, the reassurance strategy can also be understood as a reaction against other forms of policing, in particular, the intelligence-based approach that saw officers target known offenders, cultivate informants, and develop crime-mapping techniques that would provide a basis for effective intervention against crime. While such methods might have contributed to the fall in crime noted by the BCS, it has been argued that they removed the police from the public arena and reduced the symbolic authority they provided (Sparks et al., 2001). The Neighbourhood Policing Plan indicated that policing resources would be increased, with 24,000 Police Community Support Officers (PCSOs) provided by 2008, and that 12,000 police officers would be directed away from backroom activity and dedicated to street patrols (Home Office, 2005). The role of PCSOs is supposed to be one of providing reassurance through patrol work and to provide support to police officers, although in practice it is clear that their status and function have often not been adequately understood in principle or practice (Crawford et al., 2003). More detail on their role within the '**extended police family**' is provided in Chapter 8. The Neighbourhood Policing programme is one manifestation, the Home Office claims, of a more fundamental shift toward 'citizen-focused' policing. This is defined as 'a way of working in which an in-depth understanding of the needs and expectations of individuals and local communities is routinely reflected in decision-making, service delivery and practice' (Home Office, 2005: 7). The key principles of the Neighbourhood Policing Plan are outlined in Box 4.4. As Crawford argued, these developments need to be understood in the context of a wider emphasis on the development of social cohesion:

> **Public policy has tended to define contemporary crime and disorder problems in rather simplistic terms of the breakdown of informal control, moral decline and a collapse in social capital. Associated with this are a concomitant belief in the civilising and crime-preventive effects of 'cohesive communities' with strong bonds and a tendency to conflate the security needs of all urban areas as uniformly demanding the reassertion of increased visible policing. (2006: 958)**

Box 4.4

Neighbourhood policing

The purpose of neighbourhood policing is to tackle crime and fear of crime better and bring the police closer to communities. Its key principles are:

- *Visible and accessible police* – local people seeing and having regular contact with the same officers – week in and week out – who stay in the job long enough to build lasting and trusting relationships with the communities they serve.
- *Influence* – over community safety priorities in their communities which might be dealing with persistent burglaries; clearing up graffiti and vandalism or tackling open drug dealing or gun crime. Local people who are closest to the problems in their communities are often best placed to help shape and participate in the solutions to them.
- *Interventions* – joint action with communities and partners to solve problems and harness everyone's strengths.
- *Answers* – sustainable solutions to problems and feedback on results. People will know the names, numbers and email addresses of their neighbourhood policing teams. They will also know who is responsible for what in terms of reducing crime, tackling anti-social behaviour and keeping the areas where they live and work safe. The Government is legislating to make it possible for local people, through the Community Call for Action, to trigger action by the police and other partners to address acute or persistent problems of crime or anti-social behaviour.

(Home Office, 2006a: 4)

The programme seeks to reintegrate the police service into the routine activity of community life and, although the Home Office (2005) recognized the fallacy of nostalgia for a by-gone golden age of policing, the programme claims it will strengthen police relations with the public so that residents are familiar with local officers and are able to communicate with them easily. In that way, informal opportunities for consultation and accountability will be developed, as routine police work is embedded in ordinary community life.

The Neighbourhood Policing (NP) programme promises to provide for both police-community consultation and co-production. The general purpose of NP is to 'tackle crime and the fear of crime better and bring the police closer to communities' and underpinning this is the stated commitment to a 'visible and accessible police ... who stay in the job long enough to build lasting and trusting relationships with the communities they serve'. In turn, the community is envisaged as being best placed to help shape and participate in the solutions to community safety priorities and in turn needs to be empowered to hold the police and other partners to account if they do not address acute or persistent problems of crime and antisocial behaviour. Finally, the programme is seen as part of the broader movement from reactive policing to being more proactive – 'using local information and real time intelligence to better target crime hotspots, increase detections and bring more offenders to justice' (Home Office, 2006a: 4).

Important elements of the NP agenda include a re-commitment to the delivery of high-visibility front-line policing that both leads and encompasses diverse partners from among the extended police family described more fully in Chapter 8. Additionally, the programme seeks to re-establish connections between the police and local communities that were lost as the Unit Beat Policing re-organized and professionalized the service in the 1960s and 1970s. By pledging that individual officers will become familiar characters in the local landscape, the programme seeks to re-embed police into the fabric of communities. Notions of consultation and responsiveness are, as with earlier reassurance policing projects, seen as vital to the integration of police and local communities. The new policing settlement promises to enhance three core principles identified in the HMIC report (HMIC, 2001) that has shaped the development of reassurance policing: namely, visibility, familiarity and accessibility. Many of the assumptions, implicit or explicit, that underpin the Neighbourhood Policing programme have applied to community policing projects more generally. The experience of those programmes, and concerns about the viability of communities as a policing resource, have led to the identification of a range of practical and conceptual challenges for community policing, and it is to these that the following section turns.

challenges for community policing

While programmes appealing to the principles of community policing have been persistent features of global policing developments for many years, it is clear that they have faced a range of challenges and rarely have lived up to the claims made for them. In this section some of the common problems that have beset community policing will be reviewed. Some of these relate to internal policing issues, such as culture and the difficulties of reconciling contrary objectives, while others relate to the lack of a 'model community' and the problematic wider context in which community policing is introduced.

not real police work?

Research evidence suggests that police officers do not tend to rate the role of community policing very highly. Foot patrol, one of the three central planks of Neighbourhood Policing, tends to be considered by officers as a low-status aspect of policing – not a 'real' part of the job. The origins, nature and implications of police sub-culture are discussed at greater length in Chapter 5. This sub-cultural resistance to community policing cannot simply be attributed to recalcitrant or retrogressive attitudes among junior ranks. Chan (1997) has shown that police working culture needs to be understood in terms of wider institutional and organizational contexts. The failure of the police service to properly resource community policing, or to protect community police officers from being re-assigned to other duties (factors that partly explain the establishment of the PCSO as a dedicated patrol role), reinforces perceptions that community policing is marginal to the 'core' business. Pressure for officers to meet performance indicators, such as ensuring a speedy response to calls from the public, also detract from foot patrol and community policing work that does not lead to tangible results in terms of measurable 'sanctioned detections'.

Another way in which police culture may be detrimental to the principle of community policing refers not to the internal organization of the force but rather to outside relations with the general public. Reiner (1978) argued that the nature of police work – the boredom, unsociable hours, occasional periods of danger, and the routine exposure to shocking and traumatic events – cultivates a sense among officers that they are separate and isolated from broader society. He argued that this encourages the police to regard the public with some suspicion and to rely upon stereotypes of different social groups in order to understand the world outside the police station. Efforts to broaden the diversity of police staff, as discussed in Chapters 5 and 7, are intended to address some of these problems. The extent to which the legitimate professional interests of officers can be reconciled with elements of the Neighbourhood Policing Plan, such as the pledge that officers will remain in post for longer periods of time and so develop stronger relations with local people, remains to be seen.

transplant failure

As well as internal factors that have hindered the effective development of community policing programmes, a range of contextual challenges relating to the nature of contemporary communities and the broader environment in which programmes are introduced are likely to pose important challenges. Brogden and Nijhar (2005) argued that community-oriented policing (COP) has become a core component of western interventions in societies in transition. US and British government policy to developing nations, for example, have placed considerable emphasis on the importance of police reform and tackling crime to more general processes of political, social and economic development, and these initiatives have usually been framed in terms of community policing. In 'third world' nations, in post-apartheid South Africa, and post-communist Eastern Europe community policing became central to social transformation (Hills, 2000; Van der Spuy, 2000; Beck and Chistyakova, 2004). Alongside a range of problems relating to the implementation of community policing, Brogden and Nijhar (2005) state that models of COP devised and practised in the United States have been exported around the world and introduced into countries with wholly different social traditions and contexts. For these reasons they argue that:

> The four primary components of community policing in the West that are most evident in the export drive – community forums, neighbourhood watch schemes, problem-solving and beat patrolling – have not worked anything like as success-fully as appears in the international sales literature. For the most part, where such schemes have been established by the police and by local business elites in Africa and in the Indian sub-continent, they have simply exacerbated social schisms. For the most part COP materials are shoddy goods, with few health warnings attached. They have invariably not been tailored to the particular needs of African, Asian, Latin American and East European societies. (ibid.: 231)

As mentioned in Chapter 6 in relation to **human rights** and ethical policing, one reason why community policing has not transplanted effectively to developing countries is that its adoption is primarily occasioned by the need to access inter-national aid, and so the roots of community policing run shallow in these circum-stances. There is a more general conundrum, that has implications for developed and developing countries alike, which is that community policing is intended, among other things, to contribute to the development of social cohesion and capital: qualities that are important to the success of community policing itself.

_____ imperfect communities _____

Current proposals to implement Neighbourhood Policing in Britain maintain that commitment to consult with local communities will not mean simply that the police respond to those interests that are articulated in the 'loudest voices' (Home Office, 2007), but the status of public demands in the overall deter-mination of policing priorities remains ambiguous. While being seen to take seriously issues of concern to local communities will continue to be an impor-tant feature of the community policing agenda, it is clear that this does not impose absolute obligations upon local police managers. The increasing salience of various forms of social diversity might mean that local communi-ties will not produce coherent agendas or priorities to which Neighbourhood Police teams can respond. Even where there is some consensus, it might be that issues of social justice, among other things, make it proper that the police service retains professional independence so that it might not act upon certain demands. Crawford et al. (2003) noted that local communities have often demanded that police officers provide reassurance by moving on young people congregated in public spaces and that this raises important questions relating to social justice and equity. Moreover there is a danger that Neighbourhood Policing programmes repeat more general tendencies to afford a spurious 'grass-roots authenticity' to locally identified priorities (Hughes and Rowe, 2007). It might be that local residents' perceptions of issues most serious to them do not equate to actual risks or harm measured in more objective terms. Furthermore, as Lee (2007) argues, there is often a feedback loop so that community perceptions of crime and security issues iterate with agendas established by the police, local media, and broader political discourse. Hughes and Rowe (2007) describe the relational nature of local knowledge in the following terms:

> In some circumstances, police and community knowledge can exist in symbiotic relation such that one can reinforce and complement the other to produce authoritative local common sense that underpins local governance. Alternative perspectives, among hard-to-reach or marginalised groups, for example, might be driven out of local consultation processes.

policing and social cohesion

The broader remit that community policing programmes develop for the service might also raise significant challenges. As several of the definitions outlined earlier in this chapter made clear, and the Neighbourhood Policing programme reaffirms, community policing promises to engage the police in developing social cohesion. Even working in partnership with other agencies, the capacity of the police service to positively improve the quality of life of disadvantaged communities is likely to remain limited. While crime and antisocial behaviour might have serious deleterious effects on the quality of life of those living in some neighbourhoods, and the police might be able to take some steps to tackle some important causal factors, it seems unlikely that the police service will have the capacity to address structural problems that might generate insecurity. Crawford (2006) and Newburn (2003) have argued that efforts to broaden the remit of the police service reflect a more general, problematic, trend whereby central government in Britain has sought criminal justice responses to non-criminal justice problems.

conclusion: whither community policing?

Community policing faces a series of challenges in terms of the viability of the police service to meet a much wider remit that requires them to build social capital and enhance 'quality of life' issues. The idea that local communities are appropriate or viable sites for determining and promoting policing priorities has also been critically explored, and it has been suggested that this might raise profound concerns relating to social justice. In many respects these concerns, while important, represent limits to the aspirations of community policing programmes but do not mean that devolved, service-oriented, inclusive models of policing ought to be abandoned. While the 'community' might not exist in the idealized form often implied in policy statements, the partnership approaches that characterize contemporary policing developments offer opportunities for engagement that might prove worthwhile on occasion.

Further questions about the future prospects of community policing relate to the tensions that surround contradictory processes of centralization and devolution. While Neighbourhood Policing and similar programmes focus on devolving responsibility to the local level, other aspects of New Public Management have meant increasing central control by the Home Office over local police performance and agenda setting. The mechanisms by which central government has developed stronger powers to scrutinze and direct policing at the local level are outlined in Chapter 6, where the tensions between local and central police governance are explored. In more general terms it is maintained by some that while contemporary nation-states have devolved various functions to other agencies, in this context, responsibility for policing has been relinquished to local **Basic Command Units**; there has nonetheless been an increase in the regulatory power of the state which has assumed greater capacity to 'steer' the provision of services, even if it is no longer directly responsible for 'rowing' (Johnston and Shearing, 2003).

Bowling and Foster's (2002) analysis of recent developments in British policing concludes by outlining contrasting trends such that an increasing emphasis on devolution and community orientation that seems to be undermined by concurrent processes whereby the governance of the police is becoming increasingly centralized as the powers available to them are being extended. While the problems facing community policing have been outlined in this chapter, it is clear that they also need to be understood in the wider context of trends moving in other directions. For this reason, Bowling and Foster's uncertainty about how these complex patterns will unfold in the future provide a suitable note on which to end this discussion:

> On the one hand, the rise of community policing, the development of multi-agency partnerships, changing loci of responsibility, new developments in police accountability – such as the implementation of an independent police complaints system, the Human Rights Act 1998, the Race Relations (Amendment) Act 2000, and the Freedom of Information Act 2000 – together with a new willingness to take account of research findings, suggest that openness, accountability of policing to the public will increase. On the other hand, a raft of recent legislation, including the Criminal Justice and Public Order Act 1994, the Crime and Disorder Act 1998, the Regulation of Investigatory Powers Act 2000,

and the Terrorism Act 2001, has extended *policing* powers, and the sphere of police influence, in new and unwelcome directions ... These shifts mirror a greater separation of public policing functions at the national and transnational level, which has been established without any significant public discussion. (2002: 1021)

▪ ▪ chapter summary ▪

- Although community policing programmes are conceptually and operationally problematic, the principle that the police service ought to seek the consent of the community, and to meet public expectations is important in terms of the legitimacy of the police, and their operational effectiveness.

- Community policing can be defined in terms of the processes, such as devolution of power and responsibility to the local level, public consultation, and the involvement of citizens. These approaches tend to emphasize that community policing is a philosophy, rather than a programme of actions.

- Other approaches explain community policing in terms of the type of outcomes that it produces. Rather than conceiving of policing primarily in terms of crime control and law enforcement, community policing establishes outcomes relating to fear of crime, quality of service, improving life chances for local communities, and thus establishes a much broader remit for the police.

- Another approach stresses that community policing programmes have developed, in Britain, as a reaction to dissatisfaction that had developed from the late 1960s, as in the interests of efficiency and professionalism, changing police practices had led to a deterioration in community relations. Coupled with concerns about malpractice and rising crime rates, these created deteriorating prospects for the police and community policing was pursued in order to salvage police legitimacy.

- In practice, community policing often entails enhanced consultation with local communities. This can be a formal legal requirement or a matter of providing for informal contacts for officers to consult local people as part of their routine work. Many of the formal mechanisms developed in Britain have been regarded as unsuccessful in terms of holding local police to account.

- Neighbourhood Watch (NW) has been the major example of police–public co-production in Britain in recent decades. Evaluating the success of NW has proved difficult, partly because schemes vary so considerably in terms of levels and types of activity.

- Community policing has aimed to bridge the reassurance gap, whereby that declining levels of crime, noted by successive British Crime Surveys, have not been mirrored in public perceptions, which have held that crime rates continue to rise. In tandem with increasing deployment of Police Community Support Officers, the Neighbourhood Policing programme intends to promote high visibility policing, as one means of providing for public reassurance.

- In addition to providing for high visibility policing, the NP programme claims to give communities influence over local agendas, opportunities for joint interventions to tackle problems, and make police answerable.

- Community policing faces internal challenges as it has often been marginalized by dominant sub-cultural understanding of what constitutes 'real police work', which tends to be defined in narrow crime control, law enforcement terms. Such cultural values reflect a more general organizational tendency to under-resource and under-value community policing.

- Community policing projects have been exported from the USA and Britain to many developing countries. Often these have been less than successful as they have been introduced into social, political and economic contexts that are not conducive to developing civil society relations with the police service.

- Further challenges relate to the nature of communities, which tend to offer fragmented, contradictory and imperfect knowledge of local crime problems. It is unlikely that community consultation, no matter how effective, would produce a coherent programme of action that officers could operationalize.

- Community policing programmes cast the role of the police service in broad terms, often relating to enhancing social cohesion or improving the quality of life for local residents. This poses challenges, since the police service, or criminal justice agencies more widely, might not be well placed to address criminogenic factors.

- More fundamentally, the devolution of policing to local levels seems incongruous during a period in which central government control over the police service, and the public sector more widely, seems to have grown exponentially. Techniques of performance management, audit and inspection seem to run counter to stated aims of allowing priorities to be determined locally.

■ self-check ℚuestions ▬▬▬▬▬▬▬▬▬▬▬▬

1 What three elements did Skogan (2006) suggest characterize community policing initiatives in the United States?

2 How did Weatheritt suggest the term 'community policing' had been used in Britain?

3 Identify four aspects of Alderson's model of community policing.

4   What was the name of the policing model introduced alongside panda cars, two-way radios and other innovations in the late 1960s?

5   What legislation required that the police, in partnership with other agencies, conduct audits to establish the community safety needs of local communities?

6   How many people was it estimated lived in areas covered by Neighbourhood Watch schemes in 2006?

7   What did a 2001 HMIC Report establish as the three core features of reassurance policing?

8   What features of police work explain the tendency for officers to be culturally isolated from the wider community?

9   Why might local residents' perceptions of crime risks not be reliable?

10 What trend appears to contradict moves to devolve policing closer to local communities?

study Questions

1   Is community policing best understood as a philosophy or a programme?

2   Do the contradictions and fragmentation of communities fundamentally undermine community policing projects?

3   Does central government control of the police service undermine the democratic credentials of Neighbourhood Policing?

annotated further reading

The development of community policing in the Anglo-American context, in the Pacific Rim and in the European Union is reviewed by Brogden and Nijhar (2005), who identify ten myths associated with much debate of this approach to police work. Brogden and Nijhar argue that community policing models have tended to fail when transported to developing countries that do not share the social and political context of North America where they were developed.

A special edition of *Criminology and Criminal Justice* (2007, volume 7, number 4) explores the development of Neighbourhood Policing in Britain, and the implications of social diversity and central government control in efforts to reinvigorate community policing. Articles in the journal explore community policing as it applies to minority ethnic communities in rural areas; to new travellers; to lesbian, gay, bisexual and transgender communities; and to virtual communities.

Roberg, Novak and Cordner's (2005) *Police and Society* provides a good overview of the foundations and administration of the police in the United States, the behaviour of officers, and a range of controversies and challenges faced in the context of policing a diverse and fragmented society. The book contains a chapter that reviews the transition towards community policing and the associated philosophy, strategy, and tactics.

_____ : // annotated listings of links to relevant websites /_____

One of the most extensive, sustained, and researched experiments in community policing was conducted in Chicago. Data on the project, known as the Chicago Alternative Policing Strategy (CAPS), including background papers and the results of research can be found at the Institute for Policy Research at Northwestern University (http://www.northwestern.edu/ipr/publications/policing.html).

Current developments in community policing in England and Wales largely focus upon the Neighbourhood Police programme, details of which can be found at http://tinyurl.com/285ojs.

The philosophy and practice of community policing have often developed in the United States. Information on the operation and principles of many examples can be found at http://tinyurl.com/2dudaz.

5

Police culture

Contents

Although the media portrayal of police work often presents officers as the brave 'thin blue line' protecting society from threats of crime, disorder and anarchy, images of corruption, deviance, racism and sexism have become common themes in popular cultural representations of policing. Integral to the TV show *Life on Mars*, in which a contemporary cop travels back in time to the 1970s, is the lead character's impatience with the causal sexism, rule-breaking, and excessive drinking of his colleagues. While the drama relies upon the idea that modern police work has been transformed from the unreconstructed insularity and machismo of earlier periods, contemporary scandals and exposés of the 'reality' of policing often focus on the problematic working culture of the junior ranks. This chapter explores the nature of police culture and the implications that this has for the delivery of policing. In particular, the chapter does the following:

- Illustrates the nature of police culture in broad terms, and in more detail, in relation to racism, sexism, and homophobia;

- considers whether police culture originates from the socio-economic background from which officers are recruited or emerges from the nature of police work;

- examines debates about the link between police culture and police behaviour, and the significance of these debates in the context of plural policing.

key terms

deviance; discretion; ethics; homophobia; institutional change and reform; organizational sub-culture; racism; sexism

introduction

In the earlier discussion about the nature of policing and police work it was noted that policing is a contested activity that can be understood and interpreted in contrasting ways. Very often policing has been considered in narrow and relatively simple terms as law enforcement. Although sociological accounts have long emphasized that this is only a marginal aspect of police work, popular culture often represents the 'cops and robbers' tradition familiar from myriad television shows, films, music, and literature. This tendency was encapsulated in the news media's response to Sir Ian Blair's call for a debate about the proper role for the police service in twenty-first-century Britain. It was noted in Chapter 1 that Blair suggested that the proper basis for policing was more difficult to discern in an increasingly complex and fragmented society and that the police should not be left to re-invent their role in isolation – a widespread public debate was required. The reaction of sections of the news media was as simplistic as it was unsympathetic to Blair's call for dialogue and suggested that the proper role of the police was to 'bring criminals to justice'. Even a cursory consideration of this common-sense definition of policing demonstrates that it is of little practical use. Offences against the criminal law range in their nature and seriousness to an enormous degree. In 2006, newspapers and opposition parties suggested that the British Labour government had introduced more than 3000 new criminal offences since taking office in May 1997. One newspaper noted that while the criminal-ization of some activities had been uncontroversial, others seemed less of a priority (Morris, 2006):

> **It is now illegal to sell grey squirrels, impersonate a traffic warden or offer Air Traffic Control services without a licence. Creating a nuclear explosion was outlawed in 1998.**
>
> **Householders who fail to nominate a neighbour to turn off their alarm while they are away from home can be breaking the law. And it is an offence for a ship's captain to be carrying grain unless he has a copy of the International Grain Code on board.**

As was explained in Chapter 1, law enforcement perspectives of policing have often been mirrored in academic analysis of policing, which – until the past few decades – tended to focus upon legal frameworks, institutional arrange-ments, and resources. This conceptualization shifted once research into policing began to establish that individual officers had considerable scope to interpret and apply the law selectively. The 'discovery' of police discretion underpins debate about the origins, nature, and impact of police sub-culture, and is the starting point for discussion in this chapter. While many occupations and professions are known to produce particular cultural patterns that develop among the working lives of employees, discussion of the 'working personality' of police officers is particularly important because it is often held that this helps to shape the ways in which policing is applied in practice. Having reviewed the nature of officer discretion, the chapter will continue by consid-ering the origins and nature of police culture.

police discretion

With limited resources it is clear that police officers, from the most junior to the most senior, prioritize which laws to enforce and to which extent they will be enforced in particular circumstances. Reiner (2000) noted that this is both a necessary and a desirable state of affairs. Noting that it is practically impossible for the police to enforce all laws on all occasions, Reiner also highlighted that it would not be normatively acceptable for them so to do. Furthermore, the application of any law requires interpretation in the context of particular circumstances, and this inevitably entails a degree of subjectivity on the part of the officer. That officers use their judgement as they decide when to use the full extent of their legal powers and when to rely upon informal means to resolve the conflicts and disputes that they routinely face is sometimes a matter of practical consideration but – equally important – it is also desirable, as the blanket enforcement of all laws on all occasions would have a deleterious effect on public confidence in the police and the criminal justice system more generally (Wilson, 1968). As has been said, employees in many occupations are expected to exercise discretion when doing their jobs. Health-care providers consider the particular characteristics of individual patients before embarking on a programme of treatment, or deciding that none should be offered. Educators properly take into account mitigating circumstances when deciding on the grade awarded to a student. Research suggests, however, that the exercise of discretion in the delivery of policing is markedly different from other contexts for a number of reasons. First, police officers occupy an unusual – although not unique – position in that they embody the symbolic power of the sovereign state and have recourse to the legitimate use of force against fellow citizens. For many analysts this is the defining characteristic of the public police (Bittner, 1974). Although regulation and governance are increasingly diffuse and are exercised by complex and shifting networks of local, national and global actors – as outlined in more detail in Chapter 8 – it remains the case that the police officer continues to occupy a symbolic position in terms of relations of power between state and citizen. For that reason, as research evidence demonstrated that police officers use their discretion in law enforcement, concern began to be expressed that the selective application of the law undermined democratic governance (Neyroud and Beckley, 2001: x). Police officers, the conventional model held, were expected to enforce laws produced by the democratic nation state 'without fear or favour'; that they did so selectively on the basis of their own judgement, it was argued, corrupted the proper constitutional framework.

A second reason why discretion in police work is somewhat distinct from that practised by other workers also relates to the particular context of the police institution. Although the scope of information technology and the reach of performance-monitoring regimes have shone some light into the darkness, it continues to be the case that officers exercise their discretion in conditions of relative invisibility. Moreover it is junior officers, with relatively little experience, who are more likely to be deployed on routine patrol work and to have direct, possibly problematic, encounters with the public. One commentator on police work famously noted that police work is unlike other types of employment since 'the police department has the special property … that within it discretion increases as one moves down the hierarchy' (Wilson, 1968: 7).

The sheer diversity and unpredictability of policework mean that individual officers will often be exercising their discretion in circumstances distanced from their supervisors. Although police officers might have targets set in terms of the number of sanctioned detections they are required to achieve, might be encouraged to participate in foot patrol, or visit vulnerable premises or communities, they retain considerable autonomy over how they discharge their duties. Police work can be considered relatively invisible since it is carried out in places and at times removed from supervision and scrutiny of more senior officers, but how technological developments have reduced the extent of officer discretion is considered in more detail in Chapter 9. Debates about the abuse of police discretion often focus on claims that officers over-police certain communities. For example, it has been widely claimed that racist aspects of police sub-culture lead officers to stop and search young black males more often than young white males. Clearly, if this claim can be substantiated, this would constitute an abuse of police powers. In response to these concerns police organizations in Britain have, for some years, monitored officers' stop- and-search activity in an effort to identify officers who, deliberately or otherwise, disproportionately target some groups in this way. Similarly, efforts to improve the police response to domestic violence have sometimes focused on encouraging officers to arrest suspects, and not to use their discretion so as to seek an informal 'resolution' of these conflicts. Carswell (2006) noted that officers' reluctance to intervene had often been rooted in cultural perspectives on gender relations within marriage and that the private sphere was beyond the proper intervention of the state. Rowe (2007) highlighted that efforts to address these shortcomings often require an officer to arrest perpetrators, and so seek to limit, or remove altogether, discretion. Technological developments and the administrative requirements to record encounters with the public and to account for time spent on duty offer police supervisors enhanced opportunities to scrutinize police behaviour (Ericson and Haggerty, 1997). While these efforts seek to limit the scope for officers to abuse their discretion by over-policing some groups, it is much more difficult to interrogate circumstances in which officers 'turn a blind eye' or use their discretion not to invoke their full legal powers. As McLaughlin (2007b) recounts, the 2003 BBC TV documentary The Secret Policeman provided clear evidence that some police recruits continued to hold violent racist attitudes, and that police probationer training was not effectively challenging such racism. One of the key passages from the undercover exposé involved a police recruit recounting how his hatred of Asian people had led him to target an Asian man for motoring violations. Additionally, the probationary officer noted that he had used his discretion to ignore similar offences committed by a white female driver. Both of these illustrate the use of police discretion; clearly the former incident amounted to an abuse of police power since the officer's decision was based, he admitted, on extraneous factors (i.e. the ethnicity of the driver). That was a decision to intervene, though, and the procedures that the officer would have been required to complete meant that it was possible, in principle, for his supervisor to review the circumstances and details of the encounter. The second incident also involved the officer using his discretion. Again, this appears to have involved an abuse of police discretion since it too was based on the ethnicity, and maybe the gender, of the driver concerned. In this case, however, the result was a decision not to intervene and as such is beyond the scrutiny of supervisory officers who are unlikely to directly observe the officer's behaviour. It is partly due to the difficulties of reviewing police decision-making that some argue that the most effective way of ensuring that officers do not abuse their discretionary powers is to develop robust ethical frameworks that encourage officers to become reflective practitioners who can be relied upon to act professionally and responsibly. Neyroud and Beckley (2001) argued that the most effective way to prevent the abuse of police discretion is to develop the professionalism of officers by establishing a stronger ethical framework for police practice.

While the exercise of discretion is a central and legitimate aspect of police-work, it is widely held that it is often unduly influenced by working cultures that encourage stereotyping and prejudice to enter into officer decision-making in ways that are unacceptable. Long-standing concerns that the police service fail to provide an appropriate service to minority groups and to women have drawn attention to the negative impact of police culture (Rowe, 2004; Westmarland, 2002). Walklate noted the close association between discretion and police culture in the following terms:

> Police officers deal with ... discretion, and the confusion it sometimes generates, through the construction of collectively understood and often taken-for-granted norms and values, frequently referred to in the academic literature as 'cop culture'. Co-operation and solidarity have frequently been commented upon as being key features of this 'cop culture' ... On occasions, that culture has been seen as the source of all policing ills. Indeed, the solidarity engendered by it had been known to provide 'cover' for rather less than legitimate policing activities. Understanding the nature and impact of this culture on how the task of policing is performed is crucial to an understanding of how, in routine practice, the central task of policing is interpreted. (1995: 104)

the nature of police culture

The 'working personality' of the police officer has been a recurring theme in sociological studies of the police since such research began in Britain and the

United States in the early 1960s. Since then successive studies of police work, especially those in an anthropological or ethnographic tradition, have explored the ways in which officers understand the world around them and conceive their role within it (Skogan, 2006; Reiner, 1978; Punch, 1979). Not surprisingly each of these studies places a different emphasis on particular aspects of police culture and each reaches its own conclusions. However, there is a remarkable and persistent unanimity on some key features of police culture (see Box 5.1).

Box 5.1

Reiner's (2000) seven components of police sub-culture

1 a sense of mission

2 suspicion

3 isolation/solidarity

4 conservatism

5 machismo

6 pragmatism

7 racial prejudice

Writing about emerging sociological studies in the United States, Balch (1972) suggested police culture was understood in the following terms:

> In the last few years a great deal has been written about the police mentality. If we can believe everything we read in magazines, journals, and sociology books, the typical policeman is cynical, suspicious, conservative, and thoroughly bigoted. This is not a flattering picture to be sure, but it recurs again and again in the popular and 'scientific' literature on the police. Perhaps there is something about the police system itself that generates a suspicious, conservative world-view. Or perhaps certain personality types are inadvertently recruited for police work. Either explanation is plausible, and both may be correct.

Paoline et al. (2000) described police occupational culture in the following terms, relating it to the nature of police work:

> Officers cope with the danger and uncertainty of their occupational environment by *being suspicious* and *maintaining the edge* … Officers cope with the organizational environment by taking a *lay-low* or *cover-your-ass* attitude and adopting a *crimefighter* or *law enforcement* orientation …

> **The problems that officers confront in their working environment, as well as the coping mechanisms prescribed by the police culture: *social isolation* and *group loyalty* ... The dangerousness of their occupational environment prompts officers to distance themselves from the rest of society ... The unique elements of their coercive authority separate them further from the public.**

Such findings are often reflected in news media reports of police deviance. The 2003 BBC TV expose of racism among police probationers has already been referred to; more recently a similar undercover documentary portrayed police officers watching pornographic material while on duty, denigrating the account of a victim of rape, and boasting that they had driven past a man lying injured in the road because they had wanted to make it back to the police station in order to watch a major football match on TV (Channel 4, 2006). The same documentary recorded officers playing 'hide and seek' while on vehicle patrol and ignoring radio calls for help while they went to fetch take-away meals.

racism and police culture

Although not all aspects of police culture are inherently negative, the norms and values outlined here are often used to explain enduring concerns about police racism, sexism, and homophobia. In his report into the 1981 disorders in Brixton, Lord Scarman argued that the police service in Britain was not institutionally racist but that there was clearly a problem of racial prejudice among a proportion of junior officers (Scarman, 1981). Often this explanation of police racism is referred to as a 'rotten apples' perspective, which associates the problem with the negative prejudices and stereotyping of a small minority of officers that has a disproportionate impact on the organization as a whole. Although the 1950s and 1960s often have been portrayed as a 'golden age' of British policing, it is increasingly apparent that even during that hallowed era police officers displayed virulent racist attitudes toward migrants from the Caribbean, and later from the Indian sub-continent (McLaughlin, 2007a: 171). Furthermore, Whitfield (2007) demonstrates that racist attitudes during this period were not confined to retrograde junior officers but extended up to senior officers who, among other things, were privately opposed to the appointment of 'coloured' police officers.

In 2005, a Metropolitan Police officer was suspended following allegations during a trial that he racially abused a teenager arrested for threatening behaviour. The defendant recorded the officer on his mobile phone and it was claimed the constable told him that he would 'smash his Arab face in' and that he was a robber and a rapist (*Guardian*, 2005). It was also alleged that the constable also told the youth 'this is one that you won't fucking get off of at court, because I'll write it up properly'. Subsequently the officer was acquitted of charges of racially aggravated common assault, although he admitted that his conduct had been unprofessional (*Guardian*, 2007). In November 2006, Hertfordshire police disciplined 140 staff who had circulated a racist email containing footage of a black man being decapitated as he fell onto railings following a police pursuit. Eight of those disciplined were sergeants and seven, civilian supervisors (Butt, 2006), which suggests that the racist sub-cultures permeate supervisory roles. Apart from the contemporary references to information technology, such incidents litter accounts of police relations with minority ethnic communities and have done so for decades. These examples have been selected because they represent something of the wider context of debates about racism and police culture, and, more specifically, as they indicate that these concerns relate both to external relations between the police and the public, and to internal personnel matters. Prior to the publication of the **Macpherson Report** in 1999, it was often held that the nature of workplace banter and the use of racist and derogatory language more generally behind the scenes of the police station were not necessarily of primary importance. The off-stage characteristics of police sub-culture, such as sending 'inappropriate' emails, was not closely associated with the professional discharge of police duties. Whether this perspective is tenable, and the relationship between police culture and performance more generally, is considered at greater length later in this chapter.

This brief review of the debates about racism and police sub-culture reflects a tendency to consider these issues in relatively narrow terms associated with the individual deviance of police staff. Often this is demonstrated by senior officers' response, which is usually to identify and discipline those responsible and to devise strategies to ensure that such problems do not recur. The quest to develop effective psychological tests that might identify applicants to the police service who have authoritarian or prejudiced personalities is often cited by senior officers promising that the lessons of the past will be learnt. For example, it has been reported that new technologies tantalize employers with their apparent capacity to use MRI scans that can identify neural activity in parts of the brain that indicate that an individual has racist values (Russo, 2007). Sociologically such techno-solutions raise profound questions about the nature and definition of racism and whether it can be isolated to particular chemical processes in the brain or is an emergent property of social relations that develop in particular contexts and power dynamics.

While understandable in institutional terms, conceptualizing police culture only in terms of the deviant behaviour of retrograde officers and staff who transgress against official policy is of limited use. Discourse that presents racism as a pathological problem associated with flawed individuals has become commonplace in public debates about the problem. While it might appear to further antiracist agendas, the creation of racist 'folk devils' by the mass media serves to marginalize analysis of racialization in its broader social context. The condemnatory couplet of 'racist copper' has become a recurring image in popular culture representation, which serves to keep the problem of racism on the agenda but does nothing to develop an understanding in the context of cultural and institutional dynamics. The racism of police culture must also be understood more broadly in terms of the normative whiteness of police services. Efforts to promote cultural diversity, for example, through the establishment of staff associations such as the **Black Police Association** or the Muslim Police Association, have the unintended consequence of underlining the marginality and specificity of officers and civilian staff of a minority ethnic background. Affording these groups particular status re-affirms the 'whiteness' of the mainstream of police organizations. This promotes the 'balkanization' of police staff into narrow enclaves of identity politics and has created an environment in which 'cultural wars' can gain ground (McLaughlin, 2007b). Furthermore, the provision of diversity training programmes or development of tougher sanctions against racist officers and other police staff does not address some of the more fundamental challenges of re-shaping police culture so that it becomes more appropriate in an increasingly diverse social, political and cultural context.

As noted in Chapter 1, police work has, in the British context at least, had metaphorical qualities that have provided a cultural lens through which national identity has been focused. As the notions of 'Englishness' and 'Britishness' become increasingly contested and complex, police culture needs to be re-worked if the embedded problems of racialization – which go far beyond instances of police deviance – are to be addressed. The relationship between police culture and efforts to reform the service are considered further towards the end of this chapter.

sexism and police culture

Sexist attitudes and machismo have been widely noted elements of police culture and, like the other topics discussed here, have been identified as problematic both internally in terms of staff relations and equal opportunities, and externally in terms of the provision of effective service to the public. Jordan argued that police culture was a central factor underlying the failure of the service to effectively respond to victims of rape: 'The beliefs of the police occupational sub-culture have been shaped by its origins as a male-dominated organization enforcing laws designed to protect male property owners, with women being construed as part of men's property' (2004: 243).

Although minority ethnic officers have long been under-represented in the ranks of British police forces, they have not been subject to the same formal and overt barriers that have impacted upon female officers. While women had been employed as police officers in Britain and in the United States from early in the twentieth century, their employment was highly gendered and reflected stereotypes and prejudices about the role of women more generally. Their work was largely confined to dealing with other women or with children – tasks to which it was thought they were better suited than their male counterparts. During the First World War women were recruited, as volunteers, into the police service with the specific remit of protecting women and children, particularly women thought to be vulnerable due to their working in large numbers in war-related industries such as munitions production. After the war the employment of women was intended to help curb a perceived increase in prostitution (Carrier, 1988, cited in Heidensohn, 1992). Heidensohn noted that the gendered nature of women's police work represented a curious victory for those who had campaigned for the rights of female police officers. While they achieved many of their goals relating to the provision of pay and pensions, the role they conceived of for women officers perpetuated patriarchal perspectives on the status of women:

> **Police work for women was still defined, and was to remain until well after the Second World War, as a specialist field, mainly confined to moral and sexual matters and inevitably making female officers complicit in their control of their own sex in ways in which men's behaviour was not controlled. (ibid.: 52)**

It was not until the mid-1970s that female police officers achieved a degree of formal equality in policing as, in Britain, in 1975, the Sex Discrimination Act and the Equal Pay Act came into force. It was during this period that police services disbanded women's departments and integrated female officers into general police duties. Clearly the changing legal and organizational context did not wholly transform the position of women within the police service and they continue to be significantly under-represented in general terms in most police services around the world, a situation exacerbated in senior ranks, as Table 5.1 indicates.

Table 5.1   Police officer strength[1] in England and Wales,[2] by rank and gender, as at 31 March 2005

Rank	Male	Female	Total	% Female
ACPO ranks	204	23	227	10
Chief Superintendent	502	40	542	7
Superintendent	930	99	1029	10
Chief Inspector	1765	203	1968	10
Inspector	6192	746	6938	11
Sergeant	17982	2704	20686	13
Constable	85057	26347	111404	24
Total	112632	30162	142794	21

Notes:
[1]Full-time equivalents.
[2]Including NCIS, NCS and 'central service secondments'.

Source: Bibi et al. (2005: 14)

Although clearly still under-represented, there has been an increase in the number of female officers. In recent years, a number of women have been appointed to senior ranks and organizations such as the **British Association of Women Police (BAWP)** have sought to address institutional barriers to the recruitment, retention and promotion of female officers. In 2001, the BAWP launched the Gender Agenda, a programme of initiatives addressing a host of factors such as part-time working and the provision of equipment for female officers. The five key elements of the Gender Agenda are outlined in Box 5.2, which shows that the barriers to the progression of female officers often relate to cultural factors, such as the marginalization of women's voices within the service.

Box 5.2

The Gender Agenda: executive summary

We believe by focusing on the agenda the Police Service will ensure benefits for both women officers and the greater organization.

This document clearly explains the BAWP vision, values, *raison d'être* and the five long-term aims which are:

1. For the Service to demonstrate consistently that it values women officers.
2. To achieve a gender, ethnicity and sexual orientation balance across the rank structure and specialisms consistent with the proportion of women in the economically active population.
3. To have a woman's voice in influential policy fora focusing on both internal and external service delivery.
4. To develop an understanding of the competing demands in achieving a work/life balance and a successful police career.
5. To have a working environment and equipment of the right quality and standards to enable women officers to do their job professionally.

It then clearly and succinctly outlines the case for the agenda, giving the Service five good reasons why it should pursue it with vigour.

Finally, each long-term aim was broken down to give the reality of what it means: clearly identify the barriers to progress, what action needs to be undertaken to break down the barriers, examples of positive initiatives currently happening to improve the situation and finally highlight bad practice that needs to be stopped.

Source: British Association of Women Police, http://www.bawp.org/WhereWe Stand.htm

---

Just as sexism within police culture has explained the marginalization of women within the police service, and the persistence of the 'glass ceiling' that has prevented them from progressing up the **rank structure**, so too it has detracted from the quality of service offered to female crime victims. As with the relationship between racism and the paucity of the police response to victims of racist crime, there is a symbiotic relationship between the lack of female officers and the failure of the service to understand the nature and impact of sexual offences and domestic violence (Jordan, 2002; Walklate, 1995). As with efforts to tackle racism and homophobia, a key response to problems of sexism in police subculture has been to seek to recruit more female staff, and it is clear that progress has been made in this area. However, it is not simply the absence of women officers that explains the failure of the service; the police culture itself complicates the picture and makes the position more intractable. As with other minority groups within the service, evidence suggests that female officers have often sought to fit into their working environment by embracing the prevailing norms of the police working personality. In an effort to demonstrate that their primary working identity is as a police officer, not a *female* police officer, women in the service have tended to adopt the sub-cultural values predominant in the service. While this might prove an effective coping strategy for individual officers, it suggests that simply recruiting more female officers is unlikely, in and of itself, to lead to a better provision for survivors of sexual assault or domestic violence (Walklate, 1995: 112–14).

These problems of sexism and policing tend to be related to police subculture in narrow terms of officer deviance. Denigrating female victims of sexual assault, for example, or making sexist comments about colleagues in the workplace have informally tended to be tolerated within the police service, but are clearly contrary to the official policies and public statements (Brown and Heidensohn, 2000). Officers found to engage in such activities are liable to be disciplined, dismissed or required to undertake training programmes. Additionally, problems of discrimination in the police workplace reflect a failure to introduce effective equal opportunities programmes that cater, for example, for the needs of part-time staff.

As with the problem of racism, however, there are wider dimensions of police culture, not related to specific misbehaviour among officers, which perpetuate stereotypes and disadvantage female staff. Although empirically misleading, it was noted in Chapter 1 that police work is often (mis)represented by officers who stress the action, danger and excitement of their role. One consequence of this is an emphasis on the corporal demands of police work and the centrality of a strong physical presence. As has been noted, recourse to the legitimate use of force is often offered as a defining characteristic of police work, and although sociological research clearly demonstrates that force is rarely used, it has contributed to the marginalization of women, historically and contemporaneously (Westmarland, 2002). The machismo of police work is often foregrounded in news media and 'infotainment' representations of policing, which focus on tough crime-fighting, car chases, and physical confrontation. Equally, political rhetoric that surrounds competition between rivals as they lay claim to the most severe policies on law and order, often replete with language of 'cracking down on crime' and getting 'tough' on criminals, reinforces a particularly muscular police discourse. The culture of policing in these broad terms, as well as the sub-cultural properties of the working norms and values of rank-and-file officers, clearly needs to be understood and addressed if women are to be treated equally, either within the police service or as victims of crime.

_____ homophobia and police culture _____

In terms of research, publicity campaigns, and pressure group activity, the position of lesbian, gay, bisexual and transgender (LGBT) communities in relation to policing has been almost wholly overlooked until recently. Unlike visible minority ethnic and female officers, LGBT officers can choose whether to be open about their sexual orientation, although the context of homopho-bia might means that this is not a choice freely exercised. Partly for this reason there has been little systematic monitoring of the sexual orientation of police staff. Although statistical data on the status and rank of LGBT police staff are not available, there is considerable anecdotal information to suggest that homophobia has long been a central feature of police sub-culture.

Burke (1993) noted that gay and bisexual male officers have, until recently in Britain, been marginalized partly as a result of the potential criminality of their behaviour. Prior to 2000 – when the Sexual Offences (Amendment) Act equalized the age of consent for homosexual and heterosexual sexual relations – gay and bisexual men joining the force at the age of 18, the minimum starting age for police officers, faced a period of potential conflict, and risk of exposure, between their private activity and professional status as officers. In a number of the personal testimonies that Burke presents in his study, officers recall that they were sometimes inhibited from challenging homophobia among their colleagues since to do so might risk their own status. This illustrates that police sub-culture cannot be understood outside of the legal and institutional frame-work within which officers operate. The association between police sub-culture and wider aspects of the police law enforcement role has posed a particularly difficult environment for gay police officers:

> membership of any highly regulated organization which has, as part of its own remit, the control of 'sexual deviance' is likely to result in the defamation of atypical sexualities at an organizational and thus, by extension, at a personal level. In addition, whilst crises of 'ambivalent identity' are suffered by many non-heterosexuals who are learning to accept their variation, proscriptions against their orientation are often subtle, implied, and indirect, whereas the explicitness of the collective police judgement on homosexuality, the machismo sub-culture, and the manifest discrepant status of homosexual activity in British

law (with its related police activity) mean that in trying to come to terms with a non-heterosexual orientation, many gay, lesbian, and bisexual police officers are liable to find themselves conducting multiple existences and many suffer profound psychological crises as a result. (Burke, 1994: 199)

Praat and Tuffin (1996) found that police sub-culture is partly antipathetic toward LGBT officers because of the perceived deviancy of the homosexual lifestyle, which exposed them to conflicts of interest that did not pertain to other officers. Officers argued that homosexuals were not marginalized because of their sexual orientation *per se*, but since this would have a deleterious impact on their ability to discharge their duties impartially. Similar arguments have been used in respect of minority ethnic officers who, it was sometimes claimed, would act on the basis of cultural, religious or ethno-alliances (Whitfield, 2004). Even recently, in 2006, it was reported that a Metropolitan Police internal report had suggested that Muslim officers might act corruptly in seeking to assist their extended family (Laville and Muir, 2006). Such claims about the risk of minorities acting partially fail to acknowledge evidence not only of the discriminatory discretion often associated with the operational activity of the mainstream of police work but also that minority officers have been noted to over-identify with police sub-culture in order to ensure that they integrate with their colleagues.

As has been noted in the context of racism and sexism, parallels are widely drawn between the homophobia facing LGBT staff and the failure of the police service to properly respond to homophobic hate crime. Williams and Robinson (2004) outlined the relation between police sub-culture and a failure to provide effective policing to the LGBT community in the following terms:

> **The occupational culture of police officers appears to instil negative attitudes about minority individuals, especially those identifying as lesbian, gay or bisexual ... These stereotypes impact upon policing in negative ways leading to discrimination and even harassment of LGB people. This discrimination can often be identified in policing practice, most notably the over-policing of sexual behaviour between men ... Research suggests that, combined, these negative stereotypes and discriminatory policing practices have marred the relationship between the LGB community and the police. These turbulent relationships complicate police service delivery to minority and hard-to-reach groups and reduce police efficiency in monitoring the prevalence of anti-gay hate crimes and same-sex domestic violence. (2004: 274–15)**

The homophobia of police sub-culture has created reluctance on the part of LGBT people to report homophobic incidents to the police. A study by the National Advisory Group/Policing Lesbian and Gay Communities (1999, cited in Williams and Robinson, 2004: 4) found that 80 per cent of homophobic incidents are not reported. Williams and Robinson argue that this reluctance to report stems from a number of factors related to a perception that police culture is hostile to sexual minorities, including the reputation that the police do not take reports of stranger and domestic violence aimed at the LGBT community as seriously as those experienced by heterosexual victims, concern that the victim of crime will be treated as though a perpetrator, a fear of 'coming out' to the police, and a fear of retaliation, isolation and not being believed.

Given the context of on-going perceptions of homophobia within police sub-culture it is interesting to note that, in some respects, it appears that the status of sexuality has been transformed. In 2003, the annual Gay Pride Festival in London included 80 police officers, many of whom paraded in full police uniform, and recruitment stands from a number of police forces. Critics argue that such developments are little more than public relations exercises, intended to promote an image of policing that does not match reality. Similar concerns have been expressed about efforts to recruit minority ethnic staff that present a harmonious multi-ethnic workforce (Rowe, 2004). However, other, more substantive, evidence seems to suggest that the position of LGBT minorities in the police service is improving. In particular, in 2007, 13 of the top 100 'gay friendly' employers identified by the pressure group Stonewall (2007) were police services. That they were ranked highly on this index demonstrates that these police services could demonstrate good practice in terms of developing human resource policies, that they had support networks for staff, and that senior leaders championed sexual orientation diversity across the organization (Stonewall, 2007: 3). Meeting these requirements does not, of course, indicate that there is no longer a problem of homophobia in police sub-culture, and it is revealing that the vast majority of police services did not make the top 100 in this review.

the roots of police culture

Key aspects of police occupational culture have been outlined in the above sections. The reasons why these features have tended to develop and to provide a working personality that is specific to police officers have often remained implicit within these discussions. In this part of the chapter, the roots of police culture are disentangled. Fielding characterized these twin perspectives in the following terms, as he explained the emergence of studies that sought to explain police culture in terms of the working environment in which officers are situated:

> **Rather than the presumption that policing attracts malicious individuals of a punitive and reactionary bent, such work begins from the assumption that the work the police are given to do, and its institutional placing, largely accounts for the character of police practice. (1998: 5)**

Put simply, the question to be addressed in the following paragraphs is: are officers born or made? Explanations that suggest the police culture is best understood with reference to the pre-existing characteristics of those who enter the police service usually focus upon the relatively narrow socio-economic profile of entrants to the service, or on their psychological traits. Traditionally new entrants to the police service have tended to be males of school-leaving age and from a working-class background. The conservative and insular nature of police occupational culture has often been attributed to the profile of new recruits as it is held that the prejudices and preconceptions, such as those relating to minority ethnic communities, to women, and to sexual minorities, reflect the prevailing cultural norms and values of the sections of society from which police officers are recruited. Claims that the norms and values associated with police culture reflect the prevailing disposition of officers as they enter the service draw upon the notion of the 'authoritarian personality', developed by Adorno et al. (1950) after the Second World War. Colman and Gorman (1982) measured the attitudes of new recruits to the police service on a range of controversial issues, such as the death penalty and migration, and compared the results to those obtained from a control group. They concluded that newly recruited police officers were significantly more illiberal and intolerant than the control group. Although criticized on methodological and other grounds (Waddington, 1982), the notion that police officers enter the service with regressive and insular values has remained a primary explanation of police culture. This is reflected in those efforts to change problematic dimensions of police culture by re-engineering the profile of police service personnel so as to include more minority ethnic and female officers (Cashmore, 2002; Paoline et al., 2000). Some of these efforts have already been described in this chapter. Others include policies that seek to attract a broader age range of candidates for the police service, by, for example, emphasizing the importance of recruiting individuals who have experience of other occupations that might be valuable to the police service. Additionally, reconfiguring initial police training programmes so that they are delivered in partnership with universities has had the goal of exposing new recruits to a broader spectrum of experience and learning than was available in the narrow confines of police training colleges.

At the other end of the spectrum of explanations of police culture are those who suggest that it is the nature of police work itself that engenders the cultural patterns identified in this chapter. Some of the characteristics of police work that perpetuate the culture common among officers relate to practical aspects of organizational policing. Shift-work, for example, might enhance group solidarity and insularity in that it makes it more difficult for officers to form social relations outside of 'the job' (Cain, 1973). Until recently, probationer training was conducted almost exclusively in an extended period during which officers would be literally separated from the wider community as they resided in training college. Similarly, officers are required to observe certain regulations (relating to their political activity and the economic activities of their families, for example) that extend into the social and domestic spheres in ways not experienced by many other occupational groups. In addition to these institutional requirements, it has been noted that the routine environment of police work also fosters a certain cultural framework. The uncertainty facing officers as they respond to incidents, for example, is often cited as a factor that explains group loyalty. Although officers rarely experience direct physical confrontation, the possibility of doing so shapes the nature of contacts with the public and provides strong instrumental reasons why officers place value on subscribing to the occupational sub-culture and team loyalty. These pressures might make it difficult for officers to challenge aspects of police culture to which they do not subscribe, since to do so might risk their isolation from colleagues, which may, in turn, have implications for their physical well-being. Similarly, attributes of suspicion and cynicism might have important advantages in routine police work but have negative implications if they are practised in accordance with stereotyping and prejudice. The importance of understanding police sub-culture in the context of the broader operational nature of routine police work is reflected in the perspective of a gay police officer who left the policing after seven years' service:

> I have faced the violent, the armed, the unstable, the drunk, the frightened, the battered, the injured. Having been part of this environment, I understand why police-men and women need to 'belong' – to identify with, and seek the support of, their own police companions. I understand the need for the canteen culture of cynicism, gossip, jokes and stereotyping. It all helps to let off the pressure of accumulated tension. But I have also seen how this often highly charged atmosphere, created by the enormous expectations laid on the individual police officer, particularly those on the front line, can lead to a peculiar bottling-up of emotion; a creation of the tendency to deny one's true feelings and beliefs on a number of issues in order to maintain the acceptance and affirmation given by the group which is so vital in fight-ing off the pressures both from the outside, and unfortunately, sometimes from the higher, managerial ranks inside the police. (Burke, 1993: 9)

the implications of police culture

In addition to debates about the roots of police culture are controversies about the implications that police culture has for the delivery of policing. As has been demonstrated, inappropriate and unjust aspects of operational police work, related to the over-policing of some communities and the failure to provide an adequate response to the victims of some types of crime, have often been explained in terms of retrograde norms and values of frontline officers.

A long sequence of media exposés of police work has contributed to a folkloric construction of police deviance that many have argued has undermined the legitimacy and authority of the police and lessened public esteem for a once-cherished symbol of national pride (Reiner, 2000).

Although such explanations have an intuitive 'common-sense' appeal, and might be attractive to senior officers who are able to distance themselves from such portrayals, there are significant reasons why police culture might not offer a definitive basis to explain police behaviour. First, as Reiner (2000) noted, police culture is not 'monolithic, universal or unchanging' and it cannot be assumed that all officers share the values, attitudes and beliefs outlined above. As has been noted in the context of institutional racism, if the inability of certain officers to provide an effective response to racist violence is explained in terms of the institutional dynamics of racism, it needs to be clarified why some officers, part of the same institution, understand racist violence and provide an effective response to it (Souhami, 2007). Similarly with police culture: if the dynamics of police working life explain the cultural patterns outlined above, then it needs to be explained why many officers are not racist, sexist, homophobes. Clearly police culture does not provide any absolute guide to police behaviour. The presence of different strains of police culture, for example, between 'street cops' and 'management cops' (Reuss Ianni, 1982) or among those officers working in specialist departments (Innes, 2003), suggests that police culture is mediated by particular working environments. That police culture is not universally constant is illustrated by Moon's (2006) study of Korean police officers' attitudes towards community policing. In contrast to findings from research in other jurisdictions, Moon argued that Korean officers were not culturally resistant to key tenets of community policing, even though they appear to share other aspects of police culture such as machismo and sense of mission. Chan (1997) noted that police culture is not always resistant to change, and that the police working personality is not inevitably an obstacle to police reform. Chan criticized the tendency to conceive of police officers themselves as passive dupes, unwittingly coaxed into a particular cultural domain. As she points out, 'while the culture may be powerful, it is nevertheless up to individuals to accommodate or resist its influence' (1997: 66).

In addition to recognizing the heterogeneity of police sub-culture, a more fundamental question about the relation between officers' views and attitudes and their operational behaviour needs to be addressed. Waddington (1999) argued that police culture needs to be understood as a means of interpreting and rationalizing police work in a post-hoc sense, and does not necessarily play a strong causal role in terms of shaping their behaviour. He noted that police sub-culture is often discussed in highly pejorative terms, and implicitly or explicitly is portrayed both as inherently retrogressive and as determining officer action. On both these grounds Waddington argued the concept of police sub-culture needs to be fundamentally reassessed. Researchers have identified such a diversity of sub-cultures, relating to the specific contexts in which groups of officers work, that any notion of police culture as a common property shared among officers, disappears 'into a near infinity of multiple sub-cultures' (1999: 290). Moreover, Waddington challenges the notion that the cultural properties identified by researchers provide any explanation of their behaviour. On the contrary, he noted a range of studies that found considerable discrepancy between the canteen talk of officers 'off stage' and their professional behaviour. Even an early British study of routine police work in London conducted by the Policy Studies Institute (PSI) (Smith and Gray, 1983) which found considerable evidence of racism, for example, noted that this was not simply reflected in officers' behaviour. Waddington (1999: 288–9) suggested that this discrepancy between attitudes and behaviours has been widely noted:

> **The PSI researchers frankly admitted that they were surprised at the discrepancy between canteen racism and actual treatment of black people, especially victims (Smith and Gray, 1983). I too found a gap between the identification of certain protest groups as 'the opposition' and the extensive steps routinely taken to facilitate their holding peaceful protests. Equally, the widespread republicanism amongst senior Metropolitan Police officers was not evident in their excessive responsiveness to royal sensibilities (Waddington, 1994a, 1994b, 1993).**

Waddington does not suggest that consideration of police culture should be abandoned altogether. Instead, it should be 'appreciated' as a response to the 'structural contingencies' of police work, just as other forms of deviant sub-culture are interpreted (Waddington, 1999: 295). The role of sub-culture is that it allows officers to make sense of their experience and to maintain professional self-esteem. The widely noted components of police culture, such as authoritarianism and machismo, directly reflect defining attributes of police work. The former relates to the authority that officers have over the territory that they patrol; since they are the symbolic representation of the state, then this authority is real – uniquely they possess the legitimate recourse to the use of violence. For that reason, the machismo of officers is also best understood in terms of the routine features of police work. That the actual experience of violence is relatively rare is of marginal importance; the key point is that a defining characteristic of police work, shared by few other professions, is the potential for violent confrontation.

broadening the horizon: culture and policing in wider perspective

While Waddington's (1999) critique of police culture provides an important reformulation that allows some of the simplistic assumptions of much of the literature to be critically reconsidered, it too needs to be critically reconsidered on the basis of the changing terrain of policing. As we have argued in earlier chapters, and will revisit in Chapter 8, discussion of 'policing' can no longer be confined to consideration of the monopolistic institution of the state police. As the nation-state itself has been weakened by internal and external processes of privatization and globalization, policing has become an increasingly networked process of social control that engages a plethora of actors at a range of levels (Johnston and Shearing, 2003). Waddington's (1999) analysis of police culture locates the concept in terms of the broader context of public police officers as the embodiment of state sovereignty with a monopoly on the use of legitimate violence. If the state, and the public police, are no longer the sole providers of policing, several consequences arise for understanding police culture. First, the diffusion of state sovereignty among pluralized networks of private and public agencies at the local, national and international levels means, among other things, that the police officer no longer has a monopoly on the legitimate use of force. The plethora of nodes within policing networks means that the range of agencies that have some coercive power has extended dramatically in recent years. While it might be that many of these agencies do not directly use force in the implementation of their powers and continue to rely upon the public police for enforcement, this is not the always the case. The recourse to the use of force might distinguish police work from that of many other occupations but this feature is increasingly fading as other agencies have become involved in policing. If Waddington (1999) was right to suggest that the legitimate use of violence configured police sub-culture, then it seems likely that the influence of this property will extend to other professions who have a role in policing in its extended sense.

The research evidence relating to some members of the extended policing family, most notably private security guards and Police Community Support Officers, suggests that they do share some of the characteristics of police officers. For example, Johnston (2006) noted that Police Community Support Officers working for the Metropolitan Police Service shared some of the properties associated with police sub-culture, such as suspicion and racial prejudice. The extent to which other agencies enmeshed in policing networks develop occupational cultures similar to those found within the police service remains to be seen. Clearly, though, as the terrain of policing becomes more complex, debates about the nature, foundations and impact of professional cultures will need to address the concepts outlined in this chapter in this broader context.

conclusion

The concept of police culture has become a central feature of debates about the role of the police service in contemporary diverse societies. It has been used to explain the failure of the police to provide an effective service to many victims of crime and the relative failure to recruit a workforce that represents the wider population. Many of these discussions afford too much weight to the notion, and associate it too closely with the negative characteristics of a minority of deviant police officers. Furthermore, it is clear that the 'working personality' of police officers can largely be attributed to the organizational context and routine demands placed upon junior officers. Group loyalty might be a negative characteristic of police sub-culture in terms of covering up to protect colleagues but it is an understandable feature of a working environment when officers might rely upon their colleagues for support when faced with risky situations. Two fundamental conclusions can be drawn from this discussion: first, that while the concept of police culture is vital to understanding policing it provides a poor guide to police behaviour in particular circumstances. Second, if the defining characteristics of policing are increasingly shared with other agencies, then it seems likely that the cultural patterns that have emerged, partly in response to them, might themselves pervade networks of policing.

▒ ▒ chapter summary ▒

- Police **organizational sub-culture** has often been highlighted in media-driven exposés of scandals, and is a common theme in news media and fictional representations of police work.

- The 'working personality' of police officers is particularly important since it is held to influence the ways in which officers interpret the law and exercise the discretion that is a hallmark of routine police activity.

- Discretion is particularly significant in policing because officers have to interpret how they will apply the law in particular circumstances, the power that they have over fellow citizens, and the 'invisible' circumstances in which routine police work is carried out. Police culture has often been cited in explanations of the poor response the service has offered to victims of domestic and sexual violence, and the apparent over-policing of minority ethnic communities.

- Successive studies have characterized police working culture in many societies in terms of insularity, cynicism, conservatism, machismo and prejudice. Racial prejudice has been identified as a central aspect of police sub-culture in Britain for many decades. Repeated media stories have focused on allegations of officer racism that are held to hinder an effective response to victims of crime and have a negative impact on minority ethnic staff. Often these accounts explain police racism in terms of the individual deviance of a small proportion of officers and fail to account for the broader organizational context in which racism can develop.

- The failure of the police to respond to victims of domestic and sexual violence has often been attributed to a sub-culture dominated by male staff at all levels of the organization. Women have always had a gendered role within the police service and until relatively recently have been formally barred from working in certain roles. As with other marginalized groups, evidence suggests that female officers have often over-subscribed to the machismo of police sub-culture as a way of demonstrating their affinity to the service.

- The position of lesbian, gay, bisexual and transgender (LGBT) communities within the police service has received less attention than that of other marginalized groups, and there is less statistical information relating to representation of these groups within police ranks. Nonetheless, there is evidence that LGBT victims of crime are reluctant to report incidents to the police since they do not expect to be taken seriously, and may fear secondary victimization by the police.

- Whatever its nature, the roots of police culture have been explained variously in terms of the profile of those who enter the service in the first instance, or the nature of police work itself. Traditionally police officers have tended to be recruited from a relatively narrow section of the general population, and have joined the service at a relatively young age and often without more than basic educational qualifications. Commentators have argued that problematic characteristics of police sub-culture tend to reflect those of the particular demographic profile from which officers are recruited. Clearly, efforts to recruit a more diverse workforce reflect this perspective.

- Others have argued that police culture is shaped by the working environment of police work that requires quick decision-making, demands loyalty, and encourages officers to treat the public with suspicion.

- While few studies have presented alternative perspectives on the character of police sub-culture, the impact that it has on police work is more contentious. First, police culture is not singular or unchanging, and not all officers fit the description outlined. Individual police officers have agency and are not dupes influenced by an overwhelming regressive sub-culture.

- Additionally, police culture might be conceptualized as a post-hoc response to police work, rather than something that determines operational practice.

- The broader terrain of policing in the contemporary period has meant that many features associated with the public police, such as the recourse to the use of force, power over fellow citizens, and so on, are now increasingly shared with other agencies. If these characteristics of police work have, among other things, shaped the sub-culture of officers, then it might be expected that the dominant features might also become shared among diverse policing networks.

■ self-check **Questions**

1 How did Wilson famously characterize the particular character of police discretion?

2 What are the key features of police sub-culture?

3 What characterizes the 'rotten apples' perspective on police racism?

4 What was the remit of early generations of female police officers?

5 What proportion of homophobic crime has it been estimated is not reported to the police?

6 In respect of what issues did Colman and Gorman measure the attitudes of police recruits?

7 What different 'strains' of police culture have been identified?

8 In what nation did Moon suggest police sub-culture is not resistant to community policing?

9 Who conducted an early study of routine police work in London?

10 Why might an understanding of police culture need to be broadened?

■ study **Questions**

1 Why might it be problematic to present undesirable aspects of police culture in terms of the characteristics of individual deviant officers?

2 Would the recruitment of a more diverse workforce improve the quality of service the police provide to minority groups and to women?

3 Does police culture determine police behaviour?

■ ■annotated further reading ■

Reiner (2000) outlines the sociological literature on cop culture, and how it came to be regarded as a central determinant of police behaviour as studies showed that the formal rules or law enforcement codes were subject to the exercise of police discretion.

Waddington's (1999) article, 'Police (Canteen) Sub-Culture: An Appreciation', provides an important reconceptualization of sub-culture, and argues that it can be understood as a response to the demands of police work, rather than something that determines the way in which officers behave.

The relation between police sub-culture and the inadequacy of police service to victims of sexual and domestic violence is outlined in Jordan's (2004) *The Word of a Woman? Police, Rape and Belief.*

Chan's (1997) study of police culture in New South Wales explored efforts to tackle cultural problems relating to racism and corruption. She argued that the latter were more successful than the former since they were accompanied by strong management interventions that made it difficult for junior officers to decide not to comply.

:// annotated listings of links to relevant websites /

The website of the National Black Police Association (www.nbpa.co.uk) provides an array of information on racism within the police service, and campaigns and policies introduced to tackle it. The site also provides links to many other police resources, including many of the associations linked to particular constabularies. Information about the Association of Muslim Police can be found at http://tinyurl.com/2gsvva. The Christian Police Association was established in 1883 and is part of an extended worldwide network. More information can be found at http://www.cpani.com/.

The British Association of Women Police website (http://www.bawp.org/) contains more information relating to the 'gender agenda' and a host of other useful resources.

The website of the **Gay Police Association** (http://www.gay.police.uk/) contains useful updates on news items relating to homophobia, crime and policing.

6

Who guards the guards?

Discussion of the governance of policing has focused primarily on the formal democratic and legal arrangements under which police services have been regulated. Issues relating to funding and the general direction and control of police services in England and Wales have been governed by arrangements that purport to ensure operational independence and accountability to both central government and local police authorities. This chapter reviews these developments but also explores issues of accountability in broader terms, by considering, for example, efforts to promote ethical codes and human rights policing. The chapter concludes by examining the prospects for democratic accountability in a period when policing is increasingly pluralized. In particular, the chapter does the following:

- critically examines disciplinary systems intended to regulate individual police officer behaviour and broader mechanisms to provide a democratic oversight of policing;

- reviews efforts to influence policing by the promotion of professionalism, ethical and human rights;

- considers the implications of increasing diversity of agencies engaged in policing for fundamental principles of democratic accountability.

key terms

accountability; complaints; ethics; human rights; legitimacy; plural policing; police governance

introduction

The question 'Who guards the guards?' is among the oldest of political philosophy. Holding police officers to account for their (in)actions raises legal, moral, and political questions about social regulation and has important implications for the legitimacy of the police service. Reiner (2000) has argued that during the 'golden age' of British policing in the 1950s and 1960s the extent of public scrutiny of police behaviour might have been minimal compared to what has followed. Nonetheless, the image and authority of the 'bobby on the beat' during that period were secure due to, among other things, an 'almost mythical process of identification with the British people' (Reiner, 2000: 55). The ties that bound the police and the public might have loosened as strategies to hold the police to account have developed over subsequent decades.

Accountability relates to political and other processes that seek to influence the performance and priorities of the police service, systems designed to investigate complaints about police malpractice, and reviews of police performance, which may be couched in terms of statistical information about crime patterns, clear-up rates, time taken to respond to emergency calls, financial scrutiny, or public satisfaction with local policing provisions (see Box 6.1). A recurring theme of this book is the increasing importance of considering policing as a process of social regulation, which engages a diverse range of local, national and international actors. As has been done with other chapters, this discussion will begin by focusing on these issues as they relate to the public police before moving on to consider wider questions about the accountability of **plural policing**.

Box 6.1

Accountability

What does 'accountability' mean? In this discussion, it is understood in two ways: first, as holding the police to account, in terms of interrogating the actions of individual officers and, second, in terms of controlling the general direction of policing (i.e. governance). An important example of the former, in recent Britain, has been the investigation of the shooting of Jean Charles de Menezes at Stockwell tube station, London, in July 2005. The latter dimension of accountability relates to the broader control and direction of policing, in terms of funding, establishing priorities, and reviewing performance across the service as a whole.

One of the problems with many mechanisms of accountability is that they provide models for police activity based upon rules, regulations, and hierarchies of decision-making and responsibility – none of which necessarily have much influence in terms of understanding what police officers actually do. As discussed previously, police work is diverse and sometimes unpredictable and so any system based upon procedural frameworks is unlikely to cover more than a small proportion of the activities officers actually carry out. See Chapter 1 for a discussion of the unpredictable and heterogeneous nature of police work. Moreover, as was seen in the preceding chapter, police culture is often held to influence the exercise of discretion that is central to police work. Moreover, features of police culture, such as group solidarity and insularity, have often been seen to frustrate the integrity and transparency of attempts to hold individual officers to account. The implications of these challenges to the accountability of the police are considered in the following section, which discusses the investigation of police complaints.

controlling the constable

A long-term trend in the investigation of complaints against the police in Britain has been the development, over several decades, of an independent system. Until the 1964 Police Act, there was no systematic means for investigating public complaints about officer conduct. The 1964 Act continued the tradition whereby complaints were dealt with internally by forces about whom the allegation had been made. Concern about this system of self-regulation led the 1976 Police Act to establish the Police Complaints Board, under which more serious complaints were investigated by officers from another force, which was intended to ensure a degree of independence by distancing the investigator from the investigated. However, by the early 1980s a range of problems had been identified by those who advocated a more transparent system with greater independence. Among these factors a series of high-profile anti-corruption initiatives had been introduced in the late 1970s following long-term perception that the Metropolitan Police Service, and in particular some squads of detectives, were undermined by corruption. Somewhat differently, concern about police racism that surfaced, among other places, in Lord Scarman's report into the 1981 Brixton disorders noted that a greater degree of independence would enhance public confidence in the system for investigating complaints against the police. In the mid-1980s, an element of independence was introduced into the oversight of police investigations, although these continued to be carried out by police officers. As Prenzler (2000) has noted, the establishment of the Police Complaints Authority (PCA) in Britain during the mid-1980s followed an international trend towards civilian oversight of the investigation of complaints. The PCA managed the investigation of more serious complaints against the police, although these continued to be conducted by police officers. It was often held that complaints were best examined by police officers as it was they who had the necessary professional and investigatory skills. As the range of agencies involved in the conduct of investigations, in both civil and criminal matters, has extended in recent years, the notion that the police were uniquely placed to conduct such forensic examinations became increasingly untenable.

Box 6.2

The Independent Police Complaints Commission

Varies from earlier systems in a range of key respects:

- Complaints investigated by independent, non-police staff.
- 'Third parties' can register complaints.
- Complaints can be reported directly to the IPCC, not necessarily the police service subject of the complaint.
- 'Local resolution' possible if the complainant is prepared to accept an apology.
- IPCC has a 'guardianship role' to look at concerns beyond individual incidents.
- IPCC is responsible for improving public confidence in the complaints system.

In addition to local resolution, other possible outcomes arising from a complaint are:

- withdrawal, at the instigation of the complainant;
- discontinuation, if the complainant is un-cooperative or vexatious;
- formal investigation.

The 2002 Police Reform Act established a wholly independent complaints system: the Independent Police Complaints Commission (IPCC). Pressure for the creation of a wholly independent system had come from several directions: it was recommended in a report by the consultancy firm KPMG and the civil rights group Liberty, and had been urged by the Lawrence Inquiry Report, a report of the Home Affairs Committee of the House of Commons and from the European Committee for the Prevention of Torture and Inhuman or Degrading Treatment or Punishment (Harrison and Cunneen, 2000: 1). In addition to using civilians to investigate complaints, the IPCC system also differs in that it is charged with investigating complaints made against non-sworn staff employed by the police, including Police Community Support Officers and civilian staff (see Box 6.2). Arrangements introduced by the 2002 Act claim a number of other advantages over previous regimes. First, any party can record a complaint about perceived misconduct, not just the person directly 'victimized'. Witnesses or third parties can record a complaint and so start an investigation. Second, complaints can be recorded directly with the IPCC who can then pass details to the relevant police force. This means that complainants do not have to directly approach the force about which they are complaining. Both of these reforms are intended to make it less intimidating to make a complaint against the police. A third change is that a system of 'local resolution' has been introduced so that complaints can be resolved relatively quickly in cases where the complainant is content to receive a formal apology from the police service. These are most obviously intended for situations where officers have been uncivil to members of the public, who then feel satisfied with an apology and do not wish to pursue their complaint further. Research evidence on the nature of complaints against the police suggests that many fall into this category so that a speedy resolution is most appropriate. A fourth aspect that distinguishes the IPCC from previous arrangements is that it can investigate issues of concern that transcend specific allegations of misconduct against particular officers by examining matters of policy and organizational practice that give rise to public concern about policing. This is referred to as the 'guardianship role'. The Home Office (2005: 3) advised local Chief Officers that complaints about the 'direction and control' of policing will relate to at least one of the following four categories, but that these do not compromise the operational independence of Chief Officers:

- operational policing policies (where there is no issue of conduct);
- organizational decisions;
- general policing standards in the force;
- operational management decisions (where there is no issue of conduct).

The broader guardianship role extends to the complaints system itself, as the IPCC is charged with increasing public confidence in the integrity of the system itself. However, it seems that the extent to which the IPCC has been able to pursue this wider remit has been limited, perhaps by the extensive case load it has been pursuing relating to specific concerns about individual officers. While research commissioned by the IPCC suggests that public confidence has been enhanced by the independence of the new regime to investigate complaints, confidence in the system tends to be related to wider attitudes towards the police service in general: those with a negative view of the police were less likely to trust the complaints system and less inclined to make a complaint (IPCC, 2007). A common challenge to police complaints systems, Prenzler argued (2000), is to avoid 'capture' by the police service itself. There are a number of ways that this commonly occurs, he showed, including the tendency to employ former officers to investigate complaints. The IPCC system seems likely to avoid this danger, as ex-officers cannot be employed. Even so, if confidence in the complaints system itself is related to wider perspectives on the police service more generally, then it might be that the IPPC has only limited scope to enhance the reputation of the complaints system.

Figure 6.1 shows the number of complaints against individual officers recorded by the IPCC in 2005–06, and the longer-term trend, 1999–2006. Clearly there has been an increase in the number of cases recorded. This is likely to be related to changes in recording practices rather than an increase in misconduct. Since any party to an incident can log a complaint, and that these can be reported directly to the IPCC, the number recorded has increased.

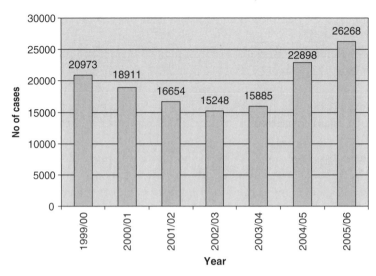

Figure 6.1 Complaint cases against the police, 1999–2006

Source: IPCC (2006: 8).

The 26,268 complainants made 36,179 allegations against police officers in 2005/06, which amounted to 256 complaints for every 1000 officers. The nature of these allegations is illustrated in Figure 6.2.

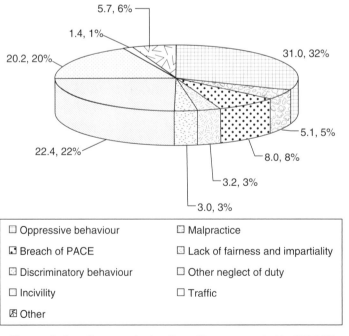

Figure 6.2 Types of allegations against police officers recorded in 2005/06

There are five potential outcomes to a complaint against the police. 'Local resolution' involves the complaint being settled via mediation between the local police service and the complainant, and may involve a local officer investigating the circumstances surrounding the complaint. With the agreement of the complainant, this process might result in an apology and the identification of measures to prevent a similar incident from recurring. IPCC (2006) data suggest that local resolution is most commonly adopted for complaints relating to a lack of fairness and impartiality and to complaints relating to traffic policing. The number of complaints resolved locally has increased steadily since the early 1980s: in 2005/06, 46 per cent of all complaints were resolved locally. Other outcomes include the withdrawal or discontinuation of the complaint, the former with the consent of the complainant and the latter in circumstances were they are uncooperative or vexatious. The IPCC can give forces permission to dispense with a complaint when there is insufficient evidence or it is judged to be an abuse of the complaints process. A small proportion of complaints are subject to formal investigation by an IPCC investigating officer. In 2005/06, 28 per cent of complaints (10,552) were formally investigated, and 12 per cent of those (1236) were substantiated.

ethics, human rights and policing

The arrangements described in the previous section provide a framework for dealing with allegations of officer misbehaviour or the inappropriate direction and control of police services locally. Essentially, they are both retrospective and negative, as they seek to redress past failures of one kind or another. Other efforts to 'guard the guards' have been developed in relation to British policing in the recent past that are future-oriented and seek to improve policing standards. This section reviews two of sets of initiatives: those that seek to encourage an ethical framework for the police service and the impact that human rights legislation has on policing.

ethics and policing

The idea of ethical policing has become increasingly salient in Britain in recent years. As a means of controlling the actions of police officers and ensuring their accountability, it might be considered that the promotion of police codes of **ethics** seeks to positively develop policing. In contrast, disciplinary frameworks, which identify and prohibit undesirable behaviour, take a relatively negative approach. If disciplinary regulations outline what officers should not do, codes of ethics tend to provide a normative framework to which they should aspire. The introduction of codes of ethics for the police needs to be understood, in the British case at least, in the wider context of a concern about standards in public life, the recent history of which can be traced back to the exposé of political 'sleaze' in the mid-1990s. Concern about political corruption and abuse of power arose after a sustained crisis of legitimacy had engulfed British policing. A series of miscarriages of justice – many of which implicated the criminal justice system in general as well as the police service in particular – coupled with incidents of public disorder and a growing sense that increased public expenditure on the police had not 'produced dividends' in terms of reducing crime combined to undermine police legitimacy (Reiner, 2000: 66–7). Advocates of ethical standards for the police often explicitly identify their potential to reverse these trends by increasing accountability and enhancing public confidence (Neyroud, 2003). This is particularly evident in the context of police reform in Northern Ireland as part of the broader peace process, which is discussed at greater length below. The development of a police code of ethics was clearly articulated in terms of the need to garner support for the police service from across the various ethno-religious communities of Northern Ireland. The PSNI Code of Ethics was launched in 2003 and replaced the previous disciplinary code that had regulated police conduct. The Code was promoted as the basis of a tacit contract between the police and the public whereby the former afford the latter respect in return for cooperation:

> **The ability of police officers to carry out their functions and duties depends on approval from the public for their existence, actions and behaviour. In simple terms, effective policing requires the support and willing co-operation of the public. Public confidence in the police is closely related to officers' attitudes and behaviour towards the public, in particular their respect for individuals' fundamental rights and freedom as enshrined in the European Convention on Human Rights. (Northern Ireland Policing Board, 2003: 4)**

The globalization of policing discourse – revisited in various contexts in this book – extends to questions of governance and accountability. Many of the ethical codes developed in liberal democratic societies provide a similar vision of the normative police officer, as the examples presented in Box 6.3 and Box 6.4 demonstrate. Both codes refer to the public and private activities of officers in ways that do not apply to most other employees. The privileged position of police officers in the information society is reflected in the stricture that notes the confidentiality of personal data contained in police systems (Ericson and Haggerty, 1997).

Box 6.3

Code of Conduct and Ethics, New South Wales Police

An employee of NSW Police must:

1 behave honestly and in a way that upholds the values and the good reputation of NSW Police whether on or off duty
2 act with care and diligence when on duty
3 know and comply with all policies, procedures and guidelines that relate to their duties
4 treat everyone with respect, courtesy and fairness
5 comply with any lawful and reasonable direction given by someone in NSW Police who has authority to give the direction
6 comply with the law whether on or off duty
7 take reasonable steps to avoid conflicts of interest, report those that can not be avoided and co-operate in their management
8 only access, use and/or disclose confidential information if required by their duties and allowed by NSW Police policy
9 not make improper use of their position or NSW Police information or resources
10 report the misconduct of other NSW Police employees.

Failure to comply with the Code of Conduct and Ethics may result in management action.

Source: http://www.police.nsw.gov.au/

Box 6.4

Code of conduct and ethics, International Association of Chiefs of Police

I will keep my private life unsullied as an example to all and will behave in a manner that does not bring discredit to me or to my agency. I will maintain courageous calm in the face of danger, scorn or ridicule; develop self-restraint; and be constantly mindful of the welfare of others. Honest in thought and deed both in my personal and official life, I will be exemplary in obeying the law and the regulations of my department. Whatever I see or hear of a confidential nature or that is confided to me in my official capacity will be kept ever secret unless revelation is necessary in the performance of my duty.

I will never act officiously or permit personal feelings, prejudices, political beliefs, aspirations, animosities or friendships to influence my decisions. With no compromise for crime and with relentless prosecution of criminals, I will enforce the law courteously and appropriately without fear or favor, malice or ill will, never employing unnecessary force or violence and never accepting gratuities.

Source: www.theiacp.org

While ethical codes might be couched broadly in normative terms and do not provide a detailed guide to activities that might result in disciplinary proceedings, it might be that these general principles are more effective in terms of regulating police behaviour than some other regulatory frameworks. A recent police scandal in New Zealand illustrates potential strengths of an ethical code relative to a disciplinary approach (see Box 6.5).

Box 6.5

Sex, scandal and police culture in New Zealand

Between 2005 and 2007, a series of court cases have tried three New Zealand police officers on charges of rape. In the first of these cases, brought against two of the three, Brad Shipton and Bob Schollum, the officers were convicted of raping a woman in 1989 and sentenced to eight years in jail. In 2006, Shipton and Schollum were tried on another charge of rape, as was an Assistant Commissioner Clint Rickards. As in the first case the trial related to historical allegations from the 1980s during which time the three were junior officers in the town of Rotorua. All three men were acquitted of the charges. It was only after their acquittal that it was revealed that Shipton and Schollum had been convicted on the earlier charges, which raised public concern about the issue of disclosing the criminal history of accused persons. In 2007, a third trial heard allegations that the three officers had kidnapped and indecently assaulted a 16-year-old girl in the early 1980s. Again, the three men were acquitted after successfully arguing that the sexual relations they had with the girl had been consensual. Shortly after their acquittal, an official inquiry into police culture was published. Following the case, Rickards stated that, since he had been acquitted, he wished to be reinstated to his position as commander of police for Auckland. Protests from women's groups and campaigners argued that the sexual abuse of power and the culture of drinking and misbehaviour that had been exposed during the case had fundamentally undermined confidence in Rickards' police credentials. The Prime Minister and the Mayor of Auckland publicly opposed Rickards' reinstatement.

The events described in Box 6.5 posed a problem for the police service since the disciplinary system was an adversarial one modelled on the court system. The Police Regulations identify behaviour that is unacceptable and the system focuses upon evidence-gathering, charges, guilt, and punishment. Although it was apparent that the officers had indulged in behaviour widely condemned as unacceptable, they had not breached particular police regulations and so there were not clear grounds to dismiss Rickards. A code of ethics, perhaps forming a part of the employment contract of each officer, might have proved a more effective means of responding to behaviour that does not meet the normative standards expected.

Advocates of ethical policing often argue that the development of such codes is an important means of enhancing the professional status of police officers. If the police service is to establish itself on professional terms similar to other public sector occupations, it needs to develop an ethical framework that mirrors those applicable in the medical professions, the legal system, or the civil service. Not only might Codes of Ethics provide a sharper management tool to deal with instances of misconduct, their development can also encourage the development of an organizational culture that allows performance monitoring and early interventions that can help officers reflect upon and improve their own practice. Neyroud (2003) argued, for example, that the development of ethical policing was a central strategy for the broader promotion of police professionalism. This would, he argued, be one method of re-shaping the exercise of police discretion so that the negative influence of police occupational sub-culture, as outlined in the previous chapter, was reduced. The traditional attempt to closely regulate officer decision-making is increasingly inappropriate to the contemporary environment, hence 'rule-bound bureaucracy' ought to be replaced by 'flexible professional practice' (Neyroud and Beckley, 2001: 86).

human rights and policing

Discussion of policing and human rights in Britain in recent years has often portrayed the latter as a politically correct restraint on the provision of effective policing. The extent of these concerns was demonstrated in a statement by the Home Secretary to the House of Commons in July 2006. The Home Secretary stressed that the government's record in tackling crime had been impressive. Crime had fallen, more offences were being brought before the courts and more police officers had been recruited. However, it was acknowledged that public perceptions did not reflect this success and this was, in large part, due to

> major issues about the way in which the Criminal Justice System currently operates and – just as importantly – the way it is perceived to operate. Too often it appears that the CJS is on the side of the offender – protecting their interests and individual rights over those of the victim and the law-abiding majority.
>
> That has to change.
>
> ...
>
> We will act to prevent human rights – which are rightly held dearly by all of us in this House – being used by offenders to secure perverse outcomes which penalise victims and the law abiding majority. (Home Office, 2006b)

Contrary to popular media-driven discourse, the argument that human rights provisions are antithetical to effective and legitimate policing does not stand up to scrutiny. The 1998 Human Rights Act effectively incorporated into British law the provisions of the European Convention on Human Rights (ECHR). The ECHR defines a series of human rights that the British state is bound to observe. Among these are the right to life (Article 2), the right not to be tortured or subject to inhuman or degrading treatment (Article 3), the right to liberty and the security of the person (Article 5), the right to a fair public hearing (Article 6), the right to freedom of expression (Article 10) and the right to peacefully assemble with others (Article 11). Very many of these provisions have implications for policing. In respect of some of the topics covered, the police were already obliged to cover the regulations set out by PACE (see Chapter 2 for more on PACE). Not only have the police had to observe controls on operational behaviour for some time, there are other reasons to reconsider the popular discourse that suggests human rights provisions shackle police officers. First, the ECHR makes very clear, by listing them in each case, that the rights identified are not absolute; there are circumstances in which they can be over-ridden. For example, individuals have the right to privacy, but Article 8 makes it clear that the need to protect an individual can be outweighed by the wider interests of society and so this right can be set aside as long as this

is in accordance with the law and is necessary in a democratic society in the interests of national security, public safety or the economic well-being of the country, for the prevention of disorder or crime, for the protection of health or morals, or for the protection of the rights and freedoms of others.

Clearly, these circumstances might include a wide range of situations in which it is permissible for the police service, or other public authorities, to conduct surveillance on those suspected of criminal activity. The test of such actions is couched in terms of the need to demonstrate that the contravention of rights in any case is necessary and proportionate. In practice, these provisions mean that police surveillance operations have to be authorized by senior officers who are required to certify that operations are justified in that the information sought cannot be gained via other means (i.e. the surveillance is 'necessary'), is reasonable in relation to the desired outcome and will not intrude upon the privacy of unrelated individuals (i.e. it is 'proportionate').

These requirements clearly seek to affect the behaviour of police officers individually and collectively and so provide a framework of police accounta-bility similar to that which governs the investigation of complaints against the police. It does not seek to restrict the activities of police officers but to limit these in ways consistent with the principles of policing in a liberal democratic society. Human rights legislation is often presented negatively, as conferring 'rights' upon criminals that restrict the ability of the police to tackle them. However, it provides an important discourse in terms of the broader mandate of a democratic police service. As Crawshaw et al. (1998: 225, cited in Sheptycki, 2000: 6) have noted, 'not only are the police required to protect human rights when exercising their powers, they are required to protect human rights as one of their functions'. Developing policing as a means of protecting and enhancing democracy and the respect of human rights has been a major component in international efforts to transform policing in transitional societies, such as countries of the former Soviet Union and South Africa. Robertson (2005) outlined the centrality of police reform to the promotion of open government and human rights in Ukraine and Russia, although she noted that such efforts might have an impact in some localities but will not improve police–public relations more widely unless there is a broader commitment to democratic reform and the rule of law. Similarly Newburn and Sparks (2004, cited in Robertson, 2005) have argued that commitment to criminal justice reform and the promotion of human rights might often be related to efforts by emerging states to gain acceptance in international forums rather than genuine commitment to change. Stenning and Shearing (2005) suggested that the pluralization of policing networks has led to a move away from a conceptualization of the police role in terms of law enforcement and crime control towards a broader remit defined in terms of the promotion of harm reduction, security and safety. One implication of this has been that policing networks are coming to be assessed against global norms. Stenning and Shearing (ibid.: 169) noted that 'acceptable policing, it is argued, is not just policing that efficiently polices a prescribed order, but policing that conforms with internationally accepted norms of civility, dignity and human rights'.

_____ policing, human rights and police reform in Northern Ireland _____

The scope for human rights discourse to transcend embedded conflicts about policing and security has been identified as a key driver of police reform in Northern Ireland. The transformation of policing in Northern Ireland has been a major component of the on-going peace process. The Independent Commission on Policing for Northern Ireland (ICPNI), chaired by Chris Patten, reported in 1999, and provided a radical agenda for the development of policing that sought to make local boards responsible for the direction of policing, in broad terms. The Commission boldly stated that the role of the police be cast in terms far beyond law enforcement and crime control:

> It is a central proposition of this report that the fundamental purpose of policing should be ... the protection and vindication of the human rights of all. Our consultations showed clear agreement across the communities in Northern Ireland that people want the police to protect their human rights from infringement by others, and to respect their human rights in the exercise of that duty. Article 28 of the

Universal Declaration of Human Rights states: 'everyone is entitled to a social and international order in which the rights and freedoms set forth in this Declaration can be fully realised'. The role of the police is to help achieve that social and international order. They must, for example, uphold the laws that safeguard the lives of citizens. There should be no conflict between human rights and policing. Policing means protecting human rights. (ICPNI, 1999: 28)

Internationally developed approaches to conflict resolution based on restorative justice have been implemented in an effort to overcome prevailing forms of informal justice exercised by Loyalist and Republican paramilitary groups (Silke and Taylor, 2000). Often these systems of informal community policing have been understood as efforts of paramilitary groups to exercise control over territories and populations. However, McEvoy and Mika (2002) noted that such explanations overlook the unpalatable truth that the swift and brutal punishments produced have often proved popular with the public. Advocacy groups such as Amnesty International and Human Rights Watch criticized punishment violence and persuaded political parties to explore other forms of criminal justice. In addition to providing a framework through which paramilitary policing could be criticized, an international discourse of human rights also created a conceptual space whereby the various parties to the conflict in Northern Ireland could engage in dialogue (McEvoy and Mika, 2002). Kempa and Johnston argued that, perhaps counter-intuitively, this process entails developing a broad political debate – including agendas on human rights – about the future of policing:

Recent experience in Northern Ireland suggests that an adaptive way forward lies in a deliberate effort to 'repoliticise' the policing debate. This does not mean encouraging partisan contests over resources and symbolic issues. It means creating opportunities for groups to come together and encouraging them to approach the policing issue in terms of broader normative questions regarding the appropriate nature of the polity in uncertain global times. (2005: 188)

As has been demonstrated in the previous paragraphs, references to ethical principles and human rights relate to debates about 'guarding the guards' in two distinct senses. First, in retrospective negative terms, both concepts provide standards against which previous police behaviour can be assessed. In this sense they contribute toward disciplinary regimes. Second, however, discussion of ethics and human rights can be used in a more progressive sense as a framework for orienting the future development of police services and policing in a broader sense. The macro-governance of the British police is further considered in the following section, before the chapter concludes by exploring the challenges of governing policing in the broader sense of a social process of regulation.

As was shown in Chapter 1, the police in Britain have always been governed by a combination of local and central agencies. Forces were established across England and Wales in the middle of the nineteenth century partly as a result of local demand for professional police institutions capable of tackling crime, and partly as a result of central government efforts to establish a standard pattern of policing across the country as a whole. The combination of central and local governance of police persisted into the twentieth century and was enshrined in the 1964 Police Act, which established the 'tripartite' arrangements for the finance and governance of the police. While the balance of powers within this arrangement might have shifted somewhat in the 40 years in which it has operated, the model continues to provide the main basis for regulating the 43 Home Office police forces in England and Wales.

The 1964 Act divides the governance of the police between three parties: the Chief Constable (or Commissioner in the case of the Metropolitan Police); the police authority, representing local citizens; and the Home Office, on behalf of central government. The Chief Constable has operational responsibility and considerable autonomy when it comes to enforcing the law in any particular situation. Case law has established, over many years, that Chief Constables can properly exercise discretion when it comes to establishing priorities and developing policy that determine how law enforcement will be operationalized in each police service area. The principle underpinning this has been the prevention of undue political interference in the application of the law. Chief Constables formulate policy and act collectively, to some degree, under the auspices of the Association of Chief Police Officers (ACPO). The power of the ACPO to determine police policy and to provide a corporate voice for chief officers raises significant questions about police accountability since it sits outside of the legislative framework established by the 1964 Act.

The other two parties, local police authorities and the Home Office, are responsible for funding the police service and for determining policy in more general terms. The police authority is a locally constituted body that provides resources and local direction to each of the 43 police forces in England and Wales. Police authorities continue the tradition of local police governance that, as we have seen, extends back many centuries in British police history. The police authority is made up of independent members, local councillors, and magistrates. They are responsible for appointing senior officers, subject to Home Office approval, and for devising local policing plans required by the 1994 Police and Magistrates' Court Act. The local sheen that continues to coat policing in Britain only barely conceals the centrality of the Home Office in determining services delivered locally. The nature and status of the local policing plans illustrate this conundrum, since they are required to 'reflect' the priorities identified in the national policing plan devised by the Home Secretary. Additionally, the work of local Basic Command Units, the component parts of the 43 constabularies, has been subject to performance assessment and micro-management coordinated centrally by the Home Office Police Standards Unit (Loveday, 2005).

The Home Office indirectly and directly has a huge influence on the British police service. The Home Secretary produces an annual policing plan that sets the broad parameters in policy terms that local police authorities and the Chief Constable have to work within. Additionally, the Home Office provides 51 per cent of funding to police forces and is able to bypass the wishes of police authorities when it comes to controversial matters such as the provision of plastic bullets and water cannon to police forces (Simey, 1982). More recently confrontation between local police authorities and the Home Office has occurred relating to the latter's efforts to remove Chief Constables deemed to be 'failing'. The Bichard Inquiry into the 2004 Soham murders made a series of criticisms about the failure of police services to effectively share intelligence about suspected sex offenders. The Humberside police held information about the sexual offences of Ian Huntley, so that he would not have been cleared to work in a school in that area. However, once he moved to Cambridgeshire, there was no mechanism whereby this information could be passed to those responsible for carrying out criminal record checks there. The Home Secretary requested that the local police authority suspend the Chief Constable. The local police authority refused to do so, and the Home Secretary threatened legal action under the 2002 Police Reform Act. The prospect of a legal battle between central and local components of the tripartite arrangement was averted by a compromise whereby the Chief Constable was allowed to return to work but the date for his retirement was brought forward. This solution did not amount to a clear-cut 'victory' – or defeat – for either party and it might be argued that it is evidence of a robust system of police governance since the dispute was resolved, albeit somewhat messily. Other recent cases illustrate circumstances in which the Home Office has been able to intervene in local policing matters. In April 2005, for example, the Home Office seconded a senior officer from West Midlands Police into Nottinghamshire Constabulary in an effort to improve the latter's performance in dealing with serious crime. This intervention followed a report from Her Majesty's Inspector of Constabulary that argued Nottinghamshire police did not make effective use of resources to tackle major crime. This illustrates a broad tendency for the Home Office, often through the auspices of the Police Standards Unit, to make interventions in local policing arrangements in order to ensure that good practice developed in some areas is adopted across all police services.

The implications that 'the central determination of ostensibly local policing' (Loveday, 2005: 275) has in terms of accountability, through police authorities, to local communities is clearly considerable. The most vivid illustration of the tensions surrounding local control and central direction of the police services of England and Wales is provided by recent proposals to merge forces, and so considerably reduce their number. An HMIC (2005) report suggested that forces in England and Wales were not able to respond effectively to the changing terrain of crime. In particular, it was argued that small forces did not have the capacity to sustain large-scale investigations and that ineffective communication between neighbouring forces hampered efforts to tackle criminal networks that operate across regional, national and international borders. Although not the only reason cited, the report made clear that a relatively large number of relatively small forces was a key concern: 'size matters: larger forces are likely to have much greater capability and resilience' (ibid.: 22). In the light of this analysis, the Home Office proposed a series of mergers of police forces, and a reduction in the overall number from 43 to 12 'strategic forces', each of a minimum of 4000 officers. These were among a series of measures contained in the 2005 Police and Justice Bill. The Home Secretary requested that local police authorities submit proposals on voluntary mergers but found widespread opposition from many quarters, including the authorities themselves (**Association of Police Authorities**, 2005). Some of those opposed to the merger proposals cited factors such as the cost of the reform, or that the logic of the analysis suggested that a better option would be to move to a single national force (Waddington, 2005). However, a major feature of the arguments about the prospect of reducing the number of forces cited the need to preserve the principles of local accountability enshrined in the 1964 tripartite structure. Speaking in July 2006 in a parliamentary debate on the Bill, for example, Lord Dholakia opposed the proposed amalgamations in these terms (Hansard, 2006):

> The question remains: are the Government ultimately proceeding to create a national police force, where the ultimate control remains with the Secretary of State? We have again and again seen centrally directed executive action to tackle local problems. Policing is essentially a local matter. The further away the decision-making process is, the more difficult it is to resolve the situation. I suspect that to achieve the best possible performance, which we all aspire to, the Government have gone overboard in demanding powers that are best left to the police authorities.

In the autumn of 2006, following the appointment of a new Home Secretary, the government announced that the amalgamation plan would be withdrawn and that the 43 local police authorities would continue their role of local oversight. While this might suggest that the principle of local accountability has continuing resonance in the context of British policing, and that central authorities do not enjoy untrammelled powers, it is clear that there has been a long-term trend towards central direction. There are a number of means by which the Home Office governs policing. As noted above, the inspection regime operated by HMIC is an important aspect of central direction, since an HMIC report that finds a particular Basic Command Unit (BCU) is failing allows the Home Secretary to intervene in the management of local policing in that area. Similarly, as Loveday (2005) has shown, the Home Office Police Standards Unit (PSU) devised a Police Performance Assessment Framework (PPAF) against which BCU performance was judged. Ultimately the PSU could assume responsibility for running a BCU judged to be failing. Furthermore, the introduction of the National Intelligence Model (NIM) has required local forces to devote considerable resources to intelligence gathering and data analysis, at the expense of providing a high level of visible policing through routine patrol work. Loveday argued that, collectively, these systems of micro-management exert:

> ... a further pressure for local forces to conform to demands and structures which are determined externally to them. As with PPAF, the NIM has introduced a strait-jacket which allows for no deviation in terms of local police procedures and objectives. (2005: 276)

The range of agencies involved in the central direction of policing had led to a position where lines of accountability were blurred, agendas overlapped and were misaligned (Home Office, 2006e). The resulting confusion had made it difficult to achieve operational and financial benefits that a more integrated approach to policing could deliver. Not only had this contributed to failings such as those noted by Bichard, the government claimed that it also reduced effectiveness in terms of service delivery more generally. For these reasons the Police and Justice Act 2006 established the National Police Improvement Agency (NPIA) to provide a more coherent national framework. In April 2007, the NPIA became responsible for oversight of the work of groups including the Police Information Technology Organisation, the PSU, and Centrex. The NIPA is tasked with providing a host of functions that will 'support' local police services, including providing evidenced-based approaches to tackling crime, information technology, and training provisions. By working closely with the police service, it is claimed, NPIA will be suitably responsive to operational requirements but, in terms of debates about increasing central government control, it is also notable that the 2006 Act gives the agency power to intervene and force Chief Constables to comply with national priorities.

All these trends suggest that the principle of local accountability that has underpinned policing in England and Wales since the nineteenth century is being steadily and stealthily eroded as the Home Office exerts ever-greater management of police services. While it is clear that, as with the public sector more generally, the demands of 'new public management' have had this effect, important qualifications to this analysis need to be made. First, advocates of local accountability need to address the evidence suggesting that police authorities have long been the junior partners within the tripartite mechanism and have never had strong democratic credentials (Jones and Newburn, 2001). While this is an argument in favour of strengthening their role just as much as a reason for abolition, many have argued that the police authorities established by the 1964 Police Act have not provided effective local accountability. McLaughlin (2007a: 180) noted that even when the 1964 Act enshrined the tripartite system, concerns were raised that 'police authorities would in any constitutional dispute be squeezed between the Home Secretary's right of veto and the Chief Constables who were entitled to ignore them'. Dixon and Smith (1998: 420) argued that critics of centralization often overlook the 'rickety and dubious' credentials of systems of local accountability, which have failed to provide meaningful accountability to local communities.

Another challenge to the centralization thesis is the countervailing tendency towards devolving policing to the local level. Over much of the period during which the power of central government has been increasing, there has been a trend in the opposite direction. The local governance of policing has been extended through the increasing integration of police forces into local crime and disorder reduction partnerships, through the devolution of police organization to the BCU level, and through a plethora of means by which consultation with local communities is supposed to inform service delivery. The Neighbourhood Policing Programme (NPP) seeks to re-integrate police officers into local communities in ways that will enhance the formal dimensions of local accountability, for example, through police–community fora. Additionally, the programme seeks to (re)engineer opportunities for informal accountability through the development of routine interactions between the public and police officers personally familiar to one another. It seems that the NPP seeks to recreate the 'mythical identification' between public and the police that Reiner argued was evident during the 'golden age' (Reiner, 2000: 55). Many of these initiatives were outlined in discussion of community policing in Chapter 4. While these devolutionary trends might not outweigh the power of central direction, it is important to avoid a deterministic perspective focused solely on centralization. The sheer diversity of provisions across community safety partnerships, for example, highlights the importance of recognizing that local networks operate with some degree of agency and that not all that is developed at the centre is reproduced locally without being filtered by local political contexts (Stenson, 2002; Hughes, 2007). A more nuanced understanding of recent developments in police governance in Britain incorporates both centralization and localization. While successive governments have sought to increase their ability to 'steer' the police service, there has been some relaxation when it comes to the business of 'rowing'. Johnston and Shearing (2003) suggest that this reflects a broader trend whereby the governance of security has shifted from central government to local actors and to public and private sector agencies that have not traditionally been responsible for policing. The challenge of governing policing in post-industrial global society is returned to in the final section of this chapter.

the rise of managerialism?

While the mechanisms for police governance have shifted and bifurcated to both central and local levels, the focus of these systems of accountability has also changed. In recent decades across much of the developed world and through much of the public sector in general and the criminal justice system in particular, the scope of regimes of accountability has shifted. This refocus is usually characterized as a transformation from a legal or public interest model of accountability to one characterized by actuarialism and a managerialist ethos (McLaughlin and Murji, 1997; Garland, 2001). Chan traced these developments in the context of Australian policing in the following terms:

> **This shift in accountability discourse and control style is partly a response to the failure of traditional legal and disciplinary procedures to control police misconduct and partly a reflection of a 'post-social' governmental rationality which favours the adoption of private-sector techniques for the administration of state agencies and an emphasis on self-regulation or a 'distantiated form of control'. (1999: 251)**

In the British context, McLaughlin (2007a) noted that the development of 'new public managerialism' sought to re-cast the public police into a 'business-like' organization that is entrepreneurial in a consumer-driven era serviced by a mixed economy of policing. One implication of these 'post-social' systems of accountability might be that the traditional emphasis on outcomes produced by the criminal justice system is subsumed beneath a managerial emphasis on achievement of targets and pursuit of places on league tables. Not only do such measures force local agencies to conform to a nationally determined model, they also act as a disincentive to innovative or creative local responses where results cannot easily be quantified (Hughes, 2007).

accountability and plural policing

The discussion so far has focused upon the public police service and how it might be held accountable, whether in terms of responding to the alleged misconduct of an individual officer or more broadly when it comes to governance and direction. However, the proliferation of agencies involved in the provision of security raises important questions about accountability in an era of plural policing. In an early study, Shearing and Stenning (1983) argued that for much of the long history of private policing in North America questions about social justice and accountability had been marginalized by a conceptualization of the sector as the junior partner to the public police. As long as the private security industry was held to be less significant, in terms of the number of people employed and the roles that they carried out, there were few concerns about regulation and it was held that this could be left to the market mechanisms in the form of contracts between security companies and their customers (Shearing and Stenning, 1983). While Shearing and Stenning demonstrated that it may never have been true that the private sector was the junior partner, the more important concern that they raised related to the increasing importance of the private sector in an era when the state monopoly on policing was rapidly unravelling. Clearly Shearing and Stenning's prediction that private policing would play an increasing role in the regulation of human relations was a prescient one. What their discussion did not anticipate, however, is the increasingly fuzzy boundary between public and private policing. It has not been the case that the role of the public sector has shrunk under the challenge of the private. As is shown in Chapter 8, the picture has become more complex than a simple binary of public and private suggests. Loader argued the need to reconsider governance in the following terms:

> **We can no longer solely concern ourselves with how the public police can be made accountable to government, whether by legal, democratic or – as has been prominent of late – managerialist means. The pluralization of policing has generated a situation in which established intra-organizational modes of accountability (and their supporting structures of thought) are rendered limited and inadequate, and where novel policing forms are fast outstripping the capacity of existing institutional arrangements to monitor and control them. The world of plural policing remains, at best, weakly or obscurely accountable. (2000: 324)**

In this final section of the chapter we will explore the nature of accountability in the context of plural policing and the various means that have been used to develop systems to regulate the mixed economy of policing. Private policing in Britain was largely unregulated until the 2001 Private Security Industry Act. The primary requirement introduced by the Act is that all personnel – officers, managers and directors of companies – be licensed. The licensing process includes a check with the Criminal Records Bureau in an effort to ensure that those with convictions are not able to operate as security personnel.

Additionally, the Act established the Security Industry Authority (SIA) that oversees the process of regulation and licensing and the provision of training that will, it is claimed, help to professionalize the industry. The Authority has powers to inspect private security businesses and check that personnel have the necessary licences. Crawford (2003: 151) argues that the voluntary nature of some aspects of the legislation and its failure to extend to companies' in-house security staff suggest that the Act's 'primary function appears to concern improving the industry's image against a background of public concern over unscrupulous and criminal operators'. Furthermore, the Act only provides oversight of individual security officers or businesses. The Act does not provide for the direction of the private security industry in broader terms such as establishing priorities or determining any wider remit in relation to social justice or community cohesion.

The end of the Cold War and the peace process in Northern Ireland might have led to an enhanced role for the security services in policing, particularly in the context of intelligence gathering and transnational organized crime. While Parliament and the government provide for the accountability of these agencies in constitutional terms, this is clearly much narrower than the systems outlined in previous sections of this chapter as they apply to the public police, (see Box 6.6). The IPCC's role has expanded to include other agencies established primarily for law enforcement purposes, such as the Serious and Organised Crime Agency (SOCA), or whose work entails elements of policing, such as HM Customs and Excise (HMCE). In respect of both SOCA and HMCE, the IPCC only deals with complaints relating to serious misconduct by individual members of staff of these agencies and does not have a broader role relating to their policies or governance.

Box 6.6

Governing the extended police family

Other parties in emerging policing networks are also subject to oversight. For example, the Regulation of Investigatory Powers Act 2000 (RIPA) established the Investigatory Powers Tribunal (IPT) to oversee surveillance and intelligence gathering. The Tribunal determines the legality of intelligence and surveillance undertaken by MI5, MI6 and GCHQ and their roles in monitoring terrorism and criminal activity. As with the SIA, the Tribunal's remit only extends to individual complaints relating to alleged infractions of the rules. The IPT does not appear to have power to hold to account services in broader terms. It does not hold agencies that have investigatory powers to account in terms of the general control and direction.

conclusion

What emerges from this review is that narrow mechanisms of accountability exist in respect to some of the agencies involved in policing networks. These tend to relate only to allegations of misconduct against specified personnel and do not extend, as with the public police, to broader questions about policies and priorities. Moreover, systems of accountability and governance have been developed to oversee specific agencies and institutions within particular jurisdictions. These regimes become increasingly unable to hold accountable policing networks as they develop in a global context. To use the language of much contemporary analysis, existing arrangements focus upon nodes rather than networks of policing. Loader (2000) argued that questions about social justice, accountability, governance and legitimacy are made more urgent in the developing environment of contemporary global policing. Prevailing systems have focused on police institutions developed in the context of modern sovereign states and as such do not translate to diverse and dispersed networks that transcend national boundaries. The response to this changing policing terrain has been the evolution of hybrid mechanisms of governance, including, among others, a reliance on licensing, registration, rules concerning insurance coverage, self-regulation, the establishment of minimum standards and marketplace accountability to customers (Wood and Shearing, 2007: 133). Loader (2000) noted that many of these mechanisms allow little or no room for consideration of fundamental principles of justice or the pursuit of the public interest. He proposed the establishment of local, regional and national policing commissions charged with controlling the public, voluntary and commercial nodes within policing networks. These commissions would hold these networks to democratic account in the interests of public justice, defined in terms of recognizing the diverse interests and demands of the public, respect for human rights, and an equitable distribution of policing resources.

▪ ▪ chapter summary ▪

- Police accountability is understood in two dimensions in this chapter. First, and most obviously, in efforts to hold individual officers to account for their (in)actions in the performance of their duties. IPCC investigations into fatal incidents involving the police are good illustrations of this form of accountability. The second aspect of accountability relates to governance in broader terms of the direction, principles, and overall performance of the police service. The values and practices of accountability in relation to plural policing and the extended police family were explored and alternative approaches based on doctrines of ethics and human rights were considered.

- Prior to the 1964 Police Act there was no systematic means for investigating complaints about officer conduct, and the response remained a matter for individual forces. The 1976 Police Act created the Police Complaints Board to oversee a system whereby serious complaints would be investigated by officers from another force; this was the first component of an independent element being introduced to the complaints system. As an increasing range of agencies become involved in investigations, arguments that the police are the only institution with the skills necessary to scrutinize public complaints becomes more difficult to sustain.

- The international trend towards the wholly independent investigation of complaints was exemplified in the 2002 Police Reform Act, which established the Independent Police Complaints Commission (IPCC). The IPCC provisions allow for the wholly independent investigation of complaints. Additionally, the IPCC model differs from previous systems as witnesses and third parties can report incidents, complaints can be registered directly with the IPCC rather than the police, complaints can be resolved locally via a formal apology, and the IPCC can investigate broader issues of complaint, beyond claims of individual officer malfeasance.

- Other approaches seek to improve British policing in more general terms by developing professional standards. Codes of ethics have been developed in an effort to promote a normative framework to which officers should aspire. Emphasizing ethical police performance has also been seen as a method to enhance police legitimacy and improve public confidence in more general terms.

- Similarly, human rights provisions have provided a framework to control police operations. While legislation enshrines the rights of the individual, principles are outlined in which these can be over-ridden. While citizens have the right to privacy, for example, the police can contravene this with surveillance operations, providing that these are 'necessary' (no alternatives are available) and 'proportionate' (in relation to the gravity of the matter at hand).

- Police reform in the context of international development has centred on the promotion of human rights. In this context, human rights agendas have not only focused on controlling what officers are permitted to do, but they also establish a range of objectives that the police are expected to secure. Commentators have suggested that these developments are indicative of a broader re-conceptualization of policing in terms of the promotion of harm reduction, security and safety. The application of these debates to police reform in Northern Ireland was examined.

- The governance of British police continues to be shaped by the 1964 Police Act, which established the tripartite system whereby the control and direction of the police are shared between central government, local police authorities, and Chief Constables. While Chief Constables have operational responsibility and independence, the local police authority and central government are responsible for financial provisions and establishing the policy and direction of police services. The bifurcation of police governance, becoming more centralized and more localized at the same time, has been much debated, although the implications of these trends for democratic oversight are not clear-cut. Government proposals to reduce the number of police services from 43 to 12, which were withdrawn in the face of widespread opposition, brought these debates about the governance of the public police into sharp focus.

- Regimes of accountability in the police service, like the public sector more generally, have increasingly centred on actuarialist models that measure officer performance in terms of criteria relating to various aspects of police work. Many have argued that this reflects a broader tendency to introduce private sector discipline into public services.

- Developments in the governance and accountability of the public police do not easily extend to the emerging context of plural policing. While legislation requires that private security personnel are licensed and the Security Industry Authority can inspect companies, concerns continue about the extent to which the sector more widely is accountable and effectively regulated. Certainly questions about the direction and control of the private security industry continue to be resolved by the market mechanism, which marginalizes public interest and social justice questions.

 ## self-check questions

1. Prior to the 2002 Police Reform Act, which agencies and groups had advocated the establishment of an independent system to investigate complaints against the police?

2. What does the 'local resolution' of a complaint against the police entail?

3. When was the Code of Ethics of the Police Service of Northern Ireland first established?

4. Under the terms of the European Convention on Human Rights, what conditions need to be met if individual rights are to be set aside?

5. What did the Patten Commission into policing in Northern Ireland suggest was the main purpose of the police?

6. From which force did the Home Office second a senior officer to improve Nottinghamshire constabulary's performance in dealing with serious crime?

7. In what way has the focus of accountability been changed by the rise of managerialism?

8. Why did Shearing and Stenning suggest that concern about the role of private security had been marginalized in the United States, prior to the 1980s?

9   What is the primary requirement of the 2001 Private Security Industry Act?

10 What concerns did Loader suggest are made more salient by the changing environment of international policing?

■ study ʔuestions ▬▬▬▬▬▬▬▬▬▬▬▬▬▬▬▬

1   What have been the key arguments in favour of developing an independent system of investigating complaints against the police?

2   How might an emphasis on ethics and human rights impact upon policing?

3   Although the position of local police authorities might have been eroded in recent years, why is it simplistic to argue there has been an unchecked process of centralization?

▬▬▬ ■ ■ annotated further reading ■ ▬▬▬▬▬

Dixon and Smith's (1998) article, 'Laying Down the Law', analyses changing combinations of systems of accountability applied to the British police. Three key cases that tested aspects of police accountability are reviewed and developments such as operational independence, liability for losses experienced by the public due to police negligence, and the increasing role of civil law proceedings against police are examined.

Neyroud and Beckley's (2001) *Policing, Ethics and Human Rights* explores the development of a human rights/ethics-based approach to policing developed in Britain in response to miscarriages of justice, and perceptions of police racism and incompetence. The book distinguishes between personal, operational and organizational ethics and argues that each of these will become increasingly important in the development of professional policing as demands on the service become increasingly complex and performance is subject to greater public scrutiny.

Loveday's (2005) article, 'The Challenge of Police Reform in England and Wales', provides a thorough account of the developing mechanisms by which the Home Office monitors, measures and directs police performance. The article considers the implications of these processes of governance in an era of reform which sees responsibility for policing increasingly devolved to local Basic Command Units.

The website of the Independent Police Complaints Commission (www.ipcc. gov.uk) contains many resources, including performance statistics, reports of specific complaints, and links to other agencies and useful police-related resources and organizations.

The role of local police authorities has come under considerable scrutiny in the light of recent controversies and aborted proposals for the merger of police services. The Association of Police Authorities website (http://tinyurl.com/yrfvxc) includes information about the role and composition of police authorities, and other publications relating to policing.

The charity Inquest was established in 1981 and provides advice and support on all aspects of deaths in custody. The Inquest website (http://tinyurl.com/22t4c5) provides a host of resources relating to general issues of procedure and practice relating to the treatment of people in detention.

7

Policing diversity

Contents

This chapter provides an overview of the recent development of the notion of 'policing diversity' in England and Wales. In addition to outlining why policing diversity has become a pre-eminent theme in current debates about policing, the chapter explores central conceptual issues and argues that increasing recognition of social diversity poses challenges to long-standing principles of 'policing by consent'. However, it argues that, taken to its logical conclusions, the concept might raise serious problems for the police service. The objectives of the chapter are:

- to outline the social and political context in which the concept of policing diversity has developed in recent times;

- to explore the widening understanding of 'diversity' issues;

- to consider why enhancing diversity is regarded as a priority for the police service;

- to reflect upon the limitations of the diversity agenda for contemporary policing.

key terms

gender; legitimacy; race and racism; racist crime; sexuality; stop and search

introduction

Although concern about police relations with sections of the community in the United Kingdom has been particularly salient since the urban unrest of the 1980s and became the defining issue of debate that followed the public inquiry into the murder of Stephen Lawrence, it is worth noting that police relations with minority ethnic groups often have been fraught since the foundation of modern police forces in the mid-nineteenth century. Similar concerns have applied in many other societies and have been a major issue in the United States, Australia, Canada and elsewhere for many decades (Barlow and Barlow, 2001; Cunneen, 2001; Baker, 2006). Historians have demonstrated that various sections of the public in Britain have been understood as problematic for the police during particular periods (Emsley, 1996; Reiner, 2000). In the early decades of the modern policing era, the 'dangerous classes' located in urban slums were widely regarded as a threat to the police and to 'respectable society' more generally (Morris, 1994). In the century or so between the foundation of the modern police and the beginning of large-scale migration to Britain from the Commonwealth, Irish people, Jews from Eastern Europe, and Arabian and African seaman, among others, were in various ways understood as difficult groups for the police (Panayi, 1996; Rowe, 1998). That concern about police relations with minority communities is often regarded as a relatively recent phenomenon is perhaps because contemporary problems are understood against the background of the perceived 'golden era' of British policing that followed the Second World War (Reiner, 2000). If a longer-term perspective is taken, then a rather different picture of police–community relations emerges. Equally, analysis of actual – rather than mythical – police relations with minority communities during the halcyon period of the 1950s and 1960s reveals a reality of prejudice and stereotyping that belies the notion that such controversies are a recent development (Whitfield, 2004; 2007).

Contemporary concerns about police relations with minority ethnic communities in Britain can be traced back to the early 1970s. Detailed histories of such relations are available elsewhere (Fryer, 1984; Keith, 1993) and will not be fully recounted here. The most significant occasion on which police relations with minority communities had a sustained impact on the national political agenda was the 1981 disorders in Brixton, South London and the subsequent Scarman Inquiry (see Box 7.1).

Box 7.1

The Scarman Report

The Scarman Inquiry into the 1981 Brixton disorders established an agenda for policing in Britain that continues to be influential a quarter of a century later ... The Brixton disorders were not the first of the urban riots of the 1980s, others had taken place a year previously in Bristol, and they were not the most serious in terms of death, injury or destruction. They did, however, become iconic; epitomising urban crisis, decay and revolt, and a synonym for troubled police–community relations. The disorders occurred over the weekend of 10–12 April 1981 and followed a week-long police initiative (Operation Swamp) designed to tackle burglary and robbery. The operation entailed 'flooding' the streets with officers instructed to stop and search, on the basis of surveillance and suspicion, as many people as possible. Some 943 people were stopped, more than half of whom were black and two-thirds were aged under 21 ... Violence eventually erupted: although on a relatively minor level that evening, it re-ignited the following afternoon and the Saturday evening saw events that Scarman (1981: 1) described in the following terms:

... the British people watched with horror and incredulity ... scenes of violence and disorder in their capital city, the like of which had not previously been seen in this century in Britain. In the centre of Brixton, a few hundred young people – most, but not all of them, black – attacked the police on the streets with stones, bricks, iron bars and petrol bombs, demonstrating to their fellow citizens the fragile basis of the Queen's peace ... These young people, by their criminal behaviour – for such, whatever their grievances or frustrations, it was – brought about a temporary collapse of law and order in the centre of an inner suburb of London.

(Continued)

In the aftermath of the disorders Lord Scarman, a senior judge, was appointed to conduct an inquiry into the circumstances of the disorders and the police response ... Perhaps the central contribution of the report was its insistence that the disorders could only be understood against the particular context of social deprivation, political marginalisation, and economic disadvantage. An inflexible and militaristic style of policing, with poor public engagement, exacerbated the situation and made worse tensions and pressures but did not solely create them ... Many of Scarman's recommendations relating to policing, for example on training, the role of community policing, lay visitors to police stations, discipline, and stop and search, established an agenda for the following decade. That some of the problems he identified were reiterated almost twenty years later in the Lawrence Inquiry suggests both that the reforms Scarman advocated were crucial and that they had not been effectively implemented. (Rowe, 2007a)

Scarman's restatement of the importance of policing by consent and commu-nity policing did not occur in a vacuum. As discussed in Chapter 4, other influ-ential commentators, perhaps most notably the former Chief Constable John Alderson, were also arguing that post-war British policing had become too isolated from the public and that officers had come to regard themselves as a group separate from society at large (Alderson, 1979). One high-profile report into police–community relations, published by Her Majesty's Inspectorate of Constabulary, notes that during the 1970s and 1980s:

> **Police force amalgamations created larger and sometimes impersonal service providers where policing strategies were decided upon, implemented and changed with a minimum of internal and external consultation. The traditional foot beat system had in many instances been replaced by unit-beat systems supported by 'panda' cars providing less continuity in personal contact between the police and the public. In many areas, particularly those within inner cities, reactive 'fire brigade' style policing had become more and more prevalent. (HMIC, 1997: 7)**

In addition to concerns that the style of policing as delivered to the public was serving to isolate officers from routine contact with members of the public, debates were also taking place about formal systems of accountability. The relative powerlessness of local police authorities *vis-à-vis* Chief Constables and the Home Secretary, within the tripartite framework laid down by the 1964 Police Act, was causing some to argue that a democratic deficit existed in governance of the police (Jefferson and Grimshaw, 1984; Scraton, 1985). These issues are discussed at greater length in Chapter 6. Whereas relations with minority ethnic communities were only one aspect of these broader debates about policing, a series of incidents involving alleged police mistreatment of black people provided many examples that fuelled arguments about the proper role of the police. Incidents of urban unrest in the mid-1980s had occurred following perceived mistreatment of black people. For example, the 1985 Broadwater Farm disorders in Tottenham, London, occurred following the death of a black woman, Cherry Groce, during a police raid on her home. While many of the allegations of police misconduct during this period related to perceived over-policing of minority communities, for example through the disproportionate use of stop and search powers, others related to under-policing, as the service failed to respond effectively to incidents of racist violence. The dichotomy between over- and under-policing of minority communities is considered further later in this chapter.

the impact of the Lawrence Inquiry

Whereas the police had been subject to a series of criticisms with regard to interaction with minority ethnic communities in Britain for several decades, there can be little doubt that the inquiry by Sir William Macpherson into the murder of Stephen Lawrence marked a significant watershed and placed issues of race and racism at the heart of debates about policing (Rowe, 2004; 2007). Although the facts of the murder of 18-year-old Lawrence are relatively straightforward and incontrovertible, the impact that the case has had in terms of policing in Britain and society's attitudes towards racism has been wide-ranging and fundamental. Because much of the discussion of particular developments in policing diversity is overtly rooted in the aftermath of the Lawrence murder and the subsequent report by Sir William Macpherson, it is important to provide an overview of the case and the developments that followed (see Box 7.2).

Box 7.2

The Stephen Lawrence case

In April 1993, Stephen Lawrence, a black teenager with ambitions of becoming an architect, was waiting for a bus in Eltham, South London, accompanied by his friend, Duwyane Brooks, when a group of white youths shouted racist abuse and charged them from across the road. The group engulfed Lawrence, stabbing him repeatedly. Brooks fled, shouting for Lawrence to follow him, which he did. Bleeding heavily, however, Lawrence collapsed some 130 yards from the scene of attack and died soon after on the pavement. The jury at the subsequent inquest into Lawrence's death returned a verdict of unlawful killing in 'a completely unprovoked

(Continued)

racist attack by five white youths'. In the years that followed the murder, two police investigations were conducted into the case by the Metropolitan Police and another, under the auspices of the Police Complaints Authority, by Kent Police. Subsequently, the Crown Prosecution Service decided against bringing a case against five suspects, which led the family of Stephen Lawrence to bring a private prosecution against the same men, a very unusual development with respect to a murder, and one that failed to bring any conviction in this case. Although the report of the official inquiry clearly rejected allegations that the failure to adequately investigate the murder was a result of police corruption or collusion, the conclusion that was arrived at offered scant comfort to the police (Macpherson, 1999):

> The conclusions to be drawn from all the evidence in connection with the investigation of Stephen Lawrence's racist murder are clear. There is no doubt but that there were fundamental errors. The investigation was marred by a combination of professional incompetence, institutional racism and a failure of leadership by senior officers. A flawed Metropolitan Police Service review failed to expose these inadequacies. The second investigation could not salvage the faults of the first investigation.
>
> At least now many of the failures and flaws are accepted. For too long the family and the public were led to believe that the investigation had been satisfactorily carried out. The belated apologies offered at this Inquiry acknowledge the truth, but there is no remedy for the grief which the unsuccessful investigation piled upon the grief caused by the murder itself.

The Macpherson Report made 70 recommendations covering a wide range of police work, including improvements to training in first-aid, the management of murder investigations, police liaison with the victims of crime, and the use of stop and search powers. While the focus here – and more widely – is on the implications that the Macpherson Report had for police relations with minority communities, it is important to note that it also found professional incompetence and a failure of leadership marred the investigation into the murder of Stephen Lawrence. Underpinning the specific recommendations was a more fundamental priority that the Home Secretary needed to improve the 'trust and confidence' that minority ethnic communities have in the police service. The Home Secretary responded by accepting the majority of the recommendations and establishing a steering group to oversee their implementation and report annually on progress made. Much of the initial political and media focus on the Report centred on the finding that the police service was institutionally racist. The Macpherson Report (1999: 6.34) defined the concept in the following terms, which have become predominant:

The collective failure of an organisation to provide an appropriate and professional service to people because of their colour, culture or ethnic origin. It can be

seen or detected in processes, attitudes and behaviour which amount to discrimination through unwitting prejudice, ignorance, thoughtlessness and racist stereotyping which disadvantages minority ethnic people.

The concept of 'institutional racism' has long been controversial, not least because it has been used to mean many different things (Singh, 2000). While the Macpherson Report finding was accepted by many senior police officers, it has subsequently been criticized on various grounds. Some have argued that the term has hampered effective policing by undermining the public reputation of the service or that it has created a climate in which officers are reluctant to intervene because they are concerned that they will be labelled as racist by newly emboldened minority communities (Hague, 2000). While there is anecdotal evidence that such concerns are expressed by officers, it is not clear that they have had a significant impact in terms of routine police work. Although it is clear, to take one example, that the number of stop and searches did fall off in the period following publication of the Macpherson Report, it is equally apparent that the use of stop and search powers has remained a central feature of police work and that the number carried out has increased again in the wake of concerns about terrorism. Issues relating to the over-representation of minority ethnic groups in police stop search data are discussed at greater length later in this chapter.

Other criticisms of the Report's use of the term 'institutional racism' suggest that, despite its apparent radical clarity, the term continues to be badly defined and contradictory. To that extent, authors such as Lea (2000) and Solomos (1999) have argued that the definition does little more than reformulate forms of indirect racism that were prohibited by the 1976 Race Relations Act. That legislation outlawed policies and procedures that had disproportionate impacts in terms of ethnicity, even where they did so unintentionally. Others have argued (Foster et al., 2005; Souhami, 2007) that police officer resistance to the charge of institutional racism and the difficulties that many have expressed in terms of responding to it, stem from a fundamental incoherence in the Report's analysis and cannot be reduced to a cultural or organizational sensitivity about racism. Souhami (2007) noted, for example, that the Report applied the term 'institutional racism' inconsistently; sometimes attributing errors to individual officers and other times to more general cultural or institutional processes. Among the arising incongruities not properly explained in the Report was how institutional racism explained the failure of some officers to properly understand that the murder was a racist attack, while other officers – part of the same institution – recognized very quickly that it was a racist murder (Lea, 2003, cited in Souhami, 2007).

_____ the development of antiracist policing _____

One of the central features of the impact that the Macpherson Report had has been in terms of the added impetus it has given to the development of policing diversity models. Prior to the publication of the report, it might be argued, the predominant policing approach was one predicated on a 'race relations' or equal opportunities model: broadly based on the provision of a similar level and style of policing to all members of society. The key focus was to ensure that minority ethnic communities received an equitable service to that delivered to all members of society. This perspective characterizes the role of the police as essentially neutral, in which officers' proper concern is to enforce the law in a professional, even-handed, and effective manner. Often the goal was to assure that officers refrained from behaving in certain ways considered to be illegal or morally and ethically undesirable. Post-Macpherson, conceptualization of the police position in respect of minority groups has become one in which antiracism is a central theme. The previous position can be characterized as one in which the police occupied a largely neutral inert role whereby social racism was a given problem to which the police responded, and members of the public, whether victims, witnesses, or suspects, were to be treated equitably and in a uniform manner. Perhaps the most significant dimension of reconceptualizing the police role has been an emphasis on policing as an explicitly antiracist activity: one in which a proactive interventionist role is taken to challenge the problem of racism. A guide to combating hate crime, published by the Association of Chief Police Officers (2000), describes the implication of antiracism in the following terms: 'To confront prejudice outside the police service and to eliminate it within it, at work, every member of staff is expected to subscribe to a code of active conduct, which requires far more than strict compliance with the law.'

Clearly, the development of antiracism as a proactive task of policing is consistent with wider changes such as the 2002 Race Relations (Amendments) Act that requires public bodies, including schools, hospitals, local authorities, and the police service, to formulate policies that will promote antiracism and actively challenge discrimination. This establishes a broader remit for individual police officers and the police service than a traditional requirement not to contravene legal or disciplinary codes. Not only does it reflect broader public policy shift in efforts to tackle racial discrimination, it also mirrors other efforts to reorientate the management of officers around positive goals and objectives rather than the negative avoidance of unacceptable practices. As shown in Chapter 8, police services internationally have developed codes of ethical practice that supplement disciplinary regulations by producing statements about the standard of behaviour that officers ought to aspire to. The promotion of antiracism within the police service places a greater onus on middle and senior ranking officers made responsible for 'delivering' on community and race relations targets, such as those relating to recruitment. Recognition that the active pursuit of good community and race relations is central to contemporary police leadership is evident in the remarks of the President of the UK **Police Superintendents Association**, who noted that 'if you are not delivering on this [policing diversity], you should not be a Basic Command Unit commander' (*Police Review*, 2001).

Efforts to develop a policing service that meets the needs of minority ethnic communities have raised more profound questions about legitimacy and efficacy in complex and fragmented societies. Although it might be argued that the notion of policing by consent has never been wholly achieved in Britain, it has provided an important discourse and an apparent source of legitimacy. In an era in which many public agencies have consciously aped private sector consumer-focused approaches to service delivery, the provision of a one-dimensional standard has been replaced by an emphasis on meeting the diverse needs of heterogeneous clients.

Partly in response to increasing political and financial scrutiny from central government, senior police officers sought to 'reconfigure the working culture of the police so as to improve the "quality" of the service it offers' (Loader and Mulcahy, 2003: 240). In addition to adopting some of the financial rigours of the private sector, policing co-opted the language of service delivery and customer satisfaction. An early example of this was the launch in 1988 of the Metropolitan Police 'Plus Programme', and the ACPO's Statement of Common Purpose and Values, both of which sought to emphasize a role for the police beyond the narrow remit of crime-fighting (Reiner, 2000: 75). The party politics of law and order in the 1990s, among other factors, meant that issues relating to policing, race and racism came under particular scrutiny. McLaughlin (2007b) argued that New Labour placed great emphasis on establishing a public inquiry into the Lawrence murder as part of broader efforts to reposition the party's stance on law and order.

two dimensions of policing diversity

As noted in the Introduction, campaign groups, media exposés, and political controversies relating to policing and race relations have centred around two tendencies that are superficially contradictory: the under-policing and the over-policing of minority ethnic communities. The latter refers to the police role in the criminalization of minority ethnic youths and the former to the failure of the service to provide an adequate service to the victims of racist harassment and violence, as epitomized by the Lawrence case. Both failures have been attributed to factors including institutional racism, police culture and the under-representation of minority ethnic people in the police service. Chapter 5 included discussion of the recruitment, retention and the promotion of minority ethnic police officers, and female and gay staff. The discussion below focuses on long-standing concern about police use of stop and search powers, as the primary illustration of the over-policing of minority ethnic officers, and the under-policing of racist incidents.

Reflecting on the position of minority ethnic communities in the criminal justice system, David Smith (1995: 1064) points out that 'among those offenders who are processed ... a considerable proportion are drawn into the net through the exercise of discretionary powers by the police, particularly stop-and-search'. Although the use of these powers is widely held to be vital to the prevention, detection, and deterrence of crime, it is also apparent that the practice of stop and search and its application to minority ethnic communities are a matter of considerable controversy, and have been for many decades. In the 1970s official statistics began to be released that suggested that black British people were more likely to be stopped and searched by the police than other sections of the community. During that period the legal basis of stop and searches lacked clarity so that officers could carry out a stop and search on the most slender of pretences. The regulation of stop and search introduced by the 1984 Police and Criminal Evidence Act was outlined in Chapter 3. In the 1970s and 1980s, anecdotal and other evidence formed a picture whereby groups of officers in certain districts would routinely and deliberately use these powers to target and harass young black people. The official inquiry report into the 1981 Brixton riots noted that the stopping and searching of young black people had been a major cause of increasing public anger with the police service in the build-up to unrest (Scarman, 1981). During this period there was a lack of authoritative statistical information about stop and search practices and claims and counter-claims were not easily scrutinized. Often allegations that stop and search was targeted in a racist manner were rebuffed in terms that suggested that it was the disproportionate involvement of young black males in forms of street crime, drug dealing, and so on, that explained police attention. Stop and search practice, it was argued, 'followed the crime' (Fitzgerald, 2000), although only 11 per cent of 'PACE stops' resulted in an arrest in 2004/05 (Home Office, 2006c).

Over subsequent decades relatively reliable and rigorous data on the distribution of stop and search across ethnic lines have developed considerably, and 'objective' quantifiable evidence is easily located in Home Office and other reports. A number of developments have broadened the evidential base against which debates about stop and search can be evaluated. Section 95 of the 1991 Criminal Justice Act required that police services collate and publish a range of information relating to ethnicity, including the ethnic profile of those who are stopped and searched under the provision of the 1984 Police and Criminal Evidence Act (PACE). These data showed that, in England and Wales in 2004/05, 15 white people per 1,000 of the resident population were stopped and searched by the police; the comparative figure for the black community was 90 in 1,000, and for Asian people it was 27 per 1,000 in the resident population. On that basis it seems that black people were six times more likely to be stopped and searched than whites, and that Asians were also over-represented in the data, although to a lesser degree.

The data also provide for a more detailed breakdown of stop and search practices that show that ethnic disparities also appear in terms of the reasons why stop and searches are conducted. Table 7.1 indicates that around half of stop and searches carried out on black or Asian people are drug-related, whereas this accounts for only 38 per cent of those conducted on white people. On the other hand, 14 per cent of stop and searches carried out on whites related to suspicions of 'going equipped' [to commit burglary or theft], which accounted for only 8 and 7 per cent of those relating to black or Asian people respectively.

Table 7.1 Percentage of stop and searches under S1 of the PACE 1984 and other legislation, by reason for stop and ethnic appearance, England and Wales, 2004/05

Reason for search	Ethnic appearance of person searched					
	White	Black	Asian	Other	Not known	Total
Stolen property	30	24	18	31	28	28
Drugs	38	51	55	40	36	41
Firearms	1	2	2	1	1	1
Offensive weapons	8	12	13	11	7	9
Going equipped	14	8	7	11	10	13
Other	8	3	4	6	16	7
Total	627,579	118,165	59,954	12,733	21,546	839,977

Source: Home Office (2006c: 28)

Such trends have appeared consistently in the Home Office data in recent years. Although the number of stop and searches in overall terms fell in the years after publication of the Macpherson Report, there has subsequently been an increase: the 839,977 cases recorded in 2004/05 represented a 14 per cent rise on the previous year. The apparent ethnic disparities identified in respect of 2004/05, however, have been a consistent feature since the data began to be collected in the mid-1990s. Official sources – such as the annual Home Office Section 95 reports – have added authority to this important element of accounts of police racism.

However, explaining patterns of police stop and search practice on the basis of these recorded statistics requires caution. First, the ethnic classification itself is problematic, since 'white' is an omnibus category that does not directly correspond to ethnicity, and 'Asian' conflates sub-groups that have sharply contrasting socio-economic profiles. Moreover, the statistics are based upon the appearance as perceived by the police officer conducting the stop and search. Clearly this introduces a problematic subjectivity to the recording process. Furthermore, the recent rise in the number of stop and searches recorded seems likely, in part at least, to be an artefact of continuing debates about the implementation of stop and search and efforts to promote good practice. As with officially recorded crime figures, the increasing number of stop and searches might be a result of changes in recording practice rather than a reflection of true prevalence. Problems with recording practices have also been identified that might explain the disparities reflected in Table 7.1 in ways that do not relate simply to police racism. Fitzgerald and Sibbit (1997) found that officers were more likely to record stop and searches conducted on minority ethnic people than on whites, in part because they were more concerned to demonstrate that they had followed procedures when dealing with the latter than they were with the former. Clearly, this means it is more likely that encounters with minority ethnic people make their way into official records than similar interactions with white people. The tendency for minorities to be treated more formally has also been noted in the context of the response of senior officers to internal matters of complaints and discipline. One reason why concerns about the performance of minority ethnic officers are more likely to activate disciplinary processes and result in formal investigation is that middle-ranking officers, most of whom are white, lack the confidence needed to resolve issues informally as they would with white officers (Morris et al., 2004).

In addition to concerns about categories and recording practices surrounding stop and search, recent research findings show that the use of alternative population benchmarks suggests a wholly different perspective in which minority ethnic communities are not over-represented. The data published annually by the Home Office are presented in terms of stop and searches per 1000 of the resident population. However, this benchmark is not the most appropriate since it is known that stop and searches tend to be conducted at particular times and in particular places. The resident population comprises all those in the police area, many of whom are unlikely to be present when and where stop and searches are likely to be performed. In response to this limitation, efforts have been made to establish a more appropriate benchmark based on those available to be stopped and searched at the times and places where this is most likely to be done. MVA and Miller (2000) compiled a benchmark of the available population in five sites and used that to determine the ethnic proportionality of stop and search. Their report suggested that this measure led to a conclusion radically at odds with the predominant narrative based upon Home Office data outlined earlier:

> The findings of this research did not suggest any general pattern of bias against those from minority ethnic backgrounds. This was true for minority ethnic groups as a whole, as well as any particular minority ethnic group. Asian people tended to be under-represented in those stopped or searched, compared to their numbers in

the available population, with some notable exceptions. The general picture for black people was mixed. For example, in Greenwich, and Chapeltown, they were mostly under-represented among those stopped or searched, yet in Hounslow and Ipswich, they were far more likely to be stopped or searched in vehicles than their available numbers would suggest. Perhaps surprisingly, the most consistent finding across sites was that white people tended to be stopped and searched at a higher rate than their numbers in the available population would predict. (ibid.: 84)

Waddington et al. (2004) reproduced MVA and Miller's methodology in Reading and in Slough. They too found that this measure of police stop and search led to an important change in prevailing explanatory frameworks. They argued that:

It seems that a very different conclusion is reached from comparing stop and search figures with the composition of the 'available population' than with residential figures ... it is difficult to see how these figures could be interpreted as an outcome of officers' stereotyping: if anything, it is white people who are disproportionately stopped and searched. (ibid.: 900)

As these studies tend to note, these findings do not end concern about racism and police stop and search (Rowe, 2004). If officers are not discriminating against minority ethnic communities available in areas where stop and search is carried out, then it seems that explanations in terms of frontline officers exercising discretion on the basis of racist stereotypes need to be rethought. However, questions about racism and discrimination still remain, since stop and search practices are concentrated on deprived areas where some minority ethnic groups are more likely to reside. Moreover, socio-economic factors, coupled in some contexts with racism, shape the availability of populations to be stopped and searched. Poverty and exclusion determine availability, in some areas; this impacts on visible minority ethnic communities and they might be over-represented in police stop and search data. In other districts, though, white communities, whether minority ethnic, such as the Irish, or otherwise, might be most affected and so have disproportionate contact with the police (Stenson and Waddington, 2007). Race and racism are crucial to understanding patterns of stop and search, but other issues, such as class and place, also need to be incorporated into a convincing explanation.

under-policing: racist violence and harassment

Concomitant concerns have recurred about the failure of the police service, and criminal justice system more widely, to provide an effective response to racist violence and harassment, and other forms of hate crime. The inadequacy of the investigation into the murder of Stephen Lawrence resonated partly because it was a compelling illustration of a much more widespread problem about which minority ethnic communities, and others, had long campaigned. The racist murder of Kelso Cochrane in 1959 was a key factor in the Notting Hill riots and an early example of a police response that served to deny that the attack was racially motivated (BBC, 2006). A common complaint has been that officers responding to incidents have tended to disregard suggestions of racist elements and instead to approach the victim's experience as an 'ordinary' offence. Similar concerns have been raised in the context of hate crimes against lesbian, gay, bisexual and transgender communities (Hall, 2005). Bowling (1998) showed that much racist violence and harassment tends to be relatively minor in character if the racist components of the offence are disregarded. His study of racist violence in the East End of London found that:

> **Incidents were frequently described [by practitioners] as being 'low level' but 'persistent' and included such incidents as criminal damage, graffiti, spreading rubbish, abusive behaviour, egg throwing, stone throwing, threatening behaviour, and 'knock-down-ginger', often forming patterns of harassing behaviour. More serious incidents such as physical assaults and arson were believed to occur, though less frequently than mundane but persistent behaviour. (ibid.: 182)**

Traditionally police officers have tended to seek relatively informal resolution of such disputes and have favoured an 'order maintenance' strategy over that of law enforcement. While this might be an appropriate response in some circumstances, it misunderstands the nature of racist victimization, which is exacerbated by routine repetition so that it forms part of the fabric of every-day life for those who experience it. As Bowling (ibid.: 280) notes, however, this type of response – where 'normal' circumstances are restored without resort to legal sanction against perpetrators – 'may simply serve to maintain the on-going process of ... victimization. If the threat of violence and occasional use of actual violence is used to intimidate, exclude, or terrorize, the balance of power between victim and perpetrator remains.'

The reactive, fire-brigade, model of policing, where officers deal with single incidents as and when they arise, has meant that the sustained and repetitive nature of racist incidents has not been sufficiently recognized. Similar problems have applied more widely and much of the thrust of the 1998 Crime and Disorder Act, 'reassurance policing' projects, and the Neighbourhood Policing programme has been to focus attention on tackling antisocial behaviour which, while not necessarily serious criminal offences, undermine the quality of life of communities affected. Additionally, a key dimension of the **problem-oriented policing** model is for officers to seek to resolve relatively minor issues before they escalate into more serious criminality (Goldstein, 1990; Leigh et al., 1996). Related to the particular point about the police failing to recognize the nature or the impact of racist incidents is the broader problem identified with problem-oriented policing, which is that officers continue to be focused on criminal incidents (Bowling, 1998).

A key contribution of the Macpherson Report (1999: 328) has been the adoption of a broader definition of a racist incident, namely that: 'a racist incident is any incident which is perceived to be racist by the victim or any other person'. This is intended to address the problematic 'gatekeeper' role of police officers who often denied that incidents were motivated by racism even in circumstances where victims and witnesses were convinced otherwise. Gordon (1990) and Hesse et al. (1992) suggest that a serious weakness in the policing of racist violence and harassment in London during the 1980s was that the police tended to deny or marginalize the racist motivation in many cases. In terms of models of crime, recording the adoption of the 'Lawrence definition' represents a shift from an evidential approach wherein officers seek proof to corroborate that an incident has occurred to a prima facia approach whereby the account of the victim is accepted without question unless there are compelling reasons not to. Once an incident is recorded in police crime databases as being racially motivated, it is 'flagged up' so that supervisory officers can ensure that the required steps are taken by frontline officers so that evidence is gathered and victims are given appropriate support (Hall, 2005). Improved reporting of racist incidents has also been encouraged by allowing third parties to accept reports and pass information onto the police. The inclusion of housing authorities, religious organizations, community groups and others in **multi-agency partnerships** able to respond to racist incidents was an early example of networked, plural policing of the kind discussed further in Chapter 8.

Home Office data clearly indicate a steady rise in racist incidents during recent years (Home Office, 2006d). Figure 7.1 shows incidents recorded by the police each year, in relation to a baseline index of 100 in 1999–2000. In these terms, the number of incidents recorded in 2004–05 was more than twenty per cent higher than in baseline year. In actual terms, the police recorded 58,000 incidents in 2004–05, much lower than the British Crime Survey estimate that 179,000 racist incidents occurred that year. Clearly this suggests that many racist incidents are not reported to the police, although increasing numbers recorded suggest that this is a problem that is being addressed. As with any crime figures, caution is required in terms of explaining these trends; the rising rates seem highly likely to reflect the broader definition of a racist incident, as mentioned above, and an increasing willingness to report incidents, made easier by the encouragement of third party reporting.

Another key development of recent years has been the introduction, in the 1998 Crime and Disorder Act, of a host of 'racially aggravated' offences. Given the Act's focus upon providing for more effective policing and local authority responses to antisocial behaviour and 'low level' offending, it is appropriate that it also provides tougher legal sanction for such offences when they are characterized by 'racial aggravation'. The 1998 Act re-writes other legislation, and introduces tougher tariffs in cases where 'racial aggravation' can be

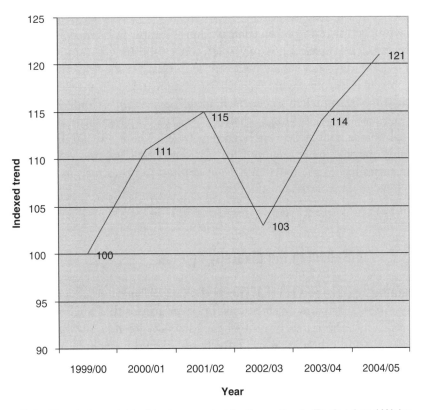

Figure 7.1 Trends in racist incidents recorded by the police in England and Wales, 1999–2000 to 2004–05

Notes:
[1]This figure shows indexed trends. The 1999/00 figure is indexed at 100. The numbers of racist incidents for each subsequent year are each expressed as a percentage of the 1999/00 figures.
[2]Revised figures for 1999/00 to 2003/04.

Source: Home Office (2006d: 6)

demonstrated. The Act defines 'racial aggravation' fairly broadly, stating in Section 28 that such an offence is:

- one motivated by racial hostility;
- or if racial hostility was demonstrated towards the victim either at the time of committing the offence, or immediately before or after.

The notion of motivation is itself open to fairly wide interpretation under Section 28 and the inclusion of the demonstration of 'racial hostility' means that such charges might be brought where the offender uses racist language or displays racist symbols (for example, on their clothing) during an offence. In these terms, then, a prosecution need not rely solely on establishing the motivation of an attack, which may be a subjective exercise in many cases, since the presence of more objective factors – what was said or demonstrated prior to, during or after an incident – are sufficient to establish 'racial aggravation' (Home Office, 1998).

Subsequent to these legal changes, related concepts of 'religious' and 'homophobic' aggravation have been developed. These indicate how problems and solutions that have emerged in relation to policing and minority ethnic communities have broadened and been applied to other marginalized groups, as the next section outlines.

broadening the diversity agenda

Developing a police service that meets the particular needs of minority ethnic communities clearly has implications for other groups that might have specific interests. While the initial impact of the 'diversity agenda' outlined above has been on race and ethnicity, it has latterly broadened to include other commu-nities of interest, such as lesbian, gay, bisexual and transgender populations, people with mental or physical disabilities, elderly people, and myriad other groups. In 2003, an HMIC report outlined the importance of recognizing the particular policing needs of a range of interest groups. While the report maintained that the police service ought to remain focused upon managing the issues relating to race and ethnicity that had been developed in the aftermath of the Macpherson Report, it suggested that other groups also had specific interests that needed to be addressed. The report highlighted 13 groups that ought to be brought into the diversity agenda, in addition to minority ethnic communities (HMIC, 2003: 62–3):

- Lesbian, gay or bisexual people
- The deaf or hard of hearing
- People with mental illness
- Gypsies/travellers
- People with disabilities
- Victims of domestic violence
- Asylum seekers
- Young people
- Older people

- Transgender people

- Those involved in child protection issues

- People from areas of poverty (the socially excluded).

It is clear that each of these groups might have particular policing needs and that different means of consultation might be necessary for effective service-delivery. However, the range of interests and needs that arise is broad, especially since any permutation of these is possible, so that it is difficult to see how they could be operationalized. While the police service has invested significant resources into providing training on issues relating to 'community and race relations', it is inconceivable that officers or support staff could be trained in any meaningful way in the complex, unpredictable, and changing patterns of diversity.

why is diversity important?

Although often not explicitly stated, a number of benefits are often alluded to by policy documents that seek to enhance the diversity of the contemporary police service. The recruitment of more minority ethnic, female, and gay officers was discussed in relation to efforts to transform police culture that were reviewed in Chapter 5. Although the police service has not always been subject to employment law that governs other institutions, it is subject to the 2000 Race Relations (Amendment) Act that requires the pursuit of policies that will promote antiracism. Avoiding legal sanctions and high-profile employment tribunals provides a negative reason why police managers might seek to promote good practice in terms of diversity and equal opportunity policies. More positively, diversity is important to contemporary policing for pragmatic operational reasons and also to preserve, regain or promote legitimacy.

Practical advantages can be considered in two respects: those relating to operational effectiveness and those that emphasize human resource advantages. As Deputy Commissioner of the Metropolitan Police, Sir Ian Blair launched the 'Protect and Respect' initiative, intended to promote diversity within the service. The programme was advanced because, Sir Ian insisted, there was a 'business case' to pursue recruitment of minority ethnic officers, and that concerns that the initiative represented a 'politically correct' agenda were misplaced. Instead he stated,

> **It is change for the most basic of business reasons. The future survival of this organisation … which needs to recruit two-thirds of its police staff over the next ten years, depends on its ability to attract and retain the most talented employees from all our communities. (*Police Review*, 2001)**

Some time later, the operational advantages of recruiting minority ethnic officers were stressed by Peter Herbert, a member of the Metropolitan Police Authority, who argued that minority ethnic officers ought to be deployed with specialist operational units of the Met, 'whether they like it or not'. This would, Herbert argued, bring operational benefits: 'How on earth are we supposed to have any insight into a terrorist group that is not from Northern Ireland without having anyone that, for example, speaks another language ... In the cause of common sense and good policing, it has got to be imposed' (Police Review, 2002). The development of the diversity agenda can be understood in terms of promoting and securing police legitimacy. As has been noted the development of a customer-focused victim-oriented management style within the police service has been related to broader developments of New Public Management (Loader and Mulcahy, 2003; McLaughlin, 2007a). Central to the discourse of policing by consent, which has surrounded the public police since the establishment of the Metropolitan Police in 1829, has been the notion that the police represent the 'citizen in uniform'. If legitimacy depends upon the police service being representative of the public, then clearly the long-term unrepresentative nature of police personnel undermines the principle of policing by consent. The recruitment of a more diverse police workforce is also seen as something of a 'litmus test' of the organizational health of the police service more generally. Efforts to celebrate the diversity of the contemporary police service can be understood as a response to media exposés of police deviance, racism and unprofessionalism, such as those outlined in Chapter 5.

the complexities of diversity

Once the principle of providing policing that meets the diverse needs of diverse communities is acknowledged, it is hard to identify where its consequences might end. Recent debates on the extent of and response to rural crime seem to indicate that rural communities have different policing needs than their urban counterparts. Other research suggests that minority ethnic communities living in rural areas experience different levels and forms of racism and discrimination compared to those in towns and cities (Chakraborti and Garland, 2004). Equally, the experience of the elderly, women, gays, and lesbians suggests that still other sets of variables need to be factored into the equation when it comes to providing policing services that reflect the diversity of the community (Williams and Robinson, 2004). In addition, those who are unemployed, have mental health problems, sleep rough, or have problems relating to addictions of various kinds are also likely to have certain specific requirements of the police. The types of 'communities at risk' (Johnston, 2000) are endless in their permutations. Clearly, for policing to be both appropriate and effective, it is vital that the complex needs of various groups are met. However, practical problems arise relating to the provision of training on the needs of diverse communities, the expectation that recruitment and retention issues will be adjusted to reflect diversity issues, and that police performance will be monitored to ensure that service provision is appropriate. As Johnston (2006) illustrated, police managers have sometimes sought to meet targets for the recruitment of minority ethnic staff by effectively employing people who lack the qualifications that would usually apply. This is a shallow and counter-productive response that focuses solely on the ethnicity of candidates.

Whether in the recruitment of staff or the development of service delivery, the identification of a particular trait as an organizing principle around which policing or any other service can be delivered is a simplistic and limited approach. It is misleading to assume that the recruitment of minority ethnic staff, for example, will lead – in and of itself – to more effective communication with diverse communities. A police officer might be of the same ethnicity as the majority of the local community in which she serves but might have very little else in common with them. Certainly, if that community lives in a deprived area, it is unlikely that a relatively well-paid public sector professional will live in the same vicinity. To assume that 'ethnic matching' police staff and local communities will provide for more effective service delivery reveals a very shallow understanding of diversity issues. Although minority groups of different kinds are likely to have certain specific needs in relation to their disproportionate experience of certain types of crime, or because they need particular types of treatment from officers, it is not necessarily the case that this will extend into all aspects of the service that they might require from the police. Put simply, diverse groups are likely to have more in common than they do apart when it comes to the provision of police service in response to many incidents. Although minority groups, for example, might have specific cultural requirements in terms of the manner in which they are dealt with, the broad framework of their needs is likely to be fairly consistent with those of the mainstream.

Diversity needs to be recognized as increasingly significant – partly because social fragmentation, which should not be exaggerated, is increasingly salient and partly because policing has become more consciously located within the service industry and so must meet the particular needs of segmented markets. Clearly the models and frameworks outlined here will continue to develop and be applied to changing constellations of communities and interest groups. The police service needs to develop a more embedded and reflective approach to diversity that recognizes that race, ethnicity, gender, sexuality, age, mental health, and so on, can shape needs and expectations in important ways. They do so without guarantee however.

In the period since the publication of the Macpherson Report the police service has developed a wide range of policies, invested significant resources, and reviewed operational practices in an effort to respond to the increasingly complex diversity agenda. With some justification, it might be argued that the scale of the response reflects the size of the problems identified. Measuring the impact that these efforts have had in terms of operational policing and the relatively intangible concept of legitimacy is difficult. Clearly, problems remain and controversies continue.

In many respects, the notion of policing diversity appears to encapsulate and further the principle of policing by consent that has informed the development of policing in Britain since the establishment of modern police forces in the first half of the nineteenth century. Although the need for some of the developments outlined above appears to indicate that policing by consent has not been achieved in practice, as an organizing principle, it has featured fairly consistently for many decades. In the past, consent was understood as a relatively straightforward concept: If the police acted in a way broadly consistent with the expectations of the public, if they used minimal force, tackled crime with reasonable effectiveness and efficiency, and treated non-criminal members of the public with courtesy and respect, it was held that consent would be forthcoming – it would be conferred upon the police for a job well done. Reiner (2000) argues that securing public consent for the police in the nineteenth century partly was the result of a deliberate set of policy decisions focusing on bureaucratic organization, the rule of law, minimal force, non-partisanship, accountability, the service role, and effectiveness (ibid.: 50–58).

The emphasis on policing diversity might be understood as a subtle renegotiation of this traditional principle because it recognizes that consent cannot be gleaned simply by treating all members of the public in the same manner. The public no longer has a consistent, or even a coherent, set of expectations for the police to fulfil. Given that society is increasingly diverse and culturally heterogeneous, the demands placed on the police are no longer straightforward, and it may be increasingly recognized that the police cannot satisfy all of the expectations placed upon them. It might be that the development of policing diversity is partly a response to the introduction of new managerialism, so that mission statements, targets, and goals feature heavily in the commitments that police organizations make to their clients and customers. Recognition of the diverse requirements of the client-base is a fairly fundamental principle of free market provision, and in an age where the police service is increasingly understood as only one provider of 'law and order' services among many, it is perhaps the case that retaining a market share requires that the service attends more carefully to the varied needs of the community. Whereas these broader trends might provide an important context that has encouraged the development of the principle of policing diversity, it is also clear that there has been a significant political agenda that has driven the type of changes outlined in this chapter.

▄ ▄ chapter summary ▄

- Police relations with minority ethnic communities have been a matter of concern and controversy in Britain for many decades. The criminalization of various minority ethnic communities has been evident since the nineteenth century and, latterly, has been a key feature of broader debates about police legitimacy.

- The 1981 Scarman Inquiry into disorders in Brixton, South London, established an agenda for the development of community policing more widely. Scarman reiterated the principle of policing by consent that continues to underpin contemporary debates about policing in a diverse society.

- In 1999, the Macpherson Report found that the police investigation of the racist murder of Stephen Lawrence had been undermined by institutional racism, professional incompetence and a failure of leadership. The Report made 70 recommendations covering training, recruitment and retention, liaison with victims of crime, the response to racist incidents, and a host of other policing issues.

- The concept of institutional racism advanced by the Macpherson Report has been criticized as replicating existing models of indirect racial discrimination, and for being inconsistent.

- The Macpherson Report contributed to the development of a model of antiracist policing, which suggested that the police service ought to play a proactive and interventionist role to confront racism. The 2000 Race Relations (Amendment) Act requires public sector organizations, including the police service, to develop measures to confront racism and promote good race relations.

- The policing diversity agenda has been developed in concert with the promotion of a service-oriented consumer-focused ethos. In addition to adopting some of the financial rigours of the private sector, policing co-opted the language of service delivery and customer satisfaction.

- Since the 1970s, a key concern among debates about police relations with minority ethnic communities has been the disproportionate use of stop and search powers. Early anecdotal evidence has been supported by statistical data that do show that, compared to their presence in the population as a whole, black people (but not all minority ethnic groups) are over-policed in terms of stop and search. More recent studies have used alternative benchmarks relating to the presence of ethnic groups at times and in places where stop and search activity is the highest. These tend to show that the ethnic disparity is in the opposite direction, so that white people are over-represented.

- Minority ethnic communities have been under-policed in terms of the policing of racist incidents. Underpinning this has been the tendency for police officers not to recognize the racist nature of incidents. Additionally has been a tendency for officers to follow an order maintenance strategy that restores 'normalcy' to relations between victims and perpetrators. In the context of racist incidents, this is likely to perpetuate victims' experience of racism. Similar concerns have been noted in the context of the police response to homophobic incidents.

- The number of racist incidents recorded by the police in England and Wales increased in the period 1999–2005. This can be attributed to heightened aware-ness in terms of police and victims, the adoption of a wider definition of what consti-tutes a racist incident, and the possibility for victims to report indirectly to the police via third parties.

- The diversity agenda established in relation to minority ethnic groups has subse-quently extended to incorporate the specific policing needs of a wide range of other 'communities of risk', including lesbian, gay, transgender and bisexual, disabled, homeless, and elderly communities.

- The tradition of policing by consent has often referred to the notion that the police are 'citizens in uniform', representing the broader society that they serve. Developing a police service that reflects the diversity of contemporary British society is pursued for operational reasons, to develop and maintain consultation, and in order to secure legitimacy.

 ■ self-check Questions

1   Why has it been assumed, mistakenly, that concerns about police relations with minority ethnic communities have only developed in recent decades?

2   Which police service conducted the second investigation into the murder of Stephen Lawrence?

3   What police policy developments in the late 1980s were associated with developing a customer-focused service delivery model of policing?

4   What three factors did the Macpherson Report suggest had marred the investigation of the murder of Stephen Lawrence?

5   How was the traditional policing strategy used in response to racist incidents characterized?

6   How many racist incidents did the British Crime Survey suggest occurred in 2004/05?

7   What legislative change, relating to racist incidents, was introduced by the 1998 Crime and Disorder Act?

8   What diverse populations were identified in a 2003 HMIC report?

9   On what basis did Sir Ian Blair defend efforts to recruit a more diverse police workforce?

10 What notion has been central to the concept of 'policing by consent'?

 ## study Questions

1   How are issues relating to policing diversity related to broader efforts to develop a 'consumer-focused' service delivery?

2   How do benchmarks of 'available' populations change explanations of the impact of stop and search on minority ethnic communities?

3   Will broadening the 'diversity agenda' result in more effective policing?

annotated further reading

Rowe's (2007c) edited collection, *Policing Beyond Macpherson*, provides a comprehensive overview of recent developments relating to policing and diversity, with particular reference to issues of race and racism. The book considers the history of police relations with minority ethnic groups in post-war Britain, the implications of 'diversity' for internal police organization and culture, the effectiveness of training in promoting diversity, the nature of institutional racism, the role of Black Police Associations, the policing of Muslim communities, 'disproportionality' and stop and search, the impact of the Lawrence case on police murder investigations, and an insider account of the police service response to the Macpherson Report.

Hall's (2005) *Hate Crime* explores the development of the concept of hate crime and the ways in which hatred and prejudice have come to be subjects of criminal law. Patterns of victimization and the characteristics of offenders are reviewed. Hall provides a thorough analysis of the moral and ethical dimensions relating to hate crimes and the practical implications of attempts to use the criminal justice system to tackle 'hate', and whether such offending is inherently more serious than other forms of crime.

Foster, Newburn and Souhami (2005) examined the impact of the Stephen Lawrence inquiry on the police service, based upon research conducted on behalf of the Home Office. They found improvements in terms of the conduct of murder investigations, the recording and monitoring of hate crimes, family liaison, and the excision of racist language among police officers. However, they also found that developments had not been introduced uniformly across the service, that reforms lacked depth, and that there was a lack of progress in tackling institutional racism in general terms.

// annotated listings of links to relevant websites

A host of reports and statistical information about policing, race and racism, and diversity issues more widely are available on the Home Office website: (http://www.homeoffice.gov.uk/equality-diversity/). This contains information about legal powers against racism and discrimination. The website of the Research Development and Statistics section contains information on race and the criminal justice system and women in the criminal justice system (http://www.homeoffice.gov.uk/rds/a-zsubjects.html).

Information about diversity issues in the Metropolitan Police, including race equalities schemes and citizen focus, is available at http://www.met.police.uk/dcf/index.htm.

The Monitoring Group provides support and advice to victims of racist violence and domestic violence, and is a research and campaign organization. Information about these issues and the particular services that the group offers can be found at http://tinyurl.com/yvg7t2.

8

Plural policing

Contents

The implications of the pluralization of policing have been referred to at various stages of the discussion so far. This chapter explores the growing importance of the private sector to current debates about policing and police work and the development of complex networks of agencies involved in crime prevention, patrol work, investigation, and reassurance policing in the UK and beyond. The objectives of the chapter are to do the following.

- explain why academic and policy debates have focused on the role of the private sector in policing;

- examine the development of a mixed economy of policing and the idea of the 'extended police family';

- consider the implications of pluralization for the conceptualization and governance of policing.

key terms

antisocial behaviour; extended police family; multi-agency partnerships; networks; new public management; pluralization; private policing; visible patrols

introduction

Most of the discussion of policing in this book has focused upon the organization and delivery of the service provided by the public police – in the context of England and Wales, analysis has centred upon the 43 constabularies directed by the Home Office and local police authorities. Chapter 1 noted that, historically, the concept of policing has been applied much more broadly in reference to a range of regulatory activities provided formally and informally by diverse providers. Although popular and political discussion of policing tends to concentrate narrowly on the powers and practices of the public police, academic interest in policing in Australasia, North America, Britain and elsewhere has become increasingly concerned with the pluralization of policing. Bayley and Shearing's (2001) review of contemporary policing developments led them to suggest that the processes of pluralization outlined in this chapter have fundamentally transformed policing:

> This involves much more than reforming the institution regarded as the police, although that is occurring as well. The key to the transformation is that policing, meaning the activity of making societies safe, is no longer carried out exclusively

by governments. Indeed, it is an open question as to whether governments are even the primary providers. Gradually, almost imperceptibly, policing has been 'multilateralized': a host of nongovernmental groups have assumed responsibility for their own protection, and a host of nongovernmental agencies have undertaken to provide security services. Policing has entered a new era, an era characterized by a transformation in the governance of security. (ibid.: 1)

Initially, from the early 1970s onward, debates about private policing questioned the role and the extent of those engaged in 'policing for profit' (South, 1988), the proper regulation of the private security companies and what relation they should have with the public police. As the discussion below illustrates, these continue to be key questions for those interested in policing in the twenty-first century but they have been supplemented by discussion of more recent forms of 'hybrid' policing that engages a range of private, public and voluntary agencies at the local, national and international level. While the private security sector continues to demand the legitimate attention of policy-makers and researchers, it seems clear that conceiving of policing in terms of a straightforward dichotomy between public and private providers fails to account for the emergence of more complex arrangements. This chapter examines the development of private policing and other aspects of the pluralization debate relating to third party policing and 'multi-agency' partnerships. In particular, analysis of the diverse 'nodes' engaged in policing indicates that 'policing' is an emergent property of the complex network of relations that exists between agencies. The implications that this has for the ways in which policing is conceptualized are considered towards the end of the chapter.

dimensions of pluralization

The first chapter outlined the distinction between the police, the public institution established, in Britain, in the early nineteenth century, and policing, a broader process of social regulation (Reiner, 2000). Traditionally, discussion of policing has referred to governance in general terms and the distinction between that and 'the police' continues to be useful in distinguishing between functions performed by different agencies. As this chapter indicates, contemporary academic and policy debate increasingly focuses upon policing in terms that include but go beyond the traditional public police forces epitomized in the 'Dixon of Dock Green' image at its height in the decades after the Second World War (Reiner, 2000; McLaughlin, 2007a). Loader (2000) charted the new policing terrain explored in this chapter, and argued that 'we inhabit a world of networked, plural policing'. Figure 8.1 indicates the five dimensions of the emerging plural policing identified by Loader (2000), who noted that the categories are porous and inter-connected:

1   policing by government: the traditional publicly funded police;

2   policing through government: activities co-ordinated and funded by the government but delivered by agencies other than the police service;

3   policing above government: transnational policing activities coordinated by international agencies;

4   policing beyond government: activities funded and delivered privately by citizens and corporations;

5   policing below government: voluntary and community activities, self-policing, and vigilantism.

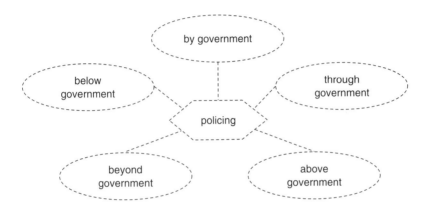

Figure 8.1   The five dimensions of plural policing

Source: Loader (2000)

private policing

the nature and extent of private policing

Much of the discussion of private policing has focused upon size and the range of functions fulfilled by the security industry. As Prenzler (2005) noted in his study of Australia, a particular focus for many researchers has been to establish the strength of the private sector in relation to the number of public police officers, suggesting that it is particularly significant that there might be more private security personnel than constables. He estimated that the growing strength of the commercial security sector suggested that the public police would be overtaken by private industry counterparts at some point in 2009.

   In Britain, various estimates of the strength of private policing have grappled with definitional and methodological problems associated with measuring a

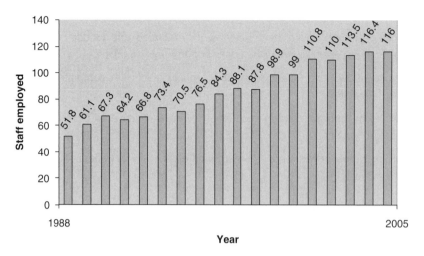

Figure 8.2 Staff employed by member firms of the British Security Industry Association, 1988–2005 ('000s)

Source: British Security Industry Association

complex, fragmented and, until recently, relatively unregulated industry. One indication of the size and scope of private policing is the membership of the British Security Industry Association (BSIA), the main professional body that represents private security companies. Figure 8.2 indicates that the number of people employed by member companies more than doubled in the period from 1988 to 2005, when 116,000 staff were employed by the 540 firms in the association. The BSIA identifies various sectors in which its members operate, including access control, the protection of cash in transit, **CCTV**, information destruction, security guarding, and the manufacture and distribution of security equipment. Collectively, the total turnover of BSIA member companies is £4.33 billion. While the number of staff employed by BSIA member companies has risen, this does not necessarily indicate an overall rise in the private security sector more generally, since it might be that a greater proportion of companies are members of BSIA and not simply that there are more companies in absolute terms. The introduction of licensing, a requirement of the Private Security Industry Act 2001, as discussed in Chapter 6, and broader efforts to professionalize the sector are likely to have increased BSIA membership, regardless of wider burgeoning of the industry. Moreover, the BSIA data does not include staff employed as in-house security by companies. Other sources, reflecting a wider definition of the private security industry, suggest a greater number of staff. Button (2002) reviewed various estimates of the size and scope of the sector and suggested that, in the early years of the twenty-first century, there were around 317,500 staff and a turnover of

£5.5 billion. As the BSIA categories indicate, many employees are engaged in the manufacture, retail and installation of security products and thus are not fulfilling traditional policing functions. Eliminating such staff from the calculation led George and Button (2000) to estimate that there were around 217,000 private sector staff employed in policing activities in 2000.

explaining the growth of private security

Although estimates of the size and scope of the private security industry vary, most research suggests that it has grown during recent years. A number of factors have contributed to this expansion. The demand for private security industry services has been fuelled by public insecurity about levels of crime and disorder, as public perceptions have not recognized falling crime rates since the mid-1990s. The 'reassurance gap' between realities and perceptions of crime trends, coupled with a responsibilization strategy that has sought to encourage the public to take steps to secure their property, have encouraged private companies to undertake tasks once considered the responsibility of the state. The public police service has been 'dethroned' and is no longer a monopoly provider (McLaughlin, 2007a). Further, wider societal trends have meant that individuals spend considerable proportions of their working and social lives in private venues rather than public spaces. As the high street has been eclipsed by the shopping mall, individuals increasingly inhabit privately owned locations that deploy private security guards in order to prevent crime and disorder, but also to provide a sanitized environment conducive to a profitable retail experience (Davis, 1990; Beck and Willis, 1995; Wakefield, 2004). Shearing and Stenning (1983) argued that the public police traditionally have not, for resource and cultural reasons, engaged in the policing of 'mass private property', and that those who own these spaces have tended to prefer to retain control over regulation.

Not only may the growth of private property be symbolically important in terms of a declining state of civic and communal interaction, it has had an important impact in terms of creating environments in which our behaviour is overseen and controlled by private security guards using the range of technologies analysed in Chapter 9. Putnam (2000) and Young (1999) have argued that the privatization and atomization of contemporary life have undermined collective identities that underpin the public provision of some goods and services. The erosion of community might be criminogenic; it also creates an environment in which private security is increasingly important as individuals seek to provide for themselves what might once have been considered the collective responsibility of the community, derogated to the public police. Similarly, the rise of 'gated communities', whereby security and reassurance can be provided – for those who can afford them – domestically by guards and patrols raises questions about social exclusion and social justice. Not only has consumerism generated the space – in some cases, literally the physical space – in which private security can flourish, it has also allowed for the commodification of security. As mentioned, public agencies have encouraged a process of responsbilization, whereby private citizens are reminded of the importance of looking out for their own, and this has been encouraged by manufacturers and retailers intent on catering to the existential need for security.

The increasing role of the private sector in the provision of policing mirrors developments in other areas of the public sector, as the role of the state has been 'hollowed out' as governments have retreated from direct provision in a host of sectors. Johnston (1992) argued that the fiscal constraints that enveloped liberal democratic states from the 1970s onwards were an important factor in promoting the role of the private sector in criminal justice, although Jones and Newburn (1998) noted that state spending on the police increased during the 1980s and that the service was not subjected to the 'rigours of the market' to anything like the same extent as other aspects of the public sector. State sovereignty has also been undermined by globalization and the fact that there are now many private corporations with more power and resources than those available to some countries. To the same end, global technologies render national boundaries more porous and less meaningful. The development of global policing networks, in response to emerging transnational problems of crime and terrorism, have required national police services to move beyond borders, as has growing emphasis on security and law and order in the context of international development, as was noted in Chapter 4. In this context the position of the nation-state has become precarious. Since the development of the public police service in the nineteenth century was closely related to the concomitant expansion of the nation-state itself, it is inevitable that contemporary shifts in the scope and function of the state impact upon patterns of policing (Shearing and Stenning, 1983).

Garland (2001) argued that the process of 'responsibilization', whereby the onus to provide for personal security is transferred from state to citizen, is a direct consequence of the changing role of the state itself. While government might continue to play a fundamental role in terms of regulation of services, and control the framework, funding and manage performance, it is no longer directly responsible for provision. In the much-cited phrase of Osborne and Gaebler (1992), the state continues to be responsible for 'steering' public services but has become disengaged from the business of 'rowing'. A host of private, voluntary and hybrid providers have assumed responsibility for the delivery of security. Garland puts it thus:

> For most of the last two centuries the state's specialist institutions of criminal justice have dominated the field, and have treated crime as a problem to be governed through the policing, prosecution and punishment of individual law-breakers. Today we see developments that enlist the activity of citizens, communities and companies ... At the same time we have seen the remarkable

expansion of a private security industry that originally grew up in the shadow of the state but which is increasingly recognized by government as a partner. (2001: 17)

Considering the expansion of the private security industry in terms of a market model, whereby public insecurity about crime and disorder increases demand and restructuring of the public sector provides new opportunities to suppliers, is a convenient characterization of recent patterns, but in practice the two may often be related. Loader (1997, cited in Jones and Newburn 1998: 104) noted that private companies have 'first to generate a demand for their products by stimulating and channelling people's anxieties and desires in particular ways'. Lee (2007) described a 'feedback loop', whereby the private security sector, and others, fuel demand for products and services by highlighting both the extent of crime risks and the ability of security companies to offer protection from them. Gated communities, for example, claim to offer a refuge from crime and insecurity by physically excluding risky people and providing an environment in which private provisions protect the comfortably off from a range of inconveniences associated with the routine interaction with the public at large. Caldeira's (2000: 234, cited in Landman and Schönteich, 2002) study of gated communities in São Paulo led him to argue that social relations in such environments are characterized by:

> suspicion and danger. Residents of all social groups have a sense of exclusion and restriction. For some, the feeling of exclusion is obvious, as they are denied access to various areas and are restricted to others. Affluent people who inhabit exclusive enclaves also feel restricted; their feelings of fear keep them away from regions and people that their mental maps of the city identify as dangerous.

The implications that discourses of private security have on civic and public relations are subject to much debate. Stenson has argued that the very concept of 'private security' is oxymoronic since it establishes individuals in relation to potential danger and, by atomizing the public, undermines the basis for collective reassurance. Similarly, Hughes (2007) has argued that policy innovation in the field of community safety is fundamentally antisocial, since strategies of risk management and crime prevention – the organizing principles of plural policing partnerships – cast citizens as potential offenders, representing a threat that must be diverted by one of a wide range of interventions. It might be wondered why, in an era in which threat, risk and danger can all, apparently, be eliminated by the purchase of the correct equipment, public concern about crime seems higher than ever.

_____ regulating the private security industry _____

Stenning (2000) has noted that private policing, internationally, has been subject to 'regulatory pluralism' embracing voluntary, statutory, and market-based forms of control. In the British context, the sector has been subject to relatively little legal regulation. Before the introduction of the Private Security Industry Act 2001, the regulation of private policing in Britain was left to the market mechanism and the requirements imposed by voluntary membership of bodies such as the BSIA and the International Private Security Association (IPSA). The BSIA and IPSA require that member companies comply with British Standards codes of practice relating to guarding and the installation of equipment. Other sectors, such as private investigations, remained largely unregulated. George and Button (1997) reviewed international approaches to the regulation of the private security sector and identified five models, moving from the least to the most intrusive. At the lower end of scale is a 'non-interventionist' approach, with no statutory requirements, followed by a 'minimum narrow' approach that requires limited checks on personnel working in specific roles. Further along the spectrum is a wider approach that requires minimum regulation of the whole sector, followed by a model that requires the comprehensive regulation of a narrow range of personnel, to the broadest category in which a wide range of regulations are applied across the sector. As Chapter 6 noted, the 2001 Private Security Industry Act introduced statutory licensing into Britain. The Security Industry Authority is empowered to inspect companies and ensure that personnel are vetted and licensed: a system that equates with George and Button's mid-range level, comprising minimal regulation of the whole sector.

Critics have argued that this light-touch regulation does not provide for meaningful accountability of an increasingly important part of the policing sector. While it might ensure that those with criminal records are not employed by security companies, it does not provide for the control and direction of the industry in more general terms. Shearing and Johnston (2003) and Loader (2000) have argued that the growth of private security reinforces social inequalities since the poor are not able to buy the same level of protection as more affluent communities. This raises the possibility that existing public police might become a provision of last resort, offering an inferior service to those unable to afford private provisions. They suggest that such an outcome is not inevitable, and that the principles of social justice and public interest can be retained via public funding being allocated to policing authorities that can act as local buyers in the marketplace of security.

private sector discipline in the public police

In addition to considering the extent and nature of the private security sector, the growing 'marketization' of policing is also evident in terms of the internal organization of the public police service which, in keeping with many other public services, has become increasing organized along quasi-market lines. Private sector discipline in the police service has been apparent in efforts to promote resource efficiency, by employing lower-cost civilian staff to perform tasks previously assigned to officers or by 'contracting out' services such as cleaning or catering. Some aspects of police services have been commercialized in recent decades; for example, revenues have been raised through encouraging local businesses to sponsor vehicles and the police has sought to recover costs through charging for certain services, such as the policing of football matches. One implication of the latter development has been to set the police service in competition with private sector stewarding companies well placed to offer services at a lower price (Garland and Rowe, 1999). Although, as Button (2002) noted, this entry into the marketplace is not wholly new, since the police service has charged for such services for many years. However, he showed that recent instances suggest that the practice is being extended to a much broader range of activities (see Box 8.1).

Box 8.1

Rent-a-cop?

Liverpool City Council … has recently 'rented' an additional 12 officers to patrol its city centre at a cost of £350,000. Some constabularies have offered their officers to local businesses for special duties, such as South Wales Police, which has hired its officers out to guard factories and business factories … It has also recently been announced that BMW, Mercedes and Lloyds UDT are to fund a complete unit of detectives in the MPS to investigate stolen vehicles … A *Sunday Times* investigation found Essex police would be willing to supply officers to police a private party for £35.40 per hour … Many other local authorities, health trusts and businesses have also purchased additional police officers. (Button, 2002: 40)

Chapter 6 examined arguments that the scrutiny of officer behaviour and force performance has been an important method by which central government control over the police service has been enhanced. In Chapter 9 the reach of information technology in the management of the police service is considered in terms of the impact that this has had on routine police work. Clearly, as in the public sector more generally, the micro-management of police performance through setting targets has enabled league tables of BCU performance to be compiled, in imitation of private sector balance sheets that measure performance in terms of profit and loss. The Conservative Government developed new public management of the police service during the early 1990s, by devising a results-based and 'customer-focused' approach to policing, that set targets, reviewed performance indicators, market-tested services, and provided a host of reviews intended to modernize the workforce (McLaughlin, 2007a). Of particular note was the Sheehy Inquiry that proposed significant changes to the rank structure, the pay structure, and terms and conditions under which officers were employed. Although many of the specific proposals that emerged during this period ran into the sand in face of considerable opposition from police representative organizations, many of the fundamental principles have been continued by New Labour's police reform programme. While the introduction of private sector discipline into the police service is couched in terms of providing efficiency and improved performance, it has also entailed important change in terms of accountability and governance, as discussed in Chapter 6. McLaughin (2007a: 185) noted that David Blunkett, the Home Secretary who introduced much of the recent reform programme in the period after 2001, was intent on confronting the 'forces of conservatism' within the police service.

third party and multi-agency policing

Not only have policing activities seeped from the public police into the private sector, they have come to be shared by a broad range of agencies within the public sector that have not traditionally been conceived of in terms of policing. The development of multi-agency community safety partnerships has drawn a host of local authority and voluntary sector organizations into networks engaged in crime prevention and public reassurance work. An early example of third party policing, in the British context, were efforts developed in the early 1980s to tackle racist harassment in public housing by the inclusion of clauses in tenancy agreements that made such behaviour grounds for eviction. In a period when the police have often failed to effectively intervene to tackle racist harassment, local authority housing departments and charitable housing associations were thus enabled to take action through the civil courts to evict tenants who breached their contracts by engaging in racist behaviour against their neighbours (Forbes, 1988). Such provisions were greatly extended by the 1996 Housing Act that not only enhanced the power of social landlords to evict those engaging in antisocial or nuisance behaviour, but also allowed them to be excluded from future housing waiting lists. Those identified as perpetrators of antisocial behaviour then are subject to sanctions drawn from an increased portfolio of interventions comprising diverse civil measures as well as traditional criminal justice. Critics have pointed out that civil law procedures require a lower standard of proof than those conducted through the criminal courts and that this might lead to punishments being imposed unfairly. Additionally, as the potential loss of housing illustrates, it might be that those who engage in problematic behaviour are not the only ones who suffer the consequences since their family members are also likely to be adversely affected. Other injustices arise since the provisions of the 1996 Housing Act do not extend to private landlords, and so those engaging in nuisance behaviour who rent outside of the public sector will not be liable to such sanctions (Crawford, 2003: 145). Hughes (2007: 128) noted that antisocial behaviour orders have tended to be applied to young people, since the average age of recipients is 16 years old, and that 'put brutally, these are the children with no chance, having been failed by their families and the care and control system'.

While these developments have raised important ethical concerns, it is clear that efforts to tackle low-level offending and incivilities through civil actions in the form of antisocial behaviour orders and voluntary agreements have greatly accelerated multi-agency policing in Britain. Central to the 1998 Crime and Disorder Act, the 'flagship' criminal justice legislation of the New Labour Government elected in 1997, was the creation of antisocial behaviour orders (ASBOs) and the establishment of a legal responsibility for crime prevention and community safety upon local authorities. Multi-agency community safety partnerships have incorporated a wide range of agencies in policing-related activities, even though their primary responsibilities lie elsewhere. The requirement for local partnerships to conduct audits of neighbourhood crime and disorder problems and to co-produce policing with community groups has extended third party policing networks to include residents associations and other voluntary organizations. Community safety partnerships are often able to allocate resources for crime prevention and other projects might provide financial incentives for community groups to seek closer relations with their 'partners' from the statutory sector. Crawford (2003) noted that the increasing emphasis on crime prevention and community safety has been an important factor driving the development of plural policing, since it is clear that a range of services need to be engaged in if preventative work is to be effective.

Patrol work has been a totemic policing activity in Britain and elsewhere and the 'bobby on the beat' has been central to discourses of policing and national identity for decades. Third parties have contributed to the provision of high visibility policing in the form of Police Community Support Officers and local authority neighbourhood wardens. Wakefield (2006) argued that long-standing policing dilemmas surrounding the provision of patrols have moved to the forefront of contemporary debates and that the identification of new providers raises the prospect of satisfying increasing public demands without placing untenable strain on police resources. Crawford and Lister (2004; 2006) have detailed the emergence of the 'mixed economy' of policing provisions and argue that patrol work has been one of the roles most clearly opened up to diverse providers. Government funding since 2000 has encouraged local authorities to establish 'street', 'neighbourhood', and 'street crime' wardens, that:

> operate exclusively in residential areas, aim to improve 'quality of life', manage housing stock and the local environment, reduce crime, fear of crime and anti-social behaviour, and build community cohesion and community development ... A central mechanism by which warden schemes seek to achieve these broad aims has been through the provision of visible patrol. By the end of December 2002, central government had funded some 419 neighbourhood wardens, 655 street wardens and 380 street crime wardens across the country. (Crawford and Lister, 2006: 167)

While these numbers are relatively small, compared to those employed as police officers and in private security, Crawford and Lister (ibid.) reported that the funding supplied to employ them had led local authorities to seek other resources; coupled with rising local demands for patrol services it seems likely that plural policing patrols will expand further. As Crawford and Lister have noted elsewhere, though, it is not clear that the greater patrol capacity of the 'extended police family' can satisfy public demands since the pluralization process has served to raise expectations to higher levels. Furthermore, it is also clear that multi-agency patrols do not provide reassurance to all sections of the community. Those who have negative experiences and perceptions of the police are unlikely to welcome additional patrols, and those living in high crime areas favour other policing methods that target known offenders. For these reasons, Wakefield (2006: 24) suggested that 'the activity of visible patrolling could ... be seen as the policing activity of choice for the citizen least troubled by crime'.

Plural policing entails not only a proliferation in terms of the range of providers, but also an expansion of legal and regulatory technologies used to deliver security and reassurance, beyond crime control or law enforcement in traditional terms. These combinations of agencies, strategies and tactics have not been restricted to efforts to tackle incivilities and antisocial behaviour, as was discussed above. Box 8.2 illustrates the network of agencies that have devised protocols to use a mixture of criminal and civil law measures to close 'crack houses' in the Royal Borough of Kensington and Chelsea. All these developments reflect the core characteristics of third party policing, conceived by Mazerolle and Ransley in the following terms:

> Police efforts to persuade or coerce organizations or non-offending persons, such as public housing agencies, property owners, parents, health and building inspectors, and business owners to take some responsibility for preventing crime or reducing crime problems ... Central ... to third party policing is the use of a range of civil, criminal and regulatory rules and laws, to engage (or force) third parties into taking some crime control responsibility. (2005: 2–3)

Box 8.2

Closing crack houses in Kensington and Chelsea

The Drug Action Team and partners established the multi-agency approach to tackling 'crack houses' in 2002. The objectives of the protocol were:

- to use community and police intelligence to identify 'crack houses' at the earliest opportunity;
- to ensure a rapid response from all partner agencies in dealing with a 'crack house' once identified;
- to minimise the risks of a 'crack house' being able to re-establish itself after closure;
- to help partnership agencies share best practice in how to counter the supply and communal consumption of Class A drugs in social housing;
- to protect the most vulnerable communities and residents from drug-related crime.

It continues to recognise that a range of interventions will be required to achieve the objectives ... these interventions may include bringing offenders to justice or using Closure Orders, civil injunctions and fast track evictions ... Changes brought about by the Anti-Social Behaviour Act 2003 give the police, the local authority and housing providers greater powers that have enabled them to reduce significantly the time taken to close 'crack houses' using Closure Orders. It also makes it easier to take enforcement action against owner-occupiers ... Police Superintendents now have the power to issue a Closure Notification ... very rapidly, depending on the level of drug activity and the nuisance or disorder being caused.

Source: The Royal Borough of Kensington and Chelsea (2006: 5–6).

networks of policing

Most discussion of pluralization of policing focuses, as this chapter has done, on the growing size and scope of the extended police family. Clearly these developments raise important questions about funding, effectiveness and regulation but some have argued that the proliferation of family members has transformed the character of policing itself, which increasingly needs to be understood as an emergent property of relations between nodal points within a policing network. Drawing on political science analysis of the transition from government to governance and Foucauldian perspectives on the diffusion of power, analysis suggests that policing has traditionally been conceptualized as the product of a particular institution ('the police'), yet it is better conceived of as a process arising from developing relations between the host of public, private and 'hybrid' agencies integrated in partnership arrangements of the kind described earlier. Wood and Shearing (2006) go so far as to argue that attention should no longer rest on policing, but on the wider network of agencies transversing national boundaries and transcending the state sphere as they seek to provide security in more general terms. They noted that the impact of pluralization goes beyond just extending the range of service providers and affects the ways in which security is 'imagined':

> Governance is not performed simply by institutions of the state, nor shaped solely by thinking originating from the state sphere. Today, ways of imagining and realizing security governance in the business sector as well as the 'third sector' (e.g. community groupings, non-governmental organizations) shape and influence the thinking of state institutions and vice versa. This is the essence of nodal governance. (ibid.: 13)

Johnston and Shearing (2003) have argued that policing ought to be reconceptualized in terms of the governance of security. Policing, whether in narrow pursuit of law enforcement or a wider provision of services, they argue, has to be understood as part of a more general process of avoiding risk and meeting the subjective and objective security needs of private citizens. They highlighted that the networks of agencies responsible for co-producing security are:

> increasingly complex. On the one hand, states continue to have a major role in security governance, the state sector of criminal justice being more extensive than other. On the other hand, a growing pluralisation of security governance is evident, estimates suggesting that commercial police outnumber public police by ratio of almost two to one in Britain, two to one in India, between two and three to one in North America, five to one in Hong Kong, and between five and seven to one in South Africa. (ibid.)

Johnston and Shearing argued that networked security in Britain has developed along five key paths. First, the state is no longer definitive in the face of private sector activity and the growing influence of the EU in shaping external border control, for example. At the subnational level, they argued, local partnerships of the kind outlined above have also shifted focus away from the nation-state, although it is also apparent that – as Chapter 6 outlined – these have been accompanied by contradictory patterns of centralization whereby the national government has introduced a performance measurement regime that affords it considerable control over local innovation. The second area that Johnston and Shearing have noted is the continuing debate over the relation between private and public interests. Controversies relating to the balance between intrusion into personal privacy and seeking to secure private interests are multiple in relation to CCTV and other technological innovations, as Chapter 9 explores. Third, the focus of policing networks is increasingly future-oriented, seeking to limit and reduce opportunities for crimes to be committed and/or identify those individuals who might be particularly criminogenic. Fourth, security governance is increasingly conducted at a distance by lay people and commercial operators, as has been demonstrated in this chapter and in Chapter 4's discussion of community policing. Fifth, security is increasingly 'distanciated' and 'embedded'; in other words, responsibility for the provision of security is transferred from the professionals working in the public sector, to communities. 'Security' becomes embedded into the routine responsibilities of a wide range of actors working in various capacities who traditionally have not had crime control or law enforcement dimensions. Bank staff, for example, are now required to report suspicious transactions that might be indicative of drug trafficking or terrorism.

Of course, many of the dimensions of 'networked' security identified by Johnston and Shearing have been noted by others who have analysed the pluralization of policing. Community involvement in multi-agency partnerships and the distanciation of security so that it comes to be embedded in the work of 'third party' actors, have all been widely discussed in this chapter. What arguments about networked policing highlight, above and beyond the proliferation of policing activities, is that these processes have not only led to a broader range of players, but that a fundamental conceptualization of the way in which the game is conducted needs to be re-thought. As Crawford (2003: 136–7) argued, these developments provide us with a 'new set of things to look at' as well as a 'new way of looking at things'. Zedner (2006) has noted, debates about pluralization have tended to focus upon charting emerging patterns and players and have paid relatively little attention to normative questions about social justice, equity, democracy and accountability.

rebirth or new paradigm?

Concerns about measuring the extent of the private security industry were outlined earlier in this chapter. Some have argued that while academic and policy interest in the sector has grown over recent decades, the plural policing arrangements identified are not of recent vintage but have been a consistent feature of British policing for centuries. In recognition of this debate Johnston's important study was entitled 'The rebirth of private policing', suggesting that the developments he was analysing mirrored earlier arrangements. Jones and Newburn (2002) argued that those who proclaimed a new paradigm of policing emerged in the last decades of the twentieth century overstate the impact and extent of the pluralization process. They based their argument on three important factors that suggest that the pluralization thesis has been overplayed. First, the long history of private policing activity demonstrates that the state has never been a monopoly provider. Policing arrangements have always been plural. Similarly, Crawford (2003) noted that the role of social landlords in the governance of the behaviour of tenants is not a new development, and it has often been argued that contemporary interventions to discipline those regarded as problematic seem to recreate distinctions between the 'deserving' and the 'undeserving' poor that informed welfare and charitable efforts in Victorian times.

Second, Jones and Newburn (2002) also argued that the evidence of pluralization is overstated, since many agencies are only lightly engaged in networks of policing and community safety, and that these continue to be dominated by the public police. The police might increasingly work in 'partnership' with other agencies but these are often not equal partners, not least because the public police continue to have relatively privileged access to information and other resources relating to local crime and disorder-related issues. As was noted in Chapter 3, an important dimension of police powers is derived from their ability to identify and define local priorities and to provide an authoritative discourse outlining the most appropriate solutions. Those partners who suggest alternative measures might be marginalized. Edwards and Hughes (2002) and Hughes (2007) have noted how social crime prevention approaches have tended to be sidelined by community-safety partnerships focused instead on enforcement measures.

Third, while Jones and Newburn (2002) acknowledged that new managerialism has transformed the conduct of police work, private sector discipline has not entirely debunked a public sector ethos. The continuing importance of public policing is also apparent in numerical terms, since, in Britain, the number of officers employed in the public sector has been rising in recent years and is higher than it has ever been. Contrary to some expectations, this increase has not been slowed by the development of Police Community Support Officers. The recent resurgence in Neighbourhood Policing has been couched in terms redolent of traditional public service. While some of the community service rhetoric might not be enacted, it does suggest opportunities for public engagement in community safety in some localities (Hughes and Rowe, 2007).

It seems that confusion reigns, as considerable evidence suggests that current developments in the pluralization of policing herald a new era of policing beyond 'the police'. New agencies and new partnerships are made and re-made in pursuit of priorities of reassurance and community safety that have not been part of the traditional police service mandate. On the other hand, it seems that this patchwork of policing arrangements – conducted through, alongside, above and below the state, as Loader's (2000) model in Figure 8.1 suggested, closely mirrors earlier, pre-modern arrangements. Zedner (2006) argued that some of this confusion can be attributed to analysts' tendencies to too readily cast developments in fundamental terms of epochal transformation. She explored a series of historical juxtapositions between pre-modern eighteenth-century criminal justice and contemporary features. Key among these were the transformation of the eighteenth-century ancestors of the contemporary extended police family, incorporating 'thief takers' – rewarded and incentivized as they were by performance-related pay – turnpike keepers, pawnbrokers and inn-keepers into the global security market of the twenty-first century. Additionally, social reformers and policy-makers of the eighteenth century saw crime prevention as a central function of the old police. While modern techniques of risk management and avoidance have been transformed by the technological sophistication they employ, they are fundamentally no different from their earlier counterparts. Zedner also drew parallels between the eighteenth-century emphasis on self-help and community-based measures to apprehend offenders and more recent trends at 'responsibilization', understood in the twenty-first century in terms of the state withdrawing from its traditional role in the provision of law and order. Contemporary trends for private citizens to club together to contract private security services, perhaps under the auspices of gated communities, are also reminiscent of pre-modern 'prosecution associations' that would offer rewards and pay for private prosecutions connected with those who had committed offences against members.

As Zedner argued, in the light of such evidence, it is tempting to dismiss current claims about the new pluralization of policing on the grounds that it is historically ignorant. To conclude, though, that since not everything is new, nothing is, misses some important points of difference between the pre-police era and the contemporary period. In particular, technological advances, some of which are outlined in Chapter 9, and globalization have significantly altered the scope of private security providers. Moreover, the continued role of the nation-state provides a distinct context that simply did not exist in earlier periods. While the twenty-first century nation-state, in many countries, has withdrawn, somewhat, from its role as primary provider of law and order, and has thus contributed to the pluralization process by vacating a series of roles now filled by voluntary, private or hybrid organizations, it continues to play an important role in terms of regulation that its eighteenth-century counterpart did not. The 'regulatory state' might have a narrower role than it once enjoyed, but it should not be assumed that it has lost power as it has relinquished various functions, since it has often assumed a central role in regulating those providers who have entered the spaces it has recently vacated. The state might have ceded certain roles to the private security industry in Britain, for example, but it continues to exert influence over it via regulation, albeit relatively 'light touch', and through contractual arrangements that underpin public–private relations.

Each chapter of this book has noted that the pluralization of policing means that concerns and debates that have surrounded the public police service need to be extended to consider a broader range of players. Early approaches to the study of the private security industry tended to regard it as the 'junior partner' to the public police, providing marginal services that supplemented the more significant business of law enforcement. In the early twenty-first century, the private sector plays a direct role in the provision of a range of policing activities and is increasingly responsible for the regulation of fellow citizens who conduct their lives on private property under the gaze of surveillance technologies that monitor their movement, shopping habits and financial practices. Furthermore, the principles of private sector market discipline have been extended to the public sector so that police managers, like their counterparts across the public sector, are engaged in managing the performance of their junior staff, budgeting, and preparing business cases to justify innovative projects that they develop. While the work of the police service might be coming to imitate the business sector, other sections of the public sector come to mirror traditional police concerns with crime prevention and community safety. Traditional animosities and tensions between police services and local government might not have been dissipated but partners from a wide range of agencies are increasingly thrown together in community safety and crime and disorder reduction partnerships. Like other kinship groups, the 'extended police family' of the twenty-first century might at times be dysfunctional or a marriage of convenience. The various partners are, for better or worse, bound together by common interests, if nothing else.

Although it is clear that the public police service never enjoyed a true monopoly position, contemporary networks are more complex than previous arrangements and consideration of policing as a social process is eclipsing analysis of the police as one agency among many. This does not necessarily mean that a fundamentally new epoch of policing is underway: such a claim might exaggerate the role of the state in both modern and late- or post-modern periods. However striking the historical parallels between policing in the eighteenth and twenty-first centuries, it should not be assumed that current developments represent a straightforward reversion to plural policing arrangements from earlier times. With this caveat in mind, a useful perspective is found in Zedner's (2006: 81) observation that the system of policing dominated by the public police service – that has come to be seen as synonymous with 'policing' in general terms – 'may come to be seen as a historical blip in a more enduring schema of policing as an array of activities undertaken by multiple private and public agencies, and individual and communal endeavours'.

- Academic and policy interest in policing during the past few decades has come increasingly to notice the role played by the private security industry. Initially much of this focus was upon charting the size of the sector, the functions that it performed, and its relation to the public police service.

- Pluralization of policing has increasingly been conceived in more complex ways than a private security–public police dichotomy. Loader (2000) suggested that it occurs by government, through government, above government, beyond government, and below government.

- Although reliable estimates are hard to find, it seems that in many countries, the private security industry outnumbers the public police to a significant degree. The notion of the private sector as a junior partner, providing minor services that complement the public police is increasingly outmoded as the private sector has proliferated and diversified.

- The expansion of private security has been explained in reference to a range of factors. The declining role of the state in the provision of goods and services to the public, partly due to fiscal constraints, has encouraged the private sector to develop. Others have argued that the growing importance of mass private property has created a context in which private policing arrangements have been preferred. Additionally, it has been argued that there has been a growing demand for private security as the public have been encouraged to take responsibility for their own security in ways not previously seen. The private sector might have played a role in encouraging an increased demand for their services.

- In Britain, the private security industry continues to be subject to only 'light touch' regulation. Until 2001, there was no statutory framework to license the sector. The 2001 Private Security Industry Act requires that individuals are vetted and allows companies to be inspected.

- More recently, debates have noted the increasing importance of private sector 'discipline' within public sector policing. This has had an effect on budgets and management and seen some commercialization of police work, as sponsors have been sought and police services have been 'hired out'.

- Pluralization has meant also that a host of other agencies that have not traditionally had law enforcement or crime control responsibilities have come to be included in policing partnerships. In the private sector, for example, banks have been given responsibility to report suspicious financial transactions that might indicate criminal activity. In the public sector, a host of agencies have been co-joined with the police service in 'multi-agency partnerships'. Until the late 1990s, local authorities did not have statutory responsibility for crime prevention. The 1998 Crime and Disorder Act contributed greatly towards the development of such partnerships by requiring councils to become involved in community safety.

- Partnerships have played a significant role in the provision of high visibility patrols, and are closely tied with the police reform process that, since 2001, has sought to 'extend the police family'. Most obviously the development of the role of Police Community Support Officer has been tied with the provision of reassurance foot patrols, but this function has also been enhanced by a range of Neighbourhood and Street Wardens who have been funded, and managed, by local government.

- Pluralization has entailed a development in the range of technologies used in policing, in particular, the use of civil provisions, such as antisocial behaviour orders and tenancy agreements, and voluntary agreements. These have been used to disrupt serious drug dealing and lower-level nuisance behaviour.

- Describing these emerging patterns in terms of networks of policing, or networks for the governance of security, focuses attention on the changing character of police work, and not just on the fact that a broader variety of actors are involved in delivery. By conceptualizing policing as an emergent property of networks of plural providers, attention is drawn to the collective impact of these arrangements and the possibility that society is becoming increasing regulated in a context where myriad bodies are charged with scrutinizing the actions of the public.

- While few doubt that private sector policing, and plural policing more generally, have become increasingly salient in policy and academic debate during recent years, there is less agreement about the extent to which this represents a funda-mental epochal shift in policing arrangements or something of a return to earlier patterns.

- The association of pluralization of policing with the growth in mass private property has led some to argue that modern policing arrangements have declined alongside the nation-state that developed with them in the early decades of the nineteenth century. The emerging networks of plural agencies that deliver policing in broad terms amount to a qualitatively new environment.

- Alternatively, others have noted that the plural policing identified in recent years is actually of long pedigree. Equally, the monopoly that the public police are held to have lost during this period was never as strong as is often suggested. Policing has always engaged diverse agencies, mixtures of public, private and voluntary providers, organized and less organized, and using a host of strategies. Claims that plural policing is a recent development also overlook the continuing primacy of the public police in new networks.

- Another perspective recognizes the similarities and continuities between pre-modern, modern, and late- or post-modern configurations. While it is true that there were private and communal policing arrangements in the eighteenth century and that these were never wholly displaced by the creation of the 'new police' in 1829, it is equally the case that current developments, in the context of globalization and technological change, mean that the private sector occupies a significantly enhanced role in the twenty-first century.

 ## ■ self-check ?uestions

1   What five dimensions of policing were outlined by Loader?

2   How many firms were members of the British Security Industry Association (BSIA) in 2005, and how many people did they employ?

3   How did Shearing and Stenning explain the growth of the private security sector?

4   How might the notion of 'responsibilization' be defined in the context of private security?

5   What body was established by the 2001 Private Security Industry Act to regulate the sector?

6   In what context did local housing authorities become involved in 'third party policing' in the 1980s?

7   What, according to Hughes, was the average age of those given antisocial behaviour orders?

8   How did Wakefield characterize police patrol work?

9   For what reasons did Jones and Newburn argue that the pluralization thesis exaggerates the transition from the public policing model?

10   Which occupations did Zedner suggest were eighteenth-century forerunners of the 'extended police family'?

 ## ■ study ?uestions

1   Does the reputed growth in private security in recent decades reinforce social, political and economic inequality?

2   What role should agencies other than the police play in the regulation of crime and antisocial behaviour?

3   Are the public police strengthened or weakened by the pluralization of policing?

▬ ▮ annotated further reading ▮

Button's (2002) *Private Policing* provides a comprehensive review of recent trends in the sector and the implications of private security in terms of its historical development, regulation, and social implications. He includes a detailed case study of the practice of private security in the context of residential patrols.

Crawford and Lister's (2006) article, 'Additional Security Patrols in Residential Areas: Notes from the Marketplace', also explores the development of pluralized residential patrol services. They argue that competition between different agencies hinders effective security provision, that it can raise unrealistic public expectations, and exacerbate local competition for limited resources.

Zedner's (2006) article in the *British Journal of Criminology* compares and contrasts elements of plural policing in the era before the establishment of the Metropolitan Police and contemporary debates. Unlike some commentators, she does not argue either that all is new in the contemporary period, or that current developments amount to a straightforward reversion to pre-modern patterns of policing. Instead Zedner examines specific aspects of current developments in their particular context and so provides a nuanced analysis of changes and continuities.

▬ ∶ // annotated listings of links to relevant websites /

The Security Industry Authority (SIA), established by the 2001 Private Security Industry Act, provides a relatively light touch regulation of the sector. The SIA website outlines its role (www.the-sia.org.uk.home) and the process by which it licenses the industry. The site addresses the nature of the licensing process that it oversees, and responds to some criticisms of the system.

The extent and long standing of the security industry are demonstrated by the breadth of topics covered by the American Society of Industrial Security, which was established in 1955 and has approximately 35,000 members organized into more than 200 'chapters' worldwide. The ASIS website, (www.asisonline.org) provides details of its work and the security industry more generally.

The website of the National Community Safety Network (www.community-safety.net/) contains a host of resources relating to the Crime and Disorder Reduction Partnerships and the growing range of agencies engaged in policing.

9

Surveillance, IT and the Future of Policing

Contents

This chapter explores the changing role of technology in contemporary policing. The impact of surveillance technology on crime and social relations is outlined and the implications that it has for policing in broader terms of social regulation are critically assessed. In particular, the chapter has the following objectives:

- to consider the extent to which technological developments transform police work, with particular reference to closed-circuit television (CCTV) and road traffic policing;

- to explore the implications that crime mapping has for intelligence-led policing and the communication of crime risks;

- to examine the impact of surveillance technology and information systems on the character of police work and the extent to which this curtails individual officer discretion.

key terms

CCTV; communication systems; discretion; 'hot spots' policing; information and intelligence; police culture; supervision; surveillance; traffic policing

introduction

Glossy visions of high tech law enforcement officers have long been a staple of fictional representations of police work. Perhaps the most prominent current example of this genre is the TV show *CSI* (Crime Scene Investigation), focusing on homicide detectives, assisted by creative and incisive technical support staff, using a dazzling array of state-of-the-art technology, combined with hugely powerful databases, to perform scientific analyses of crime scenes and victims to conclusively establish the identity of the killer, who often thought that they had planned and enacted the perfect crime. If kids TV cartoons of a certain vintage often ended with the villain ruefully lamenting that 'I'd have gotten away with it if it wasn't for those meddlesome kids', it now seems as though science and the scientist are the *bête noire* of the over-confident murderer. The CSI genre, which includes a number of factional or infotainment-style programmes that blur the reality/fiction boundary, can be criticized on a number of grounds. As with much cinematic or television crime and policing shows, it is an easy criticism to point out that 'real' cases are rarely resolved within the timeframe of a one-hour show. Moreover, guilt, or innocence, often cannot be established as a certain verifiable fact and even scientific evidence requires interpretation and explanation rarely conveyed in TV programmes. The role of technology in policing and its impact upon routine police work are considered critically in the discussion below. In the concluding section it is argued that the fictional representations reflect a more general tendency towards technological determinism, which assumes that policing can be fundamentally transformed by expanded technological capacity. Instead, enhanced information and communications technology needs to be considered in the context in which it is deployed and we note that police culture is able to resist and transform some of the potential implications of new technology.

technology in context

The ubiquity of information and communication technology in media representations of policing also marks them out from 'real' police work, which often continues to be a relatively low-tech business, even when it comes to investigations of serious criminal incidents. Innes' (2003) study of murder investigations found that the collection of forensic evidence was regarded as important to police officers, not least because of the 'symbolic' capital it brought in terms of persuading the Crown Prosecution Service to press charges. However, the value of scientific tests, DNA profiling, and so on, was limited and officers regarded it as important to also seek other forms of evidence in order to build a successful case. One limit on the value of scientific scene of crime analysis was that it took three months to get conclusive results to some of the tests used, which meant that investigating officers treated them tentatively (Innes, 2003). Understanding scientific procedures in the context of real-life investigations demonstrates the need to avoid technological determinism. That investigations do not proceed solely along the lines of the technical capacity of scientific analysis or ICT processing was further demonstrated by the Macpherson Inquiry into the police investigation of the racist murder of Stephen Lawrence in London in 1993. Although attention has focused on Macpherson's findings about institutional racism, failures in many aspects of the police investigation were also identified. Technological developments and the experience of previous investigations had led to the creation of the HOLMES (Home Office Large Major Enquiry System) computer system which allowed information to be cross-referenced and data to be retrieved. However, it was not used in the early stages of the investigation because the Deputy Investigating Officer was not trained to use it (Macpherson, 1999: 14.5). The frailty of human operatives of surveillance and IT systems is noted at various stages in the discussion that follows.

Although the current reality of policing does not mirror the technological wonders of many cop shows, politicians and policy-makers have long sought to improve the technological capacity of the police service. More effective communication systems have been regarded as an important prerequisite of improved police performance. The introduction of Unit Beat Policing in Britain in the 1960s, for example, depended on the technology of two-way radios that allowed patrolling officers to communicate more freely and meant that the beats no longer had to be drawn around the location of police telephone boxes as they had previously done (Rawlings, 2002: 200). More recently, efforts to reduce the impact of administrative duties have focused upon developing secure laptop computers that would allow officers to complete crime reports and the like without returning to police stations and disappearing from public view. Not only would this lessen the time officers take to complete routine administrative tasks, it was claimed, it would also mean that officers could complete more procedures from their patrol cars and thus promote a visible police presence on the streets. As with information technology projects in the public sector in general, it should be remembered that the promise offered by such developments has often been greater than the impact in reality. Nonetheless, the potential of hi-tech solutions to solve routine problems of police work and crime investigation continues to be emphasized. The following discussion reviews some of the main features of emerging technologies and considers their impact on the nature of police work and the broader dimensions of policing as a process of social regulation. Particular attention is paid to continuing debates about the role of surveillance technology, such as closed-circuit television (CCTV) and automatic number place recognition (ANPR) and traffic monitoring systems. The use of crime mapping as a tool in **intelligence-led policing** is then considered before the chapter concludes by reflecting upon the impact of these technological developments upon police work.

CCTV, ANPR and traffic monitoring: benevolent gaze or Big Brother?

In May 2007, a senior police officer warned that the increasing use of CCTV risked creating an Orwellian society, and that the introduction of 'cameras on every corner' was disproportionate to the problem of crime in most small towns and villages (BBC, 2007). Some months earlier, the British Information Commissioner warned of the danger of 'sleepwalking into a surveillance society' and that the exponential growth of CCTV capacity raised serious concerns about civil liberties (Evans and Mostrous, 2006). The Commissioner noted that private companies monitored individuals' on-line shopping patterns in order to develop consumer profiles and enable highly targeted advertising, that RDIF

(Radio Frequency Identification) tags are increasingly inserted into products, allowing them to be monitored when in transit, and that an increasing range of private and public agencies were developing profiles of their customers and clients. Parents, for example, were being required to pay for their children's school meals via electronic cards, which would, among other things, allow the local education authority to monitor the eating patterns and habits of pupils. At the forefront of this panoply of monitoring and surveillance infrastructure is CCTV, a field in which Britain has become a global leader, with an estimated 20 per cent of all the world's cameras. In 1999, Norris and Armstrong suggested that an individual living in urban Britain going about their routine working and social life might be captured by up to 300 cameras in 30 different systems during the course of a single day. CCTV was employed at that time on residential estates, transport networks, retail outlets, football stadia, by police and town centre managers, in schools and hospitals, in telephone boxes, and at cash machines, petrol stations, and in car parks. The ubiquity of CCTV was such, Norris and Armstrong (1999: 42) argued, that it was unlikely that an individual could avoid its electronic gaze. Since then the suppliers of CCTV have developed new inroads into the domestic security industry so that relatively cheap systems can be bought to protect private property, which suggests that the public are prone to be captured by them. One major limitation of CCTV is that it has tended to be a passive presence, able to record or monitor events but not necessarily an effective means to intervene. Indeed, Norris and Armstrong (ibid.: 166) observed CCTV operations for 600 hours, during which time police or other personnel were deployed to intervene in a situation on just 45 occasions. While their study suggested a largely passive role for CCTV, it seems that the development of interactive systems might change the way in which cameras are used. In 2007, the British media reported that the Home Office was to invest £500,000 extending a 'speaking' CCTV system across 20 towns. The piloting of the system in Middlesbrough had found that giving operators the capability to communicate with members of the public in close proximity to the cameras enhanced their efficiency. Unsurprisingly, perhaps, the media found cases of individuals who had wrongly been reprimanded by these remote voices of authority for dropping litter, or groups of youths who were commanded to disperse. The consequences for those who chose to ignore the warnings of these talking cameras are unclear; ultimately it seems likely that their capacity to enforce cooperation will result in the deployment of personnel, a limited resource that is often unlikely to be available.

assessing the impact of CCTV

Debates about the impact of CCTV have focused on a range of issues, most notably its effectiveness in terms of crime prevention and deterrence (see Box 9.1).

Although it seems that there is little definitive evidence that CCTV is effective in preventing crimes in general terms, studies have shown that it can be useful when used in bounded or limited terms, such as the monitoring of crime in car parks (Gill and Spriggs, 2005). Other debates have concentrated upon civil liberties issues or the release of deviant sexual behaviour or if footage of dangerous reckless driving has been broadcast by the entertainment media. As Jewkes (2004) has noted, CCTV images have become a staple of a genre of reality TV crime programmes that have often relied upon the thinnest of public interest grounds to defend the broadcast of salacious or gratuitous footage.

Box 9.1

Deterrence

The notion that crime prevention initiatives such as CCTV have a deterrent effect is widely claimed, and is often a matter of 'common sense'. Just as the deployment of officers or members of the extended police family on high-visibility patrol is valued since it dissuades people from taking advantage of opportunities to commit crime, so too crime prevention is often predicated on signalling the risks of offending. The counterpart to the deterrence effect is the notion of displacement, the notion that crime is not wholly prevented but is redeployed to other places, other times, or other victims, or that offenders turn their attention to other forms of crime. Although there is evidence that displacement can limit the impact of situational crime prevention, such as CCTV, most of the research evidence suggests that deterrence reduces the overall level of crime and that only a proportion is displaced.

The impact of CCTV on policing is considered in terms of the relatively narrow work of the public police and, more broadly, in relation to policing as a process of social regulation. First, the effectiveness of CCTV as an aid to crime detection is considered. Photographic records of offenders have been used by detectives since the late nineteenth century and efforts to develop effective databases of these images began with card indexes during the same period (Norris and Armstrong, 1999). Since the 1960s, British TV shows have used photofits, video stills, and e-fits of suspects in an effort to gather information about suspects from the general public, and CCTV footage has become a staple ingredient of such programmes. The overall impact of CCTV as an aid to crime detection is difficult to gauge. Footage captured by cameras has been pivotal in some high-profile cases, although the actual identification and arrest of offenders have often arisen from traditional low-tech policing, even where hi-tech developments might have contributed to the process. A good example of this followed a series of bombings in London in 1999, aimed at the gay and minority ethnic communities. During April of that year three nail bombs exploded, the first in Brixton, followed by a second attack in Brick Lane at the heart of the Asian community in the East End of London, and a third in the Admiral Duncan, a pub in Soho associated with the gay community. During the last of these attacks, three people were killed. The extent of CCTV in the capital city was evident in the investigation of these attacks, as the Metropolitan Police analysed thousands of hours of footage. Facial recognition software meant that detectives could interrogate millions of images and identify a person caught on camera in the vicinity of each incident prior to the explosions. To that extent CCTV and the computer software that supported the investigation added resources to the police investigation that would not otherwise have been possible. Subsequently, however, the perpetrator, David Copeland, was identified following a tip-off in response to publication of photographs enhanced from the CCTV images. Surveillance and information technology enabled and accelerated the course of the investigation but the police continued to rely upon information supplied by observant members of the public. Home Office-sponsored research has shown that police officers regard CCTV images as a major source of intelligence in the investigation and routinely seize footage from public and private systems in the vicinity of a criminal incident (Levesley and Martin, 2005). In addition to enhancing the capacity of the police to identify offenders, CCTV also expedites custody procedures since suspects are more likely to admit offences once presented with CCTV-derived evidence, although presumably the time spent collecting and sifting CCTV evidence needs to be offset against that saved once in the custody suite.

CCTV and the electronic gaze

In addition to evidential benefits, CCTV is also heralded as an effective means to deploy officers in the pursuit of offenders or to tackle particular crime and disorder problems. In this context, the power of CCTV to observe and monitor public space and to register problem behaviour has been enhanced by computer software that can identify incongruous activity that might warrant closer police attention. The observational capacity of CCTV was, in its early incarnations, limited by the ability of operatives, who often tended to be poorly paid and under-motivated, to physically watch over the images presented to them on screens in the control room. Subsequently, however, the development of algorithmic systems that can automatically sense movement that might be a cause of concern offers a significantly more enhanced capacity for CCTV to direct the deployment of resources to scenes of crime, disorder, traffic congestion or one of the myriad scenarios anticipated by cameras (Norris and Armstrong, 1999). Nonetheless, studies of police work do not suggest that officers are often deployed to situations identified by CCTV cameras; while the police control room plays an important role in determining the work that officers do, it seems likely that this continues to be shaped predominantly by telephone calls received from members of the public (Bayley, 1994). The benefits of CCTV in terms of the operational deployment of officers appear to be stronger in specific instances than they are in general terms. CCTV seems to play little overall role in identifying general crime problems as they occur. Many CCTV cameras are not operated directly by police staff, or by operators who have dedicated means to communicate with police services (beyond the normal phone system). Many CCTV cameras are not deployed for general reasons to detect crime problems in broad terms. It was for these reasons that Norris and Armstrong (1999) found so few deployments arising from the many hours spent observing the operation of CCTV systems.

While CCTV does not play a significant role in determining the deployment of officers on routine duties, it clearly is important to the conduct of particular policing operations. In the policing of football matches, for example, CCTV is widely used to direct officers to particular pressure points where crowds have congregated or to monitor for those individuals banned from grounds following incidents of hooliganism (Garland and Rowe, 1999). Police officers suggested to Levesley and Martin (2005: 4–5) that CCTV was most useful in dealing with public order incidents, cases of assault and theft, and was typically used in town centres on Friday and Saturday nights as pubs and clubs closed and large numbers of people spilled onto the streets. As with claims about the crime prevention properties of CCTV, it seems that the potential benefits for the police service also need to be treated with some caution. It seems that there are some evidential benefits to be gained, but these depend upon the police being able to recognize the images of offenders and the quality and forensic value of images captured on systems that vary enormously in quality. In terms of the ability of CCTV to assist in operational terms, it also seems that caution is required: research into the demands on police time rarely suggests that much crime or disorder is spotted on CCTV and then 'passed' to the police.

traffic policing and technology

A more recent technological development has been automatic number plate recognition (ANPR) systems, whereby digital cameras record vehicle registration plates and trawl databases such as the Police National Computer in an effort to identify vehicles that are reported stolen or are otherwise 'of interest' to the police. ANPR was first used in Britain as part of the development of a 'ring of steel' around the City of London, whereby technological and physical interventions were installed in an effort to safeguard London's financial centre from terrorist attack (Goold, 2004). ANPR has not been subjected to the same degree of public debate as CCTV, as described above, or the use of traffic monitoring ('speed cameras') systems, discussed below, which may be because it has widely been presented as a straightforward law enforcement tool that has no broader implications for the population at large. Box 9.2 demonstrates the way in which Thames Valley Police explain the use of APNR.

Box 9.2

Automatic Number Plate Recognition – an effective policing tool to 'deny criminals the use of the roads'

Most criminals rely on vehicles to commit crime. Automatic number plate recognition (ANPR) is a tool designed to make it far more difficult for them to use vehicles without being detected.

As a vehicle passes through an ANPR camera, it takes an image of the number plate. Those details are then fed into a system which checks them against sources such as the Police National Computer (PNC), the Driver and Vehicle Licensing Agency (DVLA), Local Force Intelligence systems and motor insurers' databases. If the number plate is matched to one of the sources, the ANPR equipment will sound an alert.

Vehicles which have sounded an alert will then be stopped by intercept team officers for further investigation. Only vehicles that are highlighted by enforcement agency databases will be stopped, so no law-abiding citizen has anything to fear from ANPR operations. Unlicensed or uninsured vehicles are likely to be seized on the spot by ANPR-equipped officers.

ANPR can be used to gather intelligence on known criminals or for post-incident crime investigation as well as for running pro-active operations using dedicated intercept teams.

ANPR cameras are located in mobile units (vans), in Roads Policing patrol cars, at dedicated fixed sites and via closed circuit television (CCTV) schemes in urban areas.

ANPR cameras are NOT 'safety' cameras, so are not used in Thames Valley to catch speeding or otherwise law-abiding motorists. Nor are they used to generate revenue for the government or other agency.

The use of ANPR by Thames Valley Police fully complies with the Data Protection Act 1998 and the Human Rights Act 1998.

(http://www.thamesvalley.police.uk/news_info/departments/anpr/index.htm)

While APNR might be presented as a neutral technology, it has raised concern about civil liberties issues and the privacy of individuals. Although the recording of vehicle registration details might not, in itself, amount to the collection of personal information, concerns have been raised that the systems can also capture images of people present in vehicles, which might bring ANPR within the remit of data protection legislation. Moreover, while ANPR cameras are often deployed in identified static positions, in other circumstances cameras might be used covertly, which means that they would require permission under the terms of the Regulation of Investigatory Powers Act (RIPA) (2000), which was discussed in Chapter 6. The Scottish Chief Surveillance Commissioner (Office of Surveillance Commissioner, 2006) suggested that the capacity of ANPR systems to capture information indiscriminately means that they would not meet the tests of proportionality required by RIPA. The use of ANPR represents another context in which the police act as knowledge or information brokers in regulatory networks that span the public and private sector, in the example in Box 9.2, by trawling motor insurers' databases for information. Technology in this context enhances and transforms the cultural attribute of suspicion that has been widely regarded as central to police work. Where once officers structured their suspicion of vehicles in terms of the age, make, and state of repair or the ascribed character of those within it, or the speed or driver's response to the presence of a patrol car, they now have recourse to technological verification of the status of all vehicles. Ericson and Haggerty (1997) suggested that the apparent scientific and objective certainty of such data both empowers officers, since it elevates their perceptions beyond 'suspicion' towards 'knowledge', and, conversely, threatens to deskill police work by removing the traditional craft aspect of patrol.

Traffic monitoring systems, particularly speed cameras, have featured in much media debate about the proper focus of policing and law enforcement in Britain in recent years and reveal much about the ways in which crime is socially constructed. Speed enforcement cameras were introduced to British roadsides from the early 1990s, although it was often found that cameras were not operative since forces either did not put film into them or did not monitor the pictures (Corbett, 2000). Debates about speed cameras have become a media staple in recent years, with concerns focusing upon the effectiveness of cameras in reducing speed, arguments about the revenue-raising role of cameras, and the impact that cameras have upon law-abiding members of the public (see Box 9.3). Corbett and Caramlau (2006) suggested that, media campaigns notwithstanding, around 75 per cent of people support the use of cameras, although concerns persist about the 'stealthy' use of cameras (i.e. those deployed in 'hidden' ways or when not adequately signposted) and the notion that cameras are used to raise revenue rather than to target speeding motorists in high-risk areas. These latter concerns suggest that the use of speed cameras have the potential to undermine police legitimacy, especially when co-joined with perceptions that the use of cameras has accompanied a reduction in the deployment of 'real' police officers. The House of Commons Transport Committee (2006) noted that technological innovation ought to enhance, rather than usurp, the role of the police officer. The Committee suggested that continuing technological developments would see a range of new measures, including 'time-distance' cameras (which record the time at which vehicles enter and exit a stretch of road and so calculate average speed), 'intelligent road studs' (planted into the road surface to gather information about road and weather conditions, traffic flow and speed), and 'intelligent speed adaptation' (which uses GPS and digital mapping to control the speed of vehicles and ensure compliance with speed limits).

Box 9.3

'Speed camera blitz on suburbs'

Until recently government policy limited cameras to accident blackspots, but new guidelines allow some on roads where safety concerns had been raised. There will be fury at the inconvenience and cost of ripping up humps – many of which have only recently been put down. But the measures would raise thousands of pounds in extra fines, fuelling claims that cameras are installed simply to raise cash. It is expected to be residents who will be caught by cameras as they drive in and out of their own homes. There are 6,000 speed cameras in Britain, and they are expected to raise £180 million this year – three times as much as 2001. Last year, more than two million drivers were fined after being caught speeding by cameras. This year, it is expected to hit three million.

(*Daily Mail*, 16 April 2004)

The tone of media coverage such as that reproduced in Box 9.3 – which raises the spectre of suburban residents being criminalized while driving in and out of their homes – reveals much about the cultural status of private cars, crime and policing in contemporary Britain. Although car 'accidents' (itself a loaded term) are usually associated with excessive speed and result in far more deaths than homicide, speeding continues to be socially constructed as a non-serious offence (Corbett, 2000). The prospects of extending the techno-logical enforcement of traffic law runs the risk of criminalizing sections of society that would not otherwise have negative contact with the police. Concern about the impact of traffic policing on relations with the public is one factor that explains the low priority police officers have often afforded traffic policing (Waddington, 1999). The deleterious impact of road policing on the legitimacy and authority afforded to the police by 'respectable' middle-class society has been noted since the expansion of car ownership in the middle of the twentieth century (Loader and Mulcahy, 2003: 114). Figure 9.1 shows that media concern about these developments is also long-standing. As early as the 1920s, Emsley noted:

Constable (to Motorist who has exceeded the speed limit). 'And I have my doubts about this being your first offence. Your face seems familiar to me.' (Doran, 1990: 36, cited in Clapton, 2004)

Figure 9.1 Policing the motorist, circa 1905

> **The development of the motor car, and its increasing availability to middle-class families, was, even by this date, bringing members of a social group, who hitherto had had virtually no contact with the police, into regular conflict with them. In the summer of 1928 the Home Secretary made a 'pressing personal appeal' to all chief constables that they should urge caution on their men in the way they behaved towards the public on the roads. Stressing the Bobby's unique qualities, his good humour and impartiality was an additional way to seek to check the new and damaging confrontations between policemen and members of the middle class on the roads. (1996: 147)**

While pleas for impartiality in the 1920s seem to be thinly veiled requests for officers to exercise their discretion to the benefit of middle-class motorists, a key concern about the use of technology to enforce traffic legislation is that that it is not possible to turn a blind eye when the observer is an automated electronic system. The impact of technology on the exercise of police discretion is discussed more fully in the penultimate section of the chapter.

crime mapping, intelligence and the regulation of policing

The technological developments described in the previous section have related to various innovations intended to regulate and survey behaviour in a range of public and private contexts. By various means they are intended to exert a deterrent effect on those who might otherwise commit crime or undertake antisocial behaviour. As has been noted, they have significant impacts on policing and police work, but these are not their primary aims. In the following discussion the focus shifts to technological regimes that have been introduced within the police environment in an effort to improve the efficiency of the police organization, to make the service more accountable, and to develop the capability to tackle crime more effectively.

crime mapping and policing

Criminological research has long shown that crime is not randomly distributed, but tends to impact disproportionately on certain populations and in specific places. A plethora of victimization surveys have demonstrated that just as a minority of offenders commit a disproportionate number of offences, so too a minority of people and locations experience relatively high levels of crime. In very narrow terms this criminological canard has formed the basis for the development of focused and targeted policing that utilizes computer software and other technology in an effort to map patterns of crime and so enable a more effective deployment of police resources. As with other technological developments described in this chapter, this does not amount to a qualitatively new form of policing, since officers have tended to rely upon conceptual maps of local areas informed by knowledge of crime problems and offenders (Keith, 1993). While collating information on the characteristics and habits of 'nominals', i.e. known offenders, has always been central to police work, developments in ICT have transformed the capacity to develop intelligence about local problems and to more effectively respond to them. Much of the recent impetus to develop policing along these lines developed from a growing realization in Britain and elsewhere in the 1970s and 1980s that traditional police patrol work appeared to have little impact upon crime rates. An assessment of traditional policing strategies of that era led Bayley (1994: 3) to the withering – and much cited – conclusion that:

> The police do not prevent crime. This is one of the best-kept secrets of modern life. Experts know it, the police know it, but the public does not know it. Yet the police pretend that they are society's best defence against crime ... This is a myth. First, repeated analysis has consistently failed to find any connection between the number of police officers and crime rates. Secondly, the primary strategies adopted by modern police have been shown to have little or no effect on crime.

One response to this counsel of despair was to utilize information technology so that police could collate data about criminal offences, use geographical information systems to pinpoint locations, and so produce local maps that enabled the identification of particular 'hot spots': areas that were particularly criminogenic. Particularly high profile applications of such approaches were developed in many US cities in the 1990s; the development of the Compstat system in New York in the 1990s proved particularly influential as it was widely imitated by other police departments in the US and was lauded by politicians, policy-makers and academics alike (Silverman, 2006) (see Box 9.4).

Box 9.4

Compstat

Essentially Compstat is a police management tool that coordinates 'up-to-date computerized crime data, crime analysis, and advanced crime mapping as the bases for regularized, interactive crime strategy meetings which hold managers accountable for specific crime strategies and solutions in their areas' (Silverman, 2006: 268). It is often used as part of a strategy whereby senior officers meet regularly to review crime patterns in their districts and are held to account on a daily or weekly basis.

The development of 'high definition' policing (McLaughlin, 2007a: 124) that Compstat and other forms of crime mapping enable has a number of implications. First, there is some evidence that it is an effective strategy in law enforcement terms. While some have argued that other factors also played a significant role in reducing crime levels in New York City in the 1990s (Bowling 1999; Stenson 2001), a more general analysis of **hot spots policing** programmes in the United States concluded that there was a positive impact in reducing crime, and that this was not at the expense of displacing crime problems to other areas (Weisburd and Braga, 2006: 232–4). However, concerns about other aspects of this form of targeted policing suggest that such success comes at a price when accompanied by aggressive tactics, such as those associated with **zero tolerance policing**. In the US context, Rosenbaum, (2006) cautioned that 'hot spots' policing is often associated with aggressive enforcement and that this can weaken police–community relations and undermine legitimacy. Furthermore, Rosenbaum argued that these technological approaches re-define crime problems in relatively narrow terms and that a geographical perspective of crime problems risks ignoring the broader dimensions of, for example, illegal drug dealing.

intelligence-led 'hot spots' policing

The same technology used to map crime for the purposes of intelligence-led policing operations has been extended, in the United States, to develop information for the public about criminal incidents and patterns in particular neighbourhoods. Often this approach is known as 'hot-spots' policing, and requires the constant profiling and mapping of local crime trends (Weisburd and Braga, 2006; Rosenbaum, 2006). The collation and communication of information about crime to third parties have become an important aspect of police work (Chan, 2001). Ericson and Haggerty (1997) delineated a wide range of public and private agencies to whom the Canadian police provided information about crime and argued that officers had become knowledge workers and 'risk communicators'. This trend is vividly illustrated by the police role in providing information about crime that is presented via the internet to provide a local cartography of crime (see Figure 9.2). Those interested in crimes reported in Chicago, for example, can visit a website and view an interactive map showing incidents by type, by date and by geographical area, down to the level of particular streets. A host of incidents are displayed and, in some cases, extended details are provided. The provision of such information is usually justified in terms of public empowerment and claims that individuals can take responsibility for their own safety on the basis of accurate and detailed knowledge. Similar arguments are made by those who campaign for the disclosure of information about convicted paedophiles in Britain (Edwards and Hughes, 2002). As Ratcliffe (2002) has outlined, such claims raise serious ethical concerns about privacy, the risk of vigilante activity, and the broader impact that such representation of crime problems can have on communities in terms of perpetuating negative perceptions that can impact upon their economic development. Moreover, they suggest a level of scientific and technological authority that might be unwarranted. Ratcliffe identified reasons why the apparent certainty of locating an incident using Geographical Information Systems technology might be misleading. Most of these relate to the real-world context in which information about criminal incidents is (mis)understood by victims and witnesses and subsequently recorded inaccurately by the police.

technology and the routines of police work

While crime mapping technology provides a platform for the strategic direction of police services, albeit one that might be imperfect, other technological innovations have shaped the routines of police work, just as they have transformed working life more generally. As was noted above, technological developments played a significant role in the development of Unit Beat Policing in Britain during the 1960s, when the introduction of Computer-Aided Dispatch (CAD) systems offered the promise of a more efficient response to demands from the public. CAD utilizes a terminal in patrol cars via which a central control room directs officers to respond to incidents reported by the public. Details of the incident, such as the address, names of those involved, previous

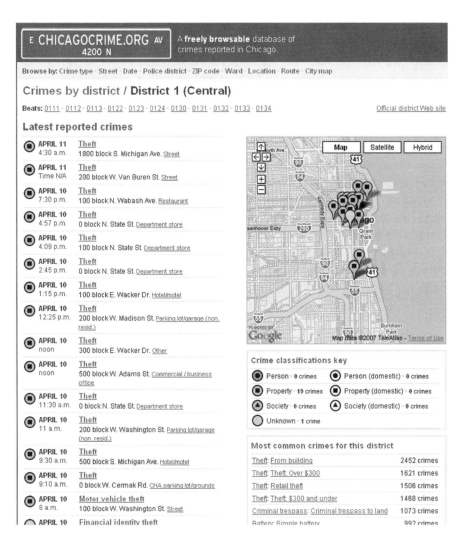

Figure 9.2 Mapping crime in Chicago

Source: http://www.chicagocrime.org/

history of the address and the caller, and the degree of priority attached to the report are transmitted to a screen in the patrol car. Manning (1992, cited in Chan, 2001) commented that the promises of increased efficiency offered by CAD, and other technological innovations, have often not been met and that they have had less impact on police practices than were forecast. However, Ericson and Haggerty (1997) found that officers regarded CAD as a positive innovation that allowed them to perform vehicle and other checks relatively quickly and securely (unlike older police radios, CAD systems are not susceptible to being monitored by illicit scanners).

An addition to technological innovations that assign officers to cases has been the development of computerized crime reporting systems into which details of incidents are entered. Although police officers have always been concerned to gather and process information about criminal and other incidents, the development of databases that store, sort and communicate such policing outputs has transformed traditional practices. In an era when the deployment of police officers and PCSOs on 'high visibility' patrol has become an imperative, the impact of computerized reporting systems on officers' time is an important concern. A Home Office study (PA Consulting Group, 2001) found that officers spent 43.1 per cent of their time engaged in 'backroom' activity, in police stations and custody suites out of public sight. Not all of this time was spent completing incident reports, but the study identified problems with IT systems that were out of date, non-intuitive and so difficult to use, did not have sufficient terminals and access points, and were prone to system failures. In addition to the limits of the systems, the study found a considerable amount of time had to be devoted to bureaucratic procedural tasks. Alongside an average of 3.5 hours spent processing individuals taken into custody, officers had to deal with myriad administrative requirements:

> **Other paperwork includes crime reports, intelligence reports, forms to log recovered property, missing person details, information required for special force initiatives as well as paperwork connected with the shift administration and the officer in question. Often one event (e.g. a crime) can trigger the recording of the same information on multiple separate records. Where forms are available electronically, little officer time is actually saved because the IT system applications are mostly antiquated and do not talk to each other. (ibid.: vi)**

Chan's (2001) study of the impact of IT on an Australian police service found similar concerns about the time that officers had to devote to computerized recording and reporting systems, and the negative consequences that this had in terms of patrol work. However, she also found that officers valued the communicative and intelligence capacity of systems and the advantages offered in terms of generating knowledge of offenders and broader crime patterns. Beyond the concerns about time and resources, Ericson and Haggerty (1997) argued that the requirements of IT-based reporting systems had become increasingly restrictive in terms of the number of fields that officers are required to complete and prescriptive in respect of the type of data that must be entered. They argued that the demands of reporting formats serve to shape not just the ways in which officers spend their time but, more significantly, play a constitutive role in the ways in which they think about crime and policing:

> **Scientization within established communication formats has the intended consequence of effecting closure and certainty in policework. It allows the officer to prospectively decide whether something should be subject to policework (whether it fits an established format), and if so, to complete the task in concrete**

and discrete terms of the formats within which they communicate. Their thinking itself becomes characterized by closure and certainty ... We observed that whenever a police officer encountered something new, the first question asked was whether a form was available to cover it. (ibid.: 383–4)

Enhancing the role of IT within the routines of police work has also impacted upon the dynamics of power relations within police services. Not only is the status of technical support staff, such as data analysts, enhanced relative to other specialist and general police staff but so too the nature and reach of supervision are affected. The ability of line managers to oversee the work of their officers is greatly enhanced by the easy availability of accessible information on the status of enquiries that an officer is assigned to. Not only does this allow for the 'performance' of officers to be inspected, and compared with that of colleagues, it can also impact upon the ways in which officers approach incidents. One consequence of this might be that the officers become relatively deskilled as they perform routine duties according to prescribed procedures and policies, secure in the knowledge that any deviation from these can quickly be identified by supervisory officers. In recent years officers have been required to identify, when inputting incident details, cases that might be hate crimes of some kind, the 'flagging' of which then prompts senior officers to ensure they have been investigated according to established guidelines. Additionally the better identification of such cases provides more effective communication of problems to other agencies involved in policing partnerships (Hall, 2005: 203–40).

the impact of technology on policing and police work

As the proceeding discussion demonstrates, technological developments have impacted upon the police service in diverse ways. Some of these have enhanced traditional features of police work, on occasion, transforming them to such an extent that they significantly affect the capacity and capability of the police service. DNA fingerprinting, for example, might be regarded as a more sophisticated version of long-established efforts to capture and collate the unique properties of individual victims or offenders. However, the scope of such technology, in terms of the increasing speed at which tests can be conducted and the range of sources from which viable samples can be extracted, transforms police investigations to the extent that it can hardly be considered in the same category as earlier incarnations such as fingerprinting. The actual and potential implications of these developments for policing and police work have been noted at various stages and this final section reviews these in a more structured discussion. The chapter concludes by arguing that the tendency towards technological determinism must be avoided, since the capabilities and prospects that they offer are dependent upon the social, institutional and cultural context in which they are deployed.

A central debate in academic discussion of the use of CCTV, ANPR and other technological innovations relates to the supposed panoptical effects of such forms of surveillance and the development of a disciplinary society. Foucault (1977) argued that systems of dispersed social control had spread beyond the penitentiary so that society itself, and the governance thereof, could be considered in panoptical terms (see Box 9.5). Along these lines, one of the key concerns about the power and reach of police surveillance technology has been that it extends the capacity of the state to monitor the previously private realm of the citizen. An early forecast of these developments was offered by Marx, who couched concerns about police surveillance in the United States in the following terms:

> Powerful new information-gathering technologies are extending ever deeper into the social fabric and to more features of the environment. Like the discovery of the atom or the unconscious, new control techniques surface bits of reality that were previously hidden or didn't contain informational clues. People are in a sense turned inside out, and what was previously invisible or meaningless is made visible and meaningful. This may involve space-age detection devices that give meaning to physical emanations based on the analysis of heat, light, pressure, motion, odour, chemicals, or psychological process, as well as the new meaning given to visible individual characteristics and behaviour when they are re-judged relative to a predictive profile based on aggregate data. (1988: 206–7)

Box 9.5

The Panopticon

Derived from the prison designs developed in the eighteenth century by Jeremy Bentham, the term 'Panopticon' refers to a system whereby the maximum degree of surveillance is derived from the minimum deployment of resources. In the context of Bentham's plans for the ideal prison this related to a system whereby prison cells were organized in tiers around the circumference of a circular prison, in the middle of which stood a tower. Each cell was open to surveillance by only a few guards who were located out of sight at the top of the central tower. In this way prisoners knew that they could be observed at any time, but were unable to know precisely when, or if, they were actually watched. One result of this efficient system of control was that prisoners internalized the disciplinary regime so that they regulated their own behaviour in the expectation that the prison guards were keeping them under observation.

The watchful gaze of CCTV has been regarded as one means of extending the 'maximum surveillance society', in which the disciplinary powers of governance are at their zenith (Cohen, 1985). The implications of these debates for policing are complex; in broad terms if the net of social control is widened and the mesh thinned, then the extension of surveillance systems will mean that the focus of the police service expands to individuals, groups and activities that would not previously have been considered the business of the police. As was noted above, this argument has been made by sections of the media in relation to road traffic policing criminalizing 'ordinary' motorists not construed as offenders. In addition, as has already been suggested, the growth of CCTV in British society has been in many and diverse directions and the technology has spread in ways so that many agencies, and individuals, have become part of a policing network. The pluralization of policing was discussed in Chapter 8, but technology and surveillance systems, such as those that encourage citizens to remotely monitor the security of their property or to consult web-sites that map local crime patterns, enlist private citizens into policing networks. Hudson (2003) argued that technological developments transform policing and security into matters of private responsibility that are related to the broader expansion of consumer culture into public services (Loader, 1999).

_____ watching the police _____

Another implication of the growth of CCTV technology, CAD systems and crime reporting regimes relates to their potential to regulate and survey police officers. In some circumstances, the power of CCTV to discipline officer behaviour is explicitly utilized, such as the use of cameras to monitor behaviour in custody suites (Newburn, 2002). On other occasions alleged police brutality has been captured on CCTV cameras. As with other potential media stories, the presence of good quality visual images makes it more likely that an item will appear in newspapers or on television (Chibnall, 1977). In 2007, for example, the British media broadcast extracts recorded on a CCTV system outside a Sheffield nightclub that purported to show an officer punching a woman who was pinned to the floor by other officers, and the case was subsequently investigated by the Independent Police Complaints Commission. High profile cases such as this might have shaped police officers' perceptions of CCTV and the ways in which it curtails the exercise of discretion. Goold's (2004: 180–1) study of policing and CCTV found that while officers claimed that they did not behave inappropriately and so had nothing to fear from surveillance, they often did recognize that their actions had been influenced:

Over two-thirds of the officers interviewed conceded that the introduction of cameras had forced them to be 'more careful' when out on patrol. Some, for

example, had heard stories of officers being prosecuted for unlawful arrest or assault on the basis of CCTV evidence – stories that had left them anxious about being watched and the possibility of their own activities being scrutinized. Others, particularly younger officers, found that being under constant surveillance made them nervous and uncomfortable. Irrespective of the reason for their concern, many of these officers had come to the conclusion that the introduction of CCTV made it essential for them to 'go by the book', or at least to create the appearance of doing so. (ibid.)

_____ micro-managing police performance _____

Technological surveillance might inhibit officers who are otherwise liable to behave inappropriately but information systems also enhance the micro-management of police performance, which impacts upon routine police work. As Ericson and Haggerty (1997) suggested, the enhanced reach of line managers, technologically enabled to review officer performance, can shape and limit the exercise of discretion. By requiring an officer to complete certain procedures, and being able to determine whether this has been done, supervisory officers can limit discretion in ways not previously possible. While this is ostensibly a retrospective review, it has anticipatory powers since officers are aware that their actions might be subject to scrutiny. As with Bentham's panoptical prison, the disciplinary capacity of surveillance affects the ways in which officers conceive of their role and exercise their powers. This is illustrated by Rowe's (2007) finding that officers' response to incidents of domestic violence adopted the principles of risk-avoidance. Partly this was based on their understanding that there was a strong likelihood of repeat victimization, which meant they ought to proactively intervene in what otherwise they might have regarded as a 'trivial' private dispute. Moreover, though, the risk of non-intervention was also understood in terms of consequences for themselves, since they anticipated that their judgement and interventions would be scrutinized by senior officers. In some cases, this meant that officers decide to intervene and arrest a perpetrator on the grounds that to do otherwise would risk their being sanctioned by senior officers. At times this was done even though the officer felt that affecting an arrest was not the most suitable way of solving the particular problem. The often-noted tendency of officers to take a non-interventionist stance in response to 'domestics' was being transformed by regulatory regimes which held officers open to scrutiny. Given that most of the routine calls that officers deal with are routed through the CAD system, much of the work that they do is subject to such inspection. The impact on routine police work is not all encompassing, however, since officers still have considerable discretion in dealing with cases brought directly to their attention while on patrol and it is more difficult to review officer response to incidents that are not first 'captured' by information systems.

Curtailing police decision-making through the use of technology and information systems has clear implications for police sub-cultures, which, has often, even if simplistically, been associated with the inappropriate exercise of discretion. Chapter 5 provides a fuller discussion of police culture. Extending the capacity of senior officers to supervise the behaviour and actions of front-line staff might make it easier, for example, to identify officers who over-police minority communities. The 'reach' of technology in this sense, however, is easily over-stated since officers inevitably retain some control over the information that is entered into computer systems in the first instance. Moreover, problems of stereotyping and discrimination cannot be solely ascribed to negative characteristics of canteen culture shared by junior ranking officers. The broader institutional framework of policing, the role and influence of plural policing beyond the public police, and the social context in which crime and policing are conceptualized must all be addressed. Micro-managing the decisions of officers on patrol will not, in isolation, prevent the inappropriate exercise of police discretion. While not providing a technological fix in terms of regulating or deterring police deviance, the changing environment in which officers work will be influenced, but not determined, by increasing use of computer-based information and communication systems. As noted above, the role of intelligence systems changes relations within police services and alters the nature and status of police knowledge (Ericson and Haggerty, 1997). Police culture, however, has never been a fixed monolithic entity that can be moulded by external technological or management regimes. Elements of police work will be transformed by the developments outlined in this chapter, just as they were in the face of technological innovations such as the police radio and the patrol car, but the direction and extent of these transformations are difficult to predict.

conclusion

Technological innovation has transformed late modern society in complex ways that continue to unfold. Many have argued that they have contributed to processes of cultural, political and economic globalization, promoted the knowledge economy, and transformed time and space. As Williams (2006) has noted, new forms of technological communication have the potential to fundamentally restructure the means by which individuals form communities and construct notions of deviance and the means to regulate human behaviour. While on-line virtual communities offer insight into possible futures that are in equal part horrifying and alluring, it is also apparent that information and communication technology has already had a significant impact on police work and crime. As with other debates about change and innovation in policing, however, there is a tendency to assume that such developments represent a fundamental epochal transformation (Jones and Newburn, 2002). The technological capacity of electronic surveillance and intelligence systems does not determine the manner in which they are used or the impact that they have in broader social terms. There are two main reasons for resisting technologically determinist views of the developments outlined in this chapter. First, police leaders and politicians have sought technological solutions to crime problems and as a means to achieve efficiency in police work since modern police services were established in the nineteenth century. The pace of technological change might have increased, with significant implications in terms of the power and reach of intelligence systems, but earlier innovations have tended to lead to evolutions in policing, rather than revolutions. The second reason for a cautious reading of these trends is that the impact of technological innovation has often been shown to be dependent upon the fallible human beings responsible for their operationalization. As has been shown in the context of CCTV, for example, the employment of poorly paid and under-motivated staff has often meant that technological capacity has not been reached in practice (Norris and Armstrong, 1999). Moreover, just as technological change presents new opportunities for crime and deviance, innovations also create avenues for 'counter-appropriation' whereby officers can find means to use, for example, mobile phones to communicate with one another beyond the sight of inspection or surveillance systems (Manning, 1996; cited in Chan, 2003). Policing will continue to be shaped by technological developments that broaden and transform networks of regulation in the global information age, and the direction and nature of this impact will be determined by the context in which it is deployed. For this reason predicting technological configurations of policing in the twenty-first century remains a risky pursuit.

▨ ▩ chapter summary ▩

- Popular cultural images misrepresent police work in a range of ways. Chief among these in contemporary fictional accounts is the genre of detective series which present policing as a highly scientific and technological profession. Academic and policy research tends to suggest that these are important components of contemporary policing but that they play only a partial role in most criminal investigations. Locating information technology in the context of real police work is a central theme of the chapter, with particular attention to CCTV and various aspects of road traffic policing.

- In addition to enhancing the investigation of crime, technology has transformed the nature of police communication and information management. This has not been a wholly recent phenomenon, however, and, again, it has been limited by 'real-world' considerations relating to funding, training, and police sub-culture.

- In Britain, CCTV has been at the forefront of new technologies that monitor a host of human interactions in residential, education, retail, business and leisure environments. In 2006, the Information Commissioner warned that Britain was 'sleepwalking into a surveillance society', and it is estimated that the country is monitored by 20 per cent of the world's cameras. The research evidence on the impact of CCTV on crime rates is not extensive, but tends to suggest that it can reduce rates of crime, without significant problems of displacement, but that this is only the case when it is applied in certain environments and in respect of certain types of crime. Although CCTV-generated images have proved very useful in investigation of some high-profile criminal cases, like other forms of technology, there is little definitive evidence of the impact it has had on detection more generally.

- CCTV can help in deploying officers and in the direction of specific policing operations, particularly relating to public disorder and theft. However, there is little evidence to suggest that it informs the deployment of officers more generally.

- ANPR technology was developed in response to threats of terrorism, and provides the police with the capacity to identify large numbers of vehicles and to retrieve information about those that might be stolen, uninsured, or associated with known offenders. It has been argued that it offers a major boost to efforts to disrupt criminal activity on the roads, although concern has been raised that it might record personal information and ought to be curtailed by the terms of the 2000 Regulation of Investigatory Powers Act.

- Social theorists and sections of the media have argued that enhanced technological traffic policing extends the reach of the police too far into the private realm and constitutes a major shift in the proper relation of the individual to the state. Arguments that the police criminalize law-abiding motorists have appeared periodically since the expansion of car ownership in Britain in the 1920s and 1930s.

- In addition to the conduct of investigation and the remote policing of motorists, technological change has also transformed the ways in which police work itself is conducted. That crime is not evenly distributed, either in terms of offenders or patterns of victimization, has led to the development of crime-mapping techniques that promise to identify locales, times, and circumstances in which criminal acts occur. Historically police work has often relied upon officers' local knowledge of offenders and crime problems but developments in ICT transform the status, reach and authority of information in police work.

- While there is some evidence that crime mapping has enabled the effective targeting of specific crime problems, concerns are also identified about the impact of aggressive police tactics on police–community relations.

- Similar technology has been used to develop 'hot spots' policing, whereby a range of plural policing agencies and wider networks provide information about criminal incidents to produce maps of local crime problems. Not only does this lead to concern about the accuracy and reliability of information provided but wider problems have been identified in terms of the impact that crime maps can have on neighbourhoods that come to be identified as particularly crime-prone.

- Beyond the identification and investigation of crime, technology has an impact upon routines of police work, particularly in terms of communication and information management. CAD systems play a central role in shaping the work that officers do, and limit the exercise of officer discretion. Requirements that officers enter data into computer systems not only means that they are removed from visible patrol work for extended periods, it also limits their discretion by requiring certain actions to be taken and decisions to be made. These trends have been central to arguments that police officers increasingly are best understood as knowledge workers.

- These developments have a range of implications for society. Many have argued that the expansion of surveillance technology pushes society into the realms of the Panopticon, whereby individual behaviour is disciplined by anticipated processes of regulation. This has various implications for the police, not least that an increasing range of agencies and individuals come to be engaged in processes of social control. It also extends surveillance of police behaviour itself, and conditions the nature in which officers exercise their discretion. The micro-management of police performance might be a useful way for senior officers to ensure that certain steps are taken in a period of victim-oriented service delivery. Moreover, however, they also have implications for the culture of police work which becomes deskilled and focused on collecting and transmitting data.

- There is a strong imperative to avoid technological determinism in considering the influence that these developments will have on crime, policing and social relations more widely. Technology is deployed into particular institutional and cultural contexts which mean that its capacity and possibilities can be resisted, deflected, or transformed in practice. Two examples illustrate the need for this caution. First, studies have often shown that CCTV operatives are a weak link in the chain of technology and their lack of application or motivation limit the power of surveillance systems. Second, there is the possibility of counter-appropriation, whereby personnel find means to use technology to resist being scrutinized, either through using systems of their own, such as mobile phones, or by finding ways and means to limit the reach of systems designed to manage their behaviour.

1   What does the acronym HOLMES stand for?

2   What percentage of the world's CCTV cameras is it estimated are deployed in Britain?

3   In relation to what three types of crime did police officers suggest CCTV was particularly effective?

4   Against what sources of information do Thames Valley Police check information gathered via ANPR?

5   What percentage of the British population support, in general terms, the use of cameras to police speeding drivers?

6   What is Compstat?

7   In Britain in the 1960s Computer-Aided Dispatch systems were introduced in the development of what model of policing?

8   Who developed a model prison that enshrined the concept of the Panopticon?

9   To what broader social and political processes do Hudson (2003) and Loader (1999) relate the development of technology in policing?

10 In which specific environment have CCTV cameras been introduced to monitor officer behaviour?

■ study ?uestions ▬▬▬▬▬▬▬▬▬▬▬▬▬▬▬▬▬▬

1   What should be the balance between civil liberty concerns about the 'right to privacy' and the security dividends associated with surveillance technology?

2   Does crime mapping provide information useful to the general public?

3   What might be the implications of technological limitations on police officer discretion?

■ ■ annotated further reading ■

Erison and Haggerty's (1997) *Policing the Risk Society* is probably the key recent study of policing and technology, not least because it argues that the development of new information and intelligence systems has importance far beyond discussions of efficiency and effectiveness. The book's central theme is that technological innovation transforms routine police work into a form of knowledge work, whereby officers are increasingly responsible for transmitting information about risk across networks of agencies engaged in policing.

Gill and Spriggs' (2005) *Assessing the Impact of CCTV* is a Home Office research study based upon an extensive study of the effectiveness of surveillance cameras in 14 sites, including town centres, residential areas, hospitals and car parks. The study used control group areas to assess the impact that CCTV had on local crime rates and examined public attitudes to the systems. The findings show a very mixed picture. CCTV proved reasonably effective in certain areas (particularly those with controlled and fixed entry and exit points, such as car parks) and in relation to certain types of crime. In other areas, such as residential locations, and in relation to crimes such as violent assault, the study suggested that CCTV had little impact.

Chan's (2001) article, 'The Technological Game: How Information Technology is Transforming Police Practice', provides a useful overview of key arguments about the role of information technology in policing since the 1960s. In particular, she argues that the impact that technology has had often has not been as anticipated and that officers have been able to resist and refocus some of the requirements placed upon them. Chan outlines findings from her own research into policing and technology in Australia and puts this into context by reviewing key themes from the wider literature which demonstrate the need for caution in considering the impact of technology on policing.

// annotated listings of links to relevant websites

The **National Policing Improvement Agency** was developed in 2004 as part of the broader government drive to reform the police. The Agency was established in 2007 in the UK and conflates the work of a host of 'support' agencies, covering resources and operational policing. The Agency's website (www.npia.police.uk/en/index.htm) includes an overview of current technological developments.

The National Institute of Justice is a sub-division of the US Department of Justice and its website (www.ojp.usdoj.gov/nij/maps/) provides a wide range of material on crime mapping and hot spots policing. The principles and practices of crime mapping are outlined in detail and supporting research is analysed. The site includes software programs used by crime analysts.

Privacy International is a pressure group campaigning on surveillance issues such as data protection, communication surveillance, border technology, ID cards, and others. The group's website (www.privacyinternational.org/index .shtml) contains a wide range of resources, including country profiles.

Answers to self-check questions

what is policing?

1 How can narrow and broader definitions of policing be characterized? [Narrow set of functions performed by the institution of the police service and the broader processes of social regulation and reproduction that govern everyday lives.]

2 What agencies, apart from the police service, play a role in regulating social life? [Among others, schools, religious groups, health providers, business sector, and the media.]

3 Why did Mawby (2003) argue that media images of policing are important? [Media accounts provide the authoritative narrative of policing for large sections of the public.]

4 Who provided a 'classic' definition of state sovereignty? [Max Weber: state sovereignty as the possession of a legitimate use of force over a given territory.]

5 Why might the 'use of force' offer only a limited understanding of the police function? [Among others, the police tend to under-utilize their potential to use force, and other agencies have coercive powers over citizens.]

6 In what, very broad, terms did Bittner (1974) define the police task? ['No human problem exists, or is imaginable, about which it could be said with finality that this certainly could not become the proper business of the police'.]

7 What proportion of public calls to the police did Bayley find were related to crime? [Seven to ten per cent.]

8 How did Ericson and Haggerty (1997) characterize police officers? ['Knowledge workers' whose primary role was to communicate risk.]

9 What two factors explain, according to research published in 2001, the significant amount of time officers spend in the police station? [Processing prisoners in custody and 'other paperwork', such as completing crime and intelligence reports, dealing with missing property and persons.]

10 What relation does the police service have to the criminal justice system more generally? [It acts as a 'gateway agency'.]

CHAPTER 2   historical origins and development of the police in England and Wales

1   What features characterized policing in England between the 1740s and 1850s? [Self-policing, community engagement in street patrols, and private sector provision of many policing services.]

2   Name the constitutional arrangement that enshrined the key features of policing from the thirteenth century until the establishment of the 'new police' in the nineteenth century. [The Statute of Winchester.]

3   To what did Sir John Fielding attribute the crime problems of the 1740s? [Illegal drinking establishments.]

4   Who addressed the Chartist rally at St Peter's Field, Manchester, in 1819 that fuelled concern about using the military to control crowds? [Henry Hunt.]

5   How did Storch characterize the role of the police in the mid-nineteenth century? ['Domestic missionaries'.]

6   What measures were introduced in an effort to overcome public suspicion of the 'new police' in the early nineteenth century? [Emphasizing the service role of the police, deploying police in uniforms distinct from the military, the appearance of the police as unarmed.]

7   What proportion of the 3000 officers recruited to the Metropolitan Police when it was established in 1829 is it estimated were still in post four years later? [Bailey suggested the figure was one-sixth.]

8   What legislation required counties to establish a police force? [The 1856 County and Borough Police Act.]

9   How do orthodox perspectives explain dissatisfaction with the use of the military to respond to political and social unrest? [Practical difficulties compounded by fears that soldiers might side with protestors and 'the mob' rather than the authorities.]

10   How do revisionist accounts tend to explain the development of the 'new police'? [In terms of the changing demands of early industrial capitalism, which required the suppression of political disorder and the greater regulation of the urban working class.]

CHAPTER 3   police powers: the legal framework

1   How did Sir Robert Mark characterize the power of the police over the citizen? [He suggested that the key feature was that police officers had the power to inconvenience citizens.]

2   What was introduced in 1912 to govern the treatment of those held in custody? [The Judges' Rules.]

3   What is the general condition for the police powers to stop and search an individual under Section 1 of PACE? [That the officer has 'reasonable suspicion' that the individual is in possession of stolen or prohibited items.]

4   How does PACE define a 'public place'? [Those places to which the public have access, whether upon payment or otherwise, but are not a dwelling.]

5   Why did the Home Office reject the Macpherson Report recommendation that police officers be required to issue a record for all stops involving members of the public? [Concerns were expressed that such a requirement would disproportionately increase bureaucracy and would discourage routine informal interactions between police and public.]

6   What documents cannot be searched under the terms of a general search warrant? [Items identified as legally privileged. For example, communication between a client and professional legal advisor, including journalistic documents, medical records, and items held in confidence for business purposes.]

7   Under what circumstances can magistrates issue a warrant for arrest? [When the identity of an offender is known but the person cannot be located or when an individual has failed to attend court in response to a summons.]

8   What conditions does PACE stipulate justify detaining an individual in custody prior to their being charged with an offence? [The detention of a person is only legal if it is necessary to allow further enquiries to be made, for example, to prevent that person from destroying evidence or interfering with witnesses.]

9   Why does a concentration on the legal powers granted to the police provide only a partial understanding of police work? [Because a focus on the legal framework of police powers reflects a jurisprudential approach to policing that fails to address the cultural and sociological determinants of police practice.]

10 How did Loader and Mulcahy characterize the power of senior police officers to identify and define crime problems? [The 'power of legitimate naming'.]

CHAPTER 4   **community policing**

1   What three elements did Skogan (2006) suggest characterize community policing initiatives in the United States? [Citizen involvement, problem-solving, and decentralization.]

2   How did Weatheritt suggest the term 'community policing' had been used in Britain? ['To denote projects of which authors approved'.]

3 Identify four aspects of Alderson's model of community policing. [To contribute to liberty, equality and fraternity; to help reconcile freedom with security and to uphold the law; to uphold and protect human rights and thus help achieve human dignity; to dispel criminogenic social conditions, through cooperative social action; to help create trust in communities; to strengthen security and feelings of security; to investigate, detect and activate the prosecution of crimes; to facilitate free movement along public thoroughfares; to curb public disorder; to deal with crises and help those in distress involving other agencies where needed.]

4 What was the name of the policing model introduced alongside panda cars, two-way radios and other innovations in the late 1960s? [Unit Beat Policing.]

5 What legislation required that the police, in partnership with other agencies, conduct audits to establish the community safety needs of local communities? [Crime and Disorder Act 1998.]

6 How many people was it estimated lived in areas covered by Neighbourhood Watch schemes in 2006? [10 million.]

7 What did a 2001 HMIC report establish as the three core features of reassurance policing? [Visibility, familiarity and accessibility.]

8 What features of police work explain the tendency for officers to be culturally isolated from the wider community? [According to Reiner 1978: the boredom, unsociable hours, occasional periods of danger, and the routine exposure to shocking and traumatic events.]

9 Why might local residents' perceptions of crime risks not be reliable? [They might not correspond to objective risks facing them.]

10 What trend appears to contradict moves to devolve policing closer to local communities? [The apparent increase in central control over the direction of policing.]

_____ CHAPTER 5 **police culture**_____

1 How did Wilson famously characterize the particular character of police discretion? ['The police department has the special property ... that within it discretion increases as one moves down the hierarchy' (Wilson, 1968: 7).]

2 What are the key features of police subculture? [A range of features are often identified: cynicism, suspicion, conservatism, sense of mission, isolation/solidarity, machismo, pragmatism, racial prejudice, orientation to action, 'covering-your-ass'.]

3 What characterizes the 'rotten apples' perspective on police racism? [The 'rotten apples' perspective associates the problem with the negative prejudices and stereotyping of a small minority of officers that has a disproportionate impact on the organization as a whole.]

4 What was the remit of early generations of female police officers? [Protecting women and children, dealing with prostitution.]

5 What proportion of homophobic crime has it been estimated is not reported to the police? [The National Advisory Group/Policing Lesbian and Gay Communities (1999) found that 80 per cent of homophobic incidents are not reported.]

6 In respect of what issues did Colman and Gorman measure the attitudes of police recruits? [The death penalty and migration.]

7 What different 'strains' of police culture have been identified? [Between 'street cops' and 'management cops', between different specialist departments, between different nations.]

8 In what nation did Moon suggest police subculture is not resistant to community policing? [Korea.]

9 Who conducted an early study of routine police work in London? [The Policy Studies Institute/Smith and Gray (1983).]

10 Why might an understanding of police culture need to be broadened? [The 'changing terrain of policing'; for example, the expansion at local, national and international levels of agencies involved in the process of policing.]

_____ CHAPTER 6 **who guards the guards?** _____

1 Prior to the 2002 Police Reform Act, which agencies and groups had advocated the establishment of an independent system to investigate complaints against the police? [The consultancy firm KPMG, the civil rights group Liberty, and the Lawrence Inquiry Report, a report of the Home Affairs Committee of the House of Commons, and the European Committee for the Prevention of Torture and Inhuman or Degrading Treatment or Punishment.]

2 What does the 'local resolution' of a complaint against the police entail? ['Local resolution' involves the complaint being settled via mediation between the local police service and the complainant, and may involve a local officer investigating the circumstances surrounding the complaint.]

3 When was the Code of Ethics of the Police Service of Northern Ireland first established? [2003.]

4 Under the terms of the European Convention on Human Rights, what conditions need to be met if individual rights are to be set aside? [In the broader public interest, but only if the breach is necessary and proportionate.]

5 What did the Patten Commission into policing in Northern Ireland suggest was the main purpose of the police? [It is a central proposition of this report that the fundamental purpose of policing should be … the protection and vindication of the human rights of all.]

6 From which force did the Home Office second a senior officer to improve Nottinghamshire constabulary's performance in dealing with serious crime? [West Midlands Police.]

7 In what way has the focus of accountability been changed by the rise of managerialism? [This refocus is usually characterized as a transformation from a legal or public-interest model of accountability to one characterized by actuarialism and a managerialist ethos.]

8 Why did Shearing and Stenning suggest that concern about the role of private security had been marginalized in the United States, prior to the 1980s? [Questions about social justice and accountability had been marginalized by a conceptualization of the private sector as the junior partner to the public police.]

9 What is the primary requirement of the 2001 Private Security Industry Act? [The primary requirement introduced by the Act is that all personnel – officers, managers and directors of companies – be licensed.]

10 What concerns did Loader suggest are made more salient by the changing environment of international policing? [Questions about social justice, accountability, governance and legitimacy.]

_____ CHAPTER 7 **policing diversity** _____

1 Why has it been assumed, mistakenly, that concerns about police relations with minority ethnic communities have only developed in recent decades? [Because of a mythical view of the golden age of policing in the 1950s and 1960s. In fact, during that period there were problems of police racism, and these can be traced back much further.]

2 Which police service conducted the second investigation into the murder of Stephen Lawrence? [Kent Police.]

3 What police policy developments in the late 1980s were associated with developing a customer-focused service delivery model of policing? [The Metropolitan Police 'Plus Programme' and ACPO's Statement of Common Purpose and Values.]

4 What three factors did the Macpherson Report suggest had marred the investigation of the murder of Stephen Lawrence [Professional incompetence, institutional racism, and a failure of leadership.]

5 How was the traditional policing strategy used in response to racist incidents characterized? [Order maintenance.]

6 How many racist incidents did the British Crime Survey suggest occurred in 2004/05? [179,000.]

7   What legislative change, relating to racist incidents, was introduced by the 1998 Crime and Disorder Act? [Racially aggravated offences.]

8   What diverse populations were identified in a 2003 HMIC report? [Lesbian, gay or bisexual people; the deaf or hard of hearing; people with mental illness; gypsies/travellers; people with disabilities; victims of domestic violence; asylum seekers; young people; older people; transgender people; those involved in child protection issues; people from areas of poverty (the socially excluded).]

9   On what basis did Sir Ian Blair defend efforts to recruit a more diverse police workforce? [That there was a 'business case' to do so, not that it was a matter of 'political correctness'.]

10 What notion has been central to the concept of 'policing by consent'? [That the police officer is a 'citizen in uniform'.]

_____ CHAPTER 8 **plural policing** _____

1   What five dimensions of policing were outlined by Loader? [Policing by government; policing through government; policing above government; policing beyond government; policing below government.]

2   How many firms were members of the British Security Industry Association (BSIA) in 2005, and how many people did they employ? [Some 540 firms and 116,000 staff.]

3   How did Shearing and Stenning explain the growth of the private security sector? [In terms of the expansion of 'mass private property'.]

4   How might the notion of 'responsibilization' be defined in the context of private security? [Whereby the onus to provide for personal security is transferred from state to citizen.]

5   What body was established by the 2001 Private Security Industry Act to regulate the sector? [The Security Industry Authority.]

6   In what context did local housing authorities become involved in 'third party policing' in the 1980s? [To tackle racist harassment in public housing by the inclusion of clauses in tenancy agreements that made such behaviour grounds for eviction.]

7   What, according to Hughes, was the average age of those given antisocial behaviour orders? [16 years.]

8   How did Wakefield characterize police patrol work? ['The activity of visible patrolling could … be seen as the policing activity of choice for the citizen least troubled by crime'.]

9 For what reasons did Jones and Newburn argue that the pluralization thesis exaggerates the transition from the public policing model? [The state was never a monopoly provider; many agencies are only loosely engaged in 'multi-agency partnerships'; private sector discipline has not debunked the public sector ethos in public policing.]

10 Which occupations did Zedner suggest were eighteenth-century forerunners of the 'extended police family'? ['Thief takers', turnpike keepers, pawnbrokers, and inn-keepers.]

CHAPTER 9 **surveillance, IT and the future of policing**

1 What does the acronym HOLMES stand for? [Home Office Large Major Enquiry System: used to cross-reference and retrieve data collated in crime investigations.]

2 What percentage of the world's CCTV cameras is it estimated are deployed in Britain? [20 per cent.]

3 In relation to what three types of crime did police officers suggest CCTV was particularly effective? [Public order offences, assault, and theft.]

4 Against what sources of information do Thames Valley Police check information gathered via ANPR? [Police National Computer (PNC), Driver and Vehicle Licensing Agency (DVLA), Local Force Intelligence systems and motor insurers' databases.]

5 What percentage of the British population support, in general terms, the use of cameras to police speeding drivers? [75 per cent.]

6 What is Compstat? [Compstat is a police management tool that coordinates 'up-to-date computerized crime data, crime analysis, and advanced crime mapping as the bases for regularized, interactive crime strategy meetings which hold managers accountable for specific crime strategies and solutions in their areas' (Silverman, 2006; 268).]

7 In Britain in the 1960s Computer-Aided Dispatch systems were introduced in the development of what model of policing? [Unit Beat Policing.]

8 Who developed a model prison that enshrined the concept of the Panopticon? [Jeremy Bentham.]

9 To what broader social and political processes do Hudson (2003) and Loader (1999) relate the development of technology in policing? [Private prudentialism, consumer culture, and neo-liberalism.]

10 In which specific environment have CCTV cameras been introduced to monitor officer behaviour? [Custody suites.]

Glossary

Accountability: relating to the legal and regulatory systems that govern the police service. While the principle of operational independence means that the police service enforces the law without political interference, the priority and general direction of policing in Britain have been overseen by arrangements that combine local and central governance. More specifically, management and auditing procedures seek to hold individual police officers to account by scrutinizing their work in an effort to promote efficiency and effectiveness. Police officers are also held to account by complaints and disciplinary systems. The prospects of accountability in an era when the role of private security and plural policing is increasingly salient are much debated.

Antisocial behaviour: low-level persistent nuisance behaviour, not all of which is criminal, traditionally has not been a high priority for police services, even though it has been a significant problem in many communities. The 1998 Crime and Disorder Act introduced a raft of measures directed at behaviour defined broadly as that which 'caused or was likely to cause harassment, alarm or distress to one or more persons'. Key among these measures have been Anti-Social Behaviour Orders (ASBOs) that seek to regulate future conduct. Police or local authorities can apply for an ASBO in the magistrates' court. Although ASBOs are civil law provisions, breaching them is a criminal offence. Anti-Social Behaviour Contracts (ABCs) are a lower-level intervention that seeks to provide a framework whereby individuals or families are offered support in return for their commitment to improved conduct.

Arrest: there are various common law and statute provisions determining the circumstances in which a person can be arrested. Essentially these fall into two categories: those conducted under the terms of a court warrant and those carried out without warrant. The former category primarily applies to circumstances in which it is necessary to force an individual to be brought to court in connection with a suspected offence that has already been committed. Arrests without warrant can be implemented in a wide variety of circumstances, some of which rely upon specific legal measures that give police officers particular powers in identified circumstances. For example, public order legislation gives constables power to arrest those wearing political uniforms. Other powers are more generally defined, so that an officer can arrest in relation to 'serious arrestable offences'. More generally yet, citizens and police officers can arrest in the case of an actual or anticipated breach of the peace. Upon arrest an individual is told the grounds on which they are detained and cautioned. They must be taken to a designated police station as soon as is practicable.

Association of Chief Police Officers (ACPO):   representative body of senior police officers, all of or above the rank of Assistant Chief Constable or their equivalent in the Metropolitan Police. Originally established as a social network, ACPO has come to play an increasingly important role as a corporate voice for the police service. It now receives some of its funding from the Home Office and has a full-time president.

Association of Police Authorities (APA):   established in 1997, the Association represents the local police authorities that form one-third of the tripartite system of police accountability. The APA plays a role in research and policy development.

Basic Command Unit (BCU):   BCUs are responsible for tackling local crime and disorder problems, for working with local partners and for delivering neighbourhood policing. Previously BCUs would have been known as divisions or sub-divisions. Each is headed by a Chief Superintendent. In 2007, there were 288 BCUs beneath the 43 police services of England and Wales.

Black Police Association (BPA):   staff association and pressure group that seeks to represent the interests of black and Asian officers and staff. The first BPA was established as a relatively informal support network in the Metropolitan Police in the mid-1990s; since then, BPAs have been established in main police service areas and a National Black Police Association acts as an umbrella group and is an important voice in public debate about policing issues. The relations of the BPA and the Police Federation, the established staff association, have sometimes been fraught. The work of BPA has been supplemented by many other groups representing particular ethnic, cultural and religious minorities within the police.

British Association for Women in Policing (BAWP):   the Association was established in 1987 and represents women officers and police civilian staff of all ranks and all police services, including the eight Scottish forces, the Police Service of Northern Ireland, the British Transport Police and others. In 2001, the BAWP launched the 'gender agenda' that details aims relating to the service and conditions facing female staff and the broader cultural landscape that has marginalized the position of women in police.

Chief Constable: the senior officer of each of the 43 police services in England and Wales, the 8 in Scotland, and the Police Service of Northern Ireland. In terms of governance and accountability, Chief Constables have operational independence in law enforcement. Chief Constables are appointed by, and accountable to, local police authorities although both matters have been subject to increased scrutiny by the Home Office.

Civilianization: in an effort to dedicate police officers to operational roles, services have sought to employ civilian staff to perform duties previously allocated to constables. Initially civilian staff were used to perform 'backroom' administrative and support duties but the range of activities have extended to include, for example, scene of crime investigations, prisoner transport, and a host of training and human resource activities.

Closed-circuit television (CCTV): surveillance and monitoring systems that provide remote visual, and occasionally audio, images of public and private spaces. As technology has advanced, facial recognition and other software has enhanced the power of CCTV systems. A central component of situational crime prevention strategies, the impact on the detection and deterrence of criminal and disorderly behaviour has been widely heralded, even though the research evidence on the effects of CCTV often tends to be equivocal. It is frequently claimed that Britain has the highest ratio of CCTV cameras to population of any country in the world.

Commissioner: the senior officer of the Metropolitan Police, with broadly similar powers and responsibilities to Chief Constables in other police services.

Consent: the doctrine of 'policing by consent' has been influential, even though the police service has always had difficult relations with significant sections of society. The need for the police service to maintain public legitimacy has been a central ethical and democratic principle, and important in terms of effectiveness since the police service require the support and cooperation of the public.

Constable: the office of constable originated during Norman times. All officers enter the police service at the level of constable and, although some statutes give specialist powers to more senior ranks, most legislation confers powers generically to those who hold the office of constable, whatever their rank. These powers are also extended to special constables.

Consultation: the principle that the police ought to consult with local communities has been central to the notion of policing by consent. The Police and Criminal Evidence Act required the establishment of Police Community Consultative Groups, designed to provide a framework for the police to elicit views from local communities. The legislative requirement for the police to consult has been enhanced by the 1998 Crime and Disorder Act that created Crime and Disorder Reduction Partnerships that have to conduct, among other things, regular audits of crime and disorder problems in local areas.

Crime control model: the principle that the primary aim of the police service ought to be to prevent and detect crime. Originally outlined by Packer, this model of the criminal justice system prioritizes the police role in arresting offenders, gathering evidence and contributing to a quick and efficient conviction. The main purpose of the police is to suppress criminal behaviour, even if this means that officers might occasionally act outside of the law or disregard the rights of suspects (see also *due process model*).

Crown Prosecution Service (CPS): independent of the police, the CPS is responsible for the prosecution of offenders. Until the CPS was established in 1986, the police prosecuted offenders.

Discretion: the translation of the 'law in books' to the 'law on the street' requires police officers to interpret complex circumstances and make judgements about the most appropriate response – all of which entails the exercise of discretion. While it is inevitable and desirable that officers exercise discretion, considerable and sustained controversies surround the extent to which this is done so inappropriately on the basis of sexist, racist, homophobic or other forms of prejudice, stereotyping and bias. Measures to influence and limit officer discretion also stem from managerial imperatives to effectively deploy resources in an effort to achieve performance targets.

Due process model: this emphasizes the importance of police officers following rules and procedures to ensure that principles of justice and equity are fulfilled. Outlined by Packer, this model applies to the criminal justice system more generally. In terms of policing, it holds that the police need to ensure suspects' rights and interests are guaranteed in order that the courts can determine innocence or guilt (see also *crime control model*).

Ethics: in policing terms, references to 'ethics' usually indicate that the service needs to recognize its broader social responsibilities. Officers are encouraged to consider the implications of their actions, beyond their responsibilities in terms of law enforcement, and the wider social and cultural context in which they exercise their powers. Codes of ethical behaviour differ from more traditional disciplinary frameworks in that they rarely proscribe behaviour considered unacceptable but instead outline normative ideals to which officers ought to aspire.

'Extended police family': a phrase developed with the police reform agenda in England and Wales in the past decade or so, it recognizes that traditional policing activities are increasingly provided by a mixture of sworn constables, Police Community Support Officers, Neighbourhood Wardens, traffic wardens, and other public and private sector agencies.

Gay Police Association (GPA): formed as the Lesbian and Gay Police Association in 1990, the GPA represents the interests of officers and staff from all sectors of the British police service. The GPA provides specific advice and support to individual members as well as acting as a pressure group within public and policy debates about general policing matters as well as more specific issues such as hate crime.

Her Majesty's Inspectorate of Constabulary (HMIC): the first inspectors of constabulary were appointed following the 1856 County and Borough Police Act. The HMIC is a Crown agency, although in practice it reports to the Home Office. The HMIC conducts inspections of the performance of all Basic Command Units as well as 'thematic' inspections that review generic matters of importance to the police service.

'Hot spots' policing: a method of organizing the deployment of police resources that recognizes that crime and disorder tend to be concentrated in certain places and occur at certain times. By using computer-aided mapping systems, police managers can make more effective use of resources, although this might mean that less-directed patrol work, popular with the public, is marginalized.

Human rights: issues relating to human rights apply to policing in two broad ways. Specifically, human rights legislation that defines relations between state and citizens has significant implications for the police service, variously described as the 'state in uniform' and the 'citizen in uniform'. For example, the human right to personal privacy shapes the circumstances in which police officers can conduct surveillance operations. More generally, domestically and internationally policing has been increasingly connected with promoting and securing human rights through ensuring the rule of law and good governance.

'Intelligence-led' policing: a model of policing that promotes effectiveness and efficiency through collecting, collating and analysing information relating to crime. Patterns and trends are examined so that police can intervene in ways that will have the most impact on offenders. Intelligence-led approaches are relatively pro-active and interventionist in contrast to more traditional reactive or 'fire-brigade' styles whereby the service responds to demands from the public.

Macpherson Report: published in 1999, the Report into the racist murder of Stephen Lawrence continues to exercise a huge influence on debates about British policing. The Report found that the police service was 'institutionally racist', and a host of policy, training, investigatory, and victim-service developments have followed in its wake. The Report also found major weaknesses in the police investigation that related to the management of the investigation, the preservation of the scene, the gathering of evidence, and other shortcomings that prevented the police from bringing the murderers to justice.

Multi-agency partnerships: a broader range of public sector agencies have assumed a role in crime prevention and community safety in recent years. A locally coordinated multi-agency approach to crime prevention had been advocated for many years before the 1998 Crime and Disorder Act placed Crime and Disorder Reduction Partnerships on a statutory footing. The inclusion of housing, education, health, fire service and other agencies from the public, private and voluntary sectors has removed the police's former pre-eminence in crime prevention, although it is often suggested they remain dominant partners amid these networks.

National Policing Improvement Agency (NPIA): established by the Police and Justice Act 2006, the NPIA became operational on 1 April 2007. The NPIA role is to spread good practice in policing, to provide expert advice to individual police services in operational and other matters (including IT, procurement, and training), and to develop international understanding of policing issues. Many units and agencies previously providing national support to the police service have been subsumed into the NPIA, such as Centrex (the police training organization) and the Police Information Technology Organisation.

Neighbourhood Policing: the devolution of policing to the level of particular neighbourhoods (coterminous with political wards) has been an important contemporary political priority. It is intended that the establishment of Neighbourhood Policing will reinvigorate contacts between local people and police officers, enhance accountability, and improve public confidence in the police service.

Organizational sub-culture: studies suggest that police work is characterized by a particular organizational sub-culture and that this can exercise a negative influence on routine policing. The disproportionate exercise of police powers is among the problems often ascribed to the nature of police sub-culture – sometimes referred to as 'canteen culture' in reference to the unofficial and informal context in which it develops. The concept has been criticized for being overly determinist and for failing to recognize the institutional context in which police officers operate.

Plural policing: while policing has never been the sole preserve of the public police service, increasing attention is paid to the proliferation and range of those who regulate social behaviour. The private security industry pre-dates the public police but the concept of plural policing reflects the wider development of 'third party' policing whereby agencies such as banks, schools, and insurance companies are made responsible for regulating and reporting on aspects of their clients' behaviour. Not only does plural policing mean new constellations of agencies, it also changes principles of policing, raising questions of legitimacy, justice and equity. Pluralization also means that policing is a property that emerges from relations and networks, rather than being the output of a particular institution (see also *private security)*.

Police and Criminal Evidence Act (PACE) 1984:   the central piece of legislation that governs the powers of the police in relation to citizens. PACE outlines the circumstances in which officers can stop and search people, search premises, seize evidence, enter premises, effect arrests and detain suspects. PACE also governs the rights of suspects, including the circumstances in which they are remanded or bailed, and the interview process.

Police and policing: the distinction between police and policing differentiates between the relatively narrow range of activities conducted by the police service and broader processes of social regulation performed more widely by a diverse range of agencies and actors. As an increasing range of public, private and civil sector organizations become involved in law enforcement, crime prevention, and community safety, policing in these broader terms has become more salient.

Police Community Support Officers (PCSOs):   auxiliary police staff who do not hold the full powers of constables but provide a visible police patrol presence. The role of the PCSO was created by the 2001 Police Reform Act and has been a major feature of the 'extended police family'. The Home Office set a target of employing 24,000 PCSOs by 2008. A framework of powers available to PCSOs is determined by the Home Office, but individual Chief Constables decide which will apply to staff in each police service area.

Police Federation: the organization that represents all officers up to and including the rank of Chief Inspector. In addition to making it illegal for police officers to strike, the 1920 Police Act created the Federation to represent the interests of frontline staff in respect of welfare, and the terms and conditions of employment. In more general terms, the Police Federation continues to be a powerful influence on the development of policing.

Police reform: the Labour Government has pursued a programme of police reform, some of which was developed by previous Conservative administrations.

The reform agenda has focused upon workforce modernization, such as the introduction of Police Community Support Officers, and measures to raise performance standards by developing a national policing plan under the auspices of the Police Standards Unit within the Home Office. These measures were introduced in the 2002 Police Reform Act.

Police service: a wide variety of police services operate in Britain. Much discussion of policing refers to 'Home Office' police services: the 43 English and Welsh services, the 8 in Scotland, and the Police Service of Northern Ireland. These constabularies are supplemented by many other specialist services that are governed and operated under other arrangements, including the British Transport Police that works on railways and transport networks, the Ministry of Defence Police that operates on UK military bases domestically and abroad, and the Royal Parks Police that patrols a small number of parks owned by the Crown.

Police Superintendents' Association: as policing has become devolved to local BCUs, the role of Superintendent has become increasingly important. The Superintendents' Association was formed in the 1950s and incorporates officers from each of the 43 services in England and Wales as well as the British Transport Police. The Association has some 1500 members.

Private security: although analysis of policing has tended to concentrate upon the role of the public-sector police, private companies have played an important role in crime prevention and control work for many decades. Reliable estimates of the size and scope of the private security industry are difficult to come by but studies tend to suggest that it is comparable, in terms of the number of staff employed in the sector, with the public police service. In an era when the development of plural policing and the 'extended police family' are high on political and policy agendas, the role of the private sector has come under increasing scrutiny (see also *plural policing*).

Problem-Oriented Policing (POP): a model of policing that encourages officers to address underlying dynamics of crime and antisocial behaviour rather than simply respond to incidents as they arise. A creative approach to resolving problems in partnership with other agencies is required by POP, which relies, partly, on mapping and analysing local crime patterns. Research suggests there are often tensions between the principles of POP and the need for police services to respond to demands for assistance from the public.

Rank structure: all police officers begin their careers at the lowest rank of constable, which means that all senior officers have served some time on the 'front line'. Ascending up the hierarchy are ranks of Sergeant, Inspector (and sometimes Chief Inspector), Superintendent (and sometimes Chief Superintendent), Assistant Chief Constable, Deputy Chief Constable, and Chief Constable. Above the rank of superintendent the position is somewhat different in the Metropolitan Police, where the senior ranks are Commander, Deputy Assistant Commissioner, Assistant Commissioner, Deputy Commissioner and Commissioner.

Reassurance policing: although crime levels have broadly fallen since the mid-1990s, public concern about crime and antisocial behaviour has not abated. In response to this 'reassurance gap', the police service, and partnership agencies, have become focused on tackling 'signal crimes', low-level offences that have a negative impact on perceptions of security. With an emphasis on consultation with the public, reassurance policing aims to provide high-visibility patrols in an effort to promote community safety.

Service role: although less high profile than crime-fighting and law enforcement, much police work is characterized in more diffuse terms of service provision. Dealing with missing persons, directing traffic, and assisting other emergency services do not directly relate to law enforcement or crime control, but account for a significant proportion of police work. The first Commissioners of the Metropolitan Police emphasized the 'service' role of the New Police in an effort to court public support and it has continued to be regarded as an important source of legitimacy.

Special constables: volunteer officers who contribute to a wide range of policing activities on a part-time basis. The role of Special Constable pre-dates modern professional policing; the current framework governing their work was established by the 1831 Special Constables Act. Special Constables have the same legal powers as other constables. In 2002, there were 11,598 'specials' in England and Wales, a total that seems to be declining as the number of Police Community Support Officers increases.

Use of force: while police officers are allowed, in general terms, to use a reasonable degree of force in the exercise of their duties, it is often held that the doctrine of the 'minimal use of force' has been central to securing the legitimacy of the British police. While frequently thought of as an unarmed police force, specialist units providing firearms support are commonly on patrol, and the range of 'less-than-lethal' weapons available to officers has increased as CS spray and 'tasers' have been deployed.

Visible patrols: as police work became professionalized and reorganized from the late 1960s onward, routine foot patrol became marginalized within police work. Although crime levels have fallen, in broad terms, since the mid-1990s, public concern about crime and disorder has not abated. Increasing the visible presence of officers on patrol has become central to efforts to provide reassurance. Non-sworn Police Community Support Officers were introduced as a dedicated cadre of patrol officers and other some local authorities provide neighbourhood wardens to fulfil similar purposes.

Zero-tolerance Policing (ZTP): usually associated with a proactive and aggressive policing strategy that prioritizes intervention against relatively minor offences in order that more serious criminal activity is pre-empted. As well as preventing small problems escalating, ZTP claims to reassure the public by providing a substantial police presence on the streets. While proponents have often claimed that ZTP successfully reduced the crime problem in New York City in the 1990s, critics maintain it has a deleterious effect on relations with marginalized communities.

References

ACPO (2003) *Police Membership of the British National Party*, press release ref: 56/03, London: ACPO.

Adorno, T.W., Frenkel-Brunswick, E., Levinson, D.J. and Sanford, R.N. (1950) *The Authoritarian Personality*, New York: Harper and Row.

Alderson, J. (1979) *Policing Freedom*, Plymouth: Macdonald and Evans.

Alderson, J. (1984) *Law and Disorder*, London: Hamish Hamilton.

Ascoli, D. (1979) *The Queen's Peace: The Origins and Development of the Metropolitan Police, 1829–1979*, London: Hamish Hamilton.

Association of Chief Police Officers (2000) *Policing Diversity*, London: ACPO.

Association of Police Authorities (2005) *Police Authorities Reject Restructuring Deadline*, London: Association of Police Authorities.

Bailey, V. (ed.) (1981) *Policing and Punishment in Nineteenth Century Britain*, London: Croom Helm.

Baker, D. (2006) *Forms of Exclusion: Racism and Community Policing in Canada*, Oshawa, Ontario: De Sitter.

Balch, R.W. (1972) 'The Police Personality: Fact or Fiction?', *The Journal of Criminal Law, Criminology, and Police Science*, 63(1): 106–19.

Banton, M. (1964) *The Policeman in the Community*, London: Tavistock Publications.

Barlow, D. and Barlow, M. (2001) *Police in a Multicultural Community: An American Story*, Illinois: Waveland Press.

Barry, N.P. (1981) *An Introduction to Modern Political Theory*, London: Macmillan.

Bauman, Z. (2000) *Community: Seeking Safety in an Insecure World*, Cambridge: Polity Press.

Baxter, J. and Koffman, L. (1985) *Police: the Constitution and the Community: A Collection of Original Essays on Issues Raised by the Police and Criminal Evidence Act 1984*, London: Professional Books.

Bayley, D. (1985) *Patterns of Policing*, Princeton, NJ: Princeton University Press.

Bayley, D. (1994) *Police for the Future*, New York: Oxford University Press.

Bayley, D. and Shearing, C. (2001) *The New Structure of Policing: Description, Conceptualization, and Research Agenda*, Washington, DC: National Institute of Justice.

BBC (2006a) 'Feeling Whose Collars', *Analysis*, BBC Radio 4, 2 March.

BBC (2006b) *Who Killed My Brother?*, BBC 2, 12 May.

BBC (2007) 'Police Chief's "Orwellian" Fears', 20 May, http://news.bbc.co.uk/2/hi/uk_news/6673579.stm

Beck, A. and Chistyakova, J. (2004) 'Closing the Gap Between the Police and the Public in Post-Soviet Ukraine: A Bridge Too Far?', *Police Practice and Research*, 5(1): 43–65.

Beck, A. and Willis, A. (1995) *Crime and Security: Managing the Risk to Safe Shopping*, Leicester: Perpetuity Press.

Bennett T. (1990) *Evaluating Neighbourhood Watch*, Aldershot: Gower.

Bibi, N., Clegg, M. and Pinto, R. (2005) *Police Service Strength: England and Wales, 31 March 2005*, London: Home Office.

Bittner, E. (1974) 'Florence Nightingale in Pursuit of Willie Sutton: A Theory of the Police', in Jacob, H. (ed.) *The Potential for Reform of Criminal Justice*, Beverly Hills: Sage Publications, pp. 17–40.

Blair, I. (2005) 'What Kind of Police Service Do We Want?', The Dimbleby Lecture, BBC 1, 16 November.

Bourdieu, P. (1991) *Language and Symbolic Power*, Cambridge: Polity Press.

Bowling, B. (1998) *Violent Racism: Victimization, Policing and Social Context*, Oxford: Oxford University Press.

Bowling, B. (1999) 'The Rise and Fall of New York Murder: Zero Tolerance or Crack's Decline?', *British Journal of Criminology*, 39(4): 531–55.

Bowling, B. and Foster, J. (2002) 'Policing and the Police', in Morgan, R., Maguire, M. and Reiner, R. (eds) *The Oxford Handbook of Criminology*, Oxford: Oxford University Press.

Brogden, M. (1982) *The Police: Autonomy and Consent*, London: Academic Press.

Brogden, M. (1999) 'Community Policing as Cherry Pie', in Mawby, R.I. *Policing Across the World: Issues for the Twenty-First Century*, London: UCL Press, pp. 167–86.

Brogden, M. and Nijhar, P. (2005) *Community Policing: National and International Models and Approaches*, Cullompton: Willan Publishing.

Brown, J. and Heidensohn, F. (2000) *Gender and Policing: Comparative Perspectives*, London: Macmillan.

Burke, M. (1993) *Coming Out of the Blue*, London: Cassell.

Burke, M. (1994) 'Homosexuality as Deviance: The Case of the Gay Police Officer', *British Journal of Criminology*, 34(2): 192–203.

Butt, R. (2006) 'Police Officers Disciplined for Email Showing Decapitation', 29 November, *Guardian*.

Button, M. (2002) *Private Policing*, Cullompton: Willan Publishing.

Cain, M. (1973) *Society and the Policeman's Role*, London: Routledge and Kegan Paul.

Caldeira, P.R. (2000) *City of Walls: Crime, Segregation and Citizenship in São Paulo*, Berkeley, CA: University of California Press.

Carswell, S. (2006) *Family Violence and the Pro-arrest Policy: A Literature Review*, Wellington: Ministry of Justice.

Cashmore, E. (2000) 'Behind the Window Dressing: Ethnic Minority Police Perspectives on Cultural Diversity', *Journal of Ethnic and Migration Studies*, 28(2): 327–41.

Cashmore, E. (2002) *The Experience of Ethnic Minority Police Officers: Final Report*, Staffordshire: Staffordshire University.

Cashmore, E. and McLaughlin, E. (eds) (1991) *Out of Order: Policing Black People*, London: Routledge.

Cassels, J. (1996) *The Role and Responsibilities of the Police*, London: Police Foundation and Policy Studies Institute.

Chakraborti, N. and Garland, J. (eds) (2004) *Rural Racism: Contemporary Debates and Perspectives*, Cullompton: Willan Publishing.

Chan, J. (1997) *Changing Police Culture: Policing in a Multiracial Society*, Cambridge: Cambridge University Press.

Chan, J. (1999) 'Governing Police Practice: Limits of the New Accountability', *British Journal of Sociology*, 50(2): 251–70.

Chan, J. (2001) 'The Technological Game: How Information Technology is Transforming Police Practice', *Criminal Justice*, 1(2): 139–59.

Chan, J. (2003) 'Policing and New Technologies', in Newburn, T. (ed.) *Handbook of Policing*, Cullompton: Willan Publishing, pp. 655–79.

Channel 4 (2006) 'Undercover Copper', *Dispatches*, 27 April.

Chibnall, S. (1977) *Law and Order News*, London: Tavistock.

Clapton, R. (2004) 'Keeping Order: Motor-Car Regulation and the Defeat of Victoria's 1905 Motor-Car Bill', *Provenance: The Journal of Public Record Office Victoria*, no. 3.

Cohen, P. (1979) 'Policing the Working Class City', in Fine, B., Kinsey, R., Lea, J., Picciotto, S. and Young, J. (eds) *Capitalism and the Rule of Law*, London: Hutchinson.

Cohen, S. (1985) *Visions of Social Control: Crime, Punishment, and Classification*, Cambridge: Polity Press.

Coleman, R. (2005) *Reclaiming the Streets: Surveillance, Social Control and the City*, Cullompton: Willan Publishing.

Coleman, R., Tombs, S. and Whyte, D. (2005) 'Capital, Crime Control and Statecraft in the Entrepreneurial City', *Urban Studies*, 42(13): 2511–30.

Colls, R. (2002) *Identity of England*, Oxford: Oxford University Press.

Colman, A. and Gorman, P. (1982) 'Conservatism, Dogmatism and Authoritarianism in British Police Officers', *Sociology*, 16(1): 1–26.

Corbett, C. (2000) 'The Social Construction of Speeding as Not "Real" Crime', *Crime Prevention and Community Safety: An International Journal*, 2(4): 33–46.

Corbett, C. and Caramlau, L. (2006) 'Gender Differences in Responses to Speed Cameras: Typology Findings and Implications for Road Safety', *Criminology and Criminal Justice*, 6(4): 411–33.

Crawford, A. (2003) 'The Pattern of Policing in the UK: Policing Beyond the Police', in Newburn, T. (ed.) *Handbook of Policing*, Cullompton: Willan Publishing, pp.136–68.

Crawford, A. (2006) '"Fixing Broken Promises?": Neighbourhood Wardens and Social Capital', *Urban Studies*, 43(5/6): 957–76.

Crawford, A. and Lister, S. (2006) 'Additional Security Patrols in Residential Areas: Notes from the Marketplace', *Policing and Society*, 16(4): 164–88.

Crawford, A., Lister, S. and Wall, D. (2003) *Great Expectations: Contracted Community Policing in New Earswick*, York: Joseph Rowntree Foundation.

Crawshaw, R., Devlin, B. and Wiliamson, T. (1998) *Human Rights and Policing: Standards for Good Behaviour and a Strategy for Change*, The Hague: Kluwer Law International.

Critchley, T. A. (1978) *A History of Police in England and Wales*, 2nd edn, London: Constable.

Cunneen, C. (2001) *Conflict, Politics and Crime: Aboriginal Communities and the Police in Australia*, Crows Nest, NSW: Allen and Unwin.

Daily Telegraph (2005) 'We Want Answers, Not Questions', 19 November, p. 24.

Davis, M. (1990) *City of Quartz: Excavating the Future in Los Angeles*, London: Verso.

Dhalech, M. (1999) *Challenging Racism in the Rural Idyll*, London: National Association of Citizens Advice Bureaux.

Dixon, B. and Smith, G. (1998) 'Laying Down the Law: The Police, the Courts and Legal Accountability', *International Journal of the Sociology of Law*, 26: 419–35.

Dixon, D. (1997) *Law in Policing*, Oxford: Oxford University Press.

Doran, A.J. (ed.) (1990) *The Punch Cartoon Album: 150 Years of Classic Cartoons*, London: Grafton.

Dunning, E., Murphy, P., Newburn, T., and Waddington, I. (1987) 'Violent Disorders in Twentieth Century Britain', in Gaskell, G. and Benewick, R. (eds) *The Crowd in Contemporary Britain*, London: Sage, pp. 19–75.

Eck, J.E. and Rosenbaum, D.P. (1994/2000) 'The New Police Order: Effectiveness, Equity and Efficiency in Community Policing', in Glensor, R.W., Correia, M.E. and Peak, K.J. (eds)

Policing Communities: Understanding Crime and Solving Problems – an Anthology, Los Angeles: Roxbury Publishing Company, pp. 30–45.

Edwards, A. (2002) 'Learning from Diversity: The Strategic Dilemmas of Community-Based Crime Control', in Hughes, G. and Edwards, A. (eds) *Crime Control and Community: the New Politics of Public Safety*, Cullompton: Willan Publishing, pp. 140–66.

Edwards, A. and Hughes, G. (eds) (2002) *Crime Control: the New Politics of Public Safety*, Cullompton: Willan Publishing.

Ekblom, P. (1986) 'Community Policing: Obstacles and Issues', in Willmott, P. (ed.) *The Debate about Community: Papers from a Seminar on Community in Social Policy*, PSI Discussion Paper 13, London: Policy Studies Institute.

Emsley, C. (1996) *The English Police: A Political and Social History*, 2nd edn, Longman: Harlow.

Emsley, C. (2003) 'The Birth and Development of the Police', in Newburn, T. (ed.) *Handbook of Policing*, Cullompton: Willan Publishing, pp. 66–83.

English, J. and Card, R. (2005) *Police Law*, 9th edn, Oxford: Oxford University Press.

Ericson, R. and Haggerty, K. (1997) *Policing the Risk Society*, Oxford: Clarendon Press.

Evans, R. and Mostrous, A. (2006) 'Spy Planes, Clothes Scanners and Secret Cameras: Britain's Surveillance Future', *Guardian*, 2 November.

Fielding, N. (1988) *Joining Forces: Police Training, Socialization and Occupational Competence*, London: Routledge.

Fielding, N. (2005) *The Police and Social Conflict,* 2nd edn, London: Glasshouse Press.

Fitzgerald, M. (2000) *Final Report into Stop and Search*, London: Metropolitan Police.

Fitzgerald, M. and Sibbit, R. (1997) *Ethnic Monitoring in Police Forces: A Beginning*, Home Office Research Study 173, London: Home Office.

Fleming, J. (2005) *'Working Together': Neighbourhood Watch, Reassurance Policing and the Potential of Partnerships*, Canberra: Australian Institute of Criminology.

Forbes, D. (1988) *Action on Racial Harassment: Legal Remedies and Local Authorities*, London: London Housing Unit and Legal Action Group.

Foster, J., Newburn, T. and Souhami, A. (2005) *Assessing the Impact of the Stephen Lawrence Inquiry*, Home Office Research Study 294, London: Home Office.

Foucault, M. (1977) *Discipline and Punish: The Birth of the Prison*, New York: Pantheon Books.

Foucault, M. (1981) *The History of Sexuality*, Harmondsworth: Penguin.

Friedman, W. (1994) 'The Community Role in Community Policing', in Rosenbaum, D.P. (ed.) *The Challenge of Community Policing: Testing the Promises*, London: Sage Publications, pp.263–9.

Fryer, P. (1984) *Staying Power: The History of Black People in Britain*, London: Pluto Press.

Garland, D. (2001) *The Culture of Control: Crime and Social Order in Contemporary Society*, Oxford: Oxford University Press.

Garland, J. and Rowe, M. (1999) 'Policing Racism at Football Matches: An Assessment of Recent Developments', *International Journal of the Sociology of Law*, 27: 251–66.

George, B. and Button, M. (1997) 'Private Security Industry Regulation: Lessons from Abroad for the United Kingdom', *International Journal of Risk, Security and Crime Prevention*, 2: 187–200.

George, B. and Button, M. (2000) *Private Security*, Leicester: Perpetuity Press.

Giddens, A. (1990) *The Consequences of Modernity*, Cambridge: Polity Press.

Gill, M. and Spriggs, A. (2005) *Assessing the Impact of CCTV*, Home Office Research Study 292, London: Home Office.

Goldstein, H. (1990) *Problem-Oriented Policing*, Philadelphia, PA: Temple University Press.

Goold, B. (2004) *CCTV and Policing: Public Area Surveillance and Police Practices in Britain*, Oxford: Oxford University Press.

Gordon, P. (1990) *Racial Violence and Harassment*, London: Runnymede Trust.

Greaves, G. (1984) 'The Brixton Disorders', in Benyon, J. (ed.) *Scarman and After: Essays Reflecting on Lord Scarman's Report, the Riots and their Aftermath*, Oxford: Pergamon Press, pp. 63–72.

Guardian (2005) 'Constable Suspended "after Racist Tirade Caught on Mobile"', 19 May.

Guardian (2007) 'Race Row Met Officer Cleared', *Guardian*, 31 January.

Hague, W. (2000) 'Where Was Jack Straw When Damilola Died?', *Sunday Telegraph*, 17 December.

Hall, N. (2005) *Hate Crime*, Cullompton: Willan Publishing.

Hansard (2005) *Parliamentary Debates*, 9 November; vol. 439, column 297.

Hansard (2006) *House of Lords Debates*, 20 June vol. 683, column 668.

Harrison, J. and Cuneen, M. (2000) *An Independent Police Complaints Commission*, London: Liberty.

Hay, D. (1975) 'Property, Authority and the Criminal Law', in Hay, D., Linebaugh, P., Winslow, C., Rule, J. and Thompson, E.P. (eds) *Albion's Fatal Tree: Crime and Society in Eighteenth Century England*, London: Penguin, pp. 17–63.

Heidensohn, F. (1992) *Women in Control? The Role of Women in Law Enforcement*, Oxford: Clarendon Press.

Her Majesty's Inspectorate of Constabulary (1997) *Winning the Race: Embracing Diversity*, London: Home Office.

Her Majesty's Inspectorate of Constabulary (2001) *Open All Hours: A Thematic Inspection Report on the Role of Police Visibility and Accessibility in Public Reassurance*, London: Home Office.

Her Majesty's Inspectorate of Constabulary (2003) *Diversity Matters*, London: Home Office.

Her Majesty's Inspectorate of Constabulary (2005) *Closing the Gap: A Review of 'Fitness for Purpose' of the Current Structure of Policing in England and Wales*, London: Home Office.

Hesse, B., Rai, D.K., Bennett, C. and McGilchrist, P. (1992) *Beneath the Surface: Racial Harassment*, Aldershot: Avebury.

Hills, A. (2000) *Policing Africa: Internal Security and the Limits of Liberalization*, Boulder, CO: Lynne Rienner.

Home Office (1991) *Safer Communities: The Local Delivery of Crime Prevention through the Partnership Approach*, London: Home Office.

Home Office (1998) *Introductory Guide to the Crime and Disorder Act*, London: Home Office.

Home Office (2000) *A Guide to the Criminal Justice System in England and Wales*, London: Home Office.

Home Office (2005a) *Guidance on the Handling of Complaints Relating to the Direction and Control of a Police Force by a Chief Officer,* Home Office Circular 19/2005, London: Home Office.

Home Office (2005b) *Neighbourhood Policing: Your Police; Your Community; Our Commitment*, London: Home Office.

Home Office (2006a) *Neighbourhood Policing: Progress Report*, London: Home Office.

Home Office (2006b) *Oral Statement by the Home Secretary, Dr John Reid, on Rebalancing the Criminal Justice System – 20 July 2006*, London: Home Office.

Home Office (2006c) *Statistics on Race and the Criminal Justice System 2005*, London: Home Office.

Home Office (2006d) *Race and the Criminal Justice System: An Overview to the Complete Statistics, 2004–05*, London: Home Office.

Home Office (2006e) *The National Police Improvement Agency: Regulatory Assessment Impact*, London: Home Office.

Home Office (2007) *Neighbourhood Policing*, http://www.homeoffice.gov.uk/

House of Commons Transport Committee (2006) *Roads Policing and Technology: Getting the Right Balance, Tenth Report of Session 2005–06*, London: House of Commons.

Hudson, B. (2003) *Justice in the Risk Society: Challenging and Re-affirming Justice in Late Modernity*, London: Sage.

Hughes, G. (2007) *The Politics of Crime and Community*, London: Palgrave.

Hughes, G. and Rowe, M. (2007) 'Neighbourhood Policing and Community Safety: Researching the Instabilities of the Local Governance of Crime, Disorder and Security in Contemporary UK', *Criminology and Criminal Justice*, 7(4): 317–46.

Independent Commission on Policing for Northern Ireland (1999) *A New Beginning: Policing in Northern Ireland*, Belfast: Northern Ireland Office.

Independent Police Complaints Commission (2006) *Police Complaints: Statistics for England and Wales 2005/06*, London: IPCC.

Independent Police Complaints Commission (2007) *Public Perceptions of the Police Complaints System*, London: IPCC.

Innes, M. (2003) *Investigating Murder: Detective Work and the Police Response to Criminal Homicide*, Oxford: Oxford University Press.

Innes, M. (2004) 'Reinventing Tradition? Reassurance, Neighbourhood Security and Policing', *Criminal Justice*, 4(2): 151–71.

Jason-Lloyd, L. (2005) *An Introduction to Policing and Police Powers*, 2nd edn, London: Cavendish Publishing Limited.

Jefferson, T. and Grimshaw, R. (1984) *Controlling the Constable: Police Accountability in England and Wales*, London: Methuen.

Jewkes, Y. (2004) *Media and Crime*, London: Sage.

Johnston, L. (1992) *The Rebirth of Private Policing*, London: Routledge.

Johnston, L. (2000) *Policing Britain: Risk, Security and Governance*, London: Longman.

Johnston, L. (2006) 'Diversifying Police Recruitment? The Deployment of Police Community Support Officers in London', *The Howard Journal*, 45(4): 388–402.

Johnston, L. and Shearing, C. (2003) *Governing Security: Explorations in Policing and Justice*, London: Routledge.

Jones, T. and Newburn, T. (1998) *Private Security and Public Policing*, Oxford: Clarendon Press.

Jones, T. and Newburn, T. (2001) *Widening Access: Improving Police Relations with Hard to Reach Groups*, Police Research Series Paper 138, London: Home Office.

Jones, T. and Newburn, T. (2002) 'The Transformation of Policing?', *British Journal of Criminology*, 42(1): 129–46.

Jordan, J. (2002) 'Will Any Woman Do?: Police, Gender and Rape Victims', *Policing: An International Journal of Police Strategies and Management*, 25(2): 319–44.

Jordan, J. (2004) *The Word of a Woman? Police, Rape and Belief*, London: Palgrave.

Judge, A. (1986) 'The Provisions in Practice', in Benyon, J. and Bourn, C. (eds) *Police: Powers, Proprieties and Procedures*, Oxford: Pergamon Press, pp. 175–82.

Keith, M. (1988) 'Squaring the Circles? Consultation and Inner-City Policing', *New Community*, 15(1): 63–77.

Keith, M. (1993) *Race, Riots, and Policing: Lore and Disorder in a Multiracial Society*, London: Macmillan.

Kempa, M. and Johnston, L. (2005) 'Inclusive Plural Policing in Britain', *Australian and New Zealand Journal of Criminology*, 38(2): 181–91.

Klockars, C. (1985) *The Idea of Police*, Beverly Hills: Sage Publications.

Koffman, L. (1985) 'Safeguarding the Rights of the Citizen', in Baxter, J. and Koffman, L. (eds) *Police: the Constitution and the Community: a Collection of Original Essays on*

Issues Raised by the Police and Criminal Evidence Act 1984, London: Professional Books, pp. 11–37.

Landman, K. and Schönteich, M. (2002) 'Urban Fortresses: Gated Communities as a Reaction to Crime', *African Security Review,* 11(4): 71–85.

Laville, S. and Muir, H. (2006) 'Secret Report Brands Muslim Police Corrupt', *Guardian*, 10 June.

Lea, J. (2000) 'The Macpherson Report and the Question of Institutional Racism', *Howard Journal of Criminal Justice*, 39(3): 219–33.

Lea, J. (2003) 'Institutional Racism in Policing: The Macpherson Report and its Consequences', in Matthews, R. and Young, J. (eds) *The New Politics of Crime and Punishment*, Cullompton: Willan Publishing.

Lea, J. and Young, J. (1993) *What Is to Be Done about Law and Order?*, London: Pluto Press.

Lee, M. (2007) *Inventing Fear of Crime*, Cullompton: Willan Publishing.

Lee, W.L. Melville (1901) *A History of Police in England*, London: Methuen.

Leigh, A., Read, T. and Tilley, N. (1996) *Problem Oriented Policing: Brit Pop*, Crime Detection and Prevention Series Paper 75, London: Home Office.

Leigh, L.H. (1985) *Police Powers in England and Wales*, London: Butterworth.

Levesley, T. and Martin, A. (2005) *Police Attitudes to and Use of CCTV*, Home Office On-line Report 09/05, London: Home Office.

Loader, I. (1997) 'Policing and the Social: Questions of Symbolic Power', *British Journal of Sociology*, 48(1): 1–18.

Loader, I. (1999) 'Consumer Culture and the Commodification of Policing and Security', *Sociology*, 33: 373–92.

Loader, I. (2000) 'Plural Policing and Democratic Governance', *Socio-Legal Studies*, 9(3): 323–45.

Loader, I. and Mulcahy, A. (2001a) 'The Power of Legitimate Naming: Part I Chief Constables as Social Commentators in Post-War England', *British Journal of Criminology*, 41: 41–55.

Loader, I. and Mulcahy, A. (2001b) 'The Power of Legitimate Naming: Part II Making Sense of the Elite Police Voice', *British Journal of Criminology*, 41: 42–65.

Loader, I. and Mulcahy, A. (2003) *Policing and the Condition of England: Memory, Politics and Culture*, Oxford: Oxford University Press.

Loveday, B. (2005) 'The Challenge of Police Reform in England and Wales', *Public Money and Management*, 25(5): 275–81.

Lukes, S. (1974) *Power: A Radical View*, London: Macmillan.

Macpherson, Sir W. (1999) *The Stephen Lawrence Inquiry: Report of an Inquiry by Sir William Macpherson of Cluny*, CM 4262–1, London: HMSO.

Manning, P.K. (1992) 'Information Technologies and the Police', in Tonry, M. and Morris, N. (eds) *Modern Policing: Crime and Justice, a Review of the Research,* vol. 15, Chicago: University of Chicago Press. pp. 349–98.

Manning, P.K. (1996) 'Information Technology in the Police Context: the "Sailor" Phone', *Information Systems Research*, 7(1): 52–62.

Marlow, J. (1971) *The Peterloo Massacre*, London: Panther.

Marx, G.T. (1988) *Undercover: Police Surveillance in America*, Berkeley, CA: University of California Press.

Mawby, R.I. (1999) *Policing Across the World: Issues for the Twenty-First Century*, London: UCL Press.

Mawby, R.I. (2003a) 'Competing the "Half-Formed Picture"? Media Images of Policing', in Mason, P. (ed.) *Criminal Visions: Media Representations of Crime and Justice*, Cullompton: Willan Publishing, pp. 214–37.

Mawby, R.I. (2003b) 'Models of Policing', in Newburn, T. (ed.) *Handbook of Policing*, Cullompton: Willan Publishing, pp. 15–40.

Mazerolle, L. and Ransely, J. (2005) *Third Party Policing*, Cambridge: Cambridge University Press.

McEvoy, K. and Mika, H. (2002) 'Restorative Justice and the Critique of Informalism in Northern Ireland', *British Journal of Criminology*, 42: 534–62.

McLaughlin, E. (1991) 'Police Accountability and Black People: into the 1990s', in Cashmore, E. and McLaughlin, E. (eds) *Out of Order? Policing Black People*, London: Routledge, pp. 109–33.

McLaughlin, E. (2005) 'From Reel to Ideal: The Blue Lamp and the Popular Cultural Construction of the English Bobby', *Crime, Media, Culture*, 1(1): 11–30.

McLaughlin, E. (2007a) *The New Policing*, London: Sage.

McLaughlin, E. (2007b) 'Diversity or Anarchy? The Post-Macpherson Blues', in Rowe, M. (ed.) *Policing Beyond Macpherson*, Cullompton: Willan Publishing.

McLaughlin, E. and Murji, K. (1997) 'The Future Lasts a Long Time: Public Policework and the Managerialist Paradox', in Francis, P., Davies, P. and Jupp, V. (eds) *Policing Futures*, Basingstoke: Macmillan.

Moon, B. (2006) 'The Influence of Organizational Socialization on Police Officers' Acceptance of Community Policing', *Policing: An International Journal of Police Strategies and Management*, 29(4): 704–22.

Moore, M.H. (1992) 'Problem-Solving and Community Policing', in Tonry, M. and Morris, N. (eds) *Modern Policing*, Chicago: University of Chicago Press, pp. 99–158.

Morgan, R. and Newburn, T. (1997) *The Future of Policing*, Oxford: Clarendon Press.

Morris, L. (1994) *Dangerous Classes: The Underclass and Social Citizenship*, London: Routledge.

Morris, N. (2006) 'Blair's "Frenzied Law Making": A New Offence for Every Day Spent in Office', *Independent* online, 16 August, (http://news.independent.co.uk/uk/politics/article 1219484.ece, accessed 23 January 2007).

Morris, Sir W., Burden, Sir A. and Weekes, A. (2004) *The Case for Change: People in the Metropolitan Police Service, the Report of the Morris Inquiry*, London: Metropolitan Police Authority.

MVA and Miller, J. (2000) *Profiling Populations Available for Stop and Search*, Police Research Series Paper 131, London: Home Office.

National Advisory Group/Policing Lesbian and Gay Communities (1999), *Breaking the Chains of Hate*, NAGS: Manchester.

Neiderhoffer, A. (1969) *Behind the Shield: The Police in Urban Society*, New York: Anchor Books.

Newburn, T. (2002) 'The Introduction of CCTV into a Custody Suite: Some Reflections on Risk, Surveillance and Policing', in Crawford, A. (ed.) *Crime and Insecurity: The Governance of Safety in Europe*, Cullompton: Willan Publishing, pp. 260–73.

Newburn, T. (2003) 'Policing Since 1945', in Newburn, T. (ed.) *Handbook of Policing*, Cullompton: Willan Publishing, pp. 84–105.

Newburn, T. and Sparks, R. (2004) *Criminal Justice and Political Cultures: National and International Dimensions of Crime Control*, Cullompton: Willan Publishing.

Neyroud, P. (2003) 'Police and Ethics', in Newburn, T. (ed.) *Handbook of Policing,* Cullompton: Willan Publishing. pp. 578–602

Neyroud, P. and Beckley, A. (2001) *Policing, Ethics and Human Rights*, Cullompton: Willan Publishing.

Norris, C. and Armstrong, G. (1999) *The Maximum Surveillance Society: The Rise of CCTV*, Oxford: Berg.

Northern Ireland Policing Board (2003) *Code of Ethics for the Police Service of Northern Ireland*, Belfast: Northern Ireland Policing Board.

Office of Surveillance Commissioner (2006) *Annual Report of the Chief Surveillance Commissioner to the Prime Minister and to Scottish Ministers for 2005–2006*, Edinburgh: Office of Surveillance Commissioner.

Osborne, D. and Gaebler, T. (1992) *Reinventing Government: How the Entrepreneurial Spirit Is Transforming the Public Sector*, New York: NY Plume.

Oxford, K. (1986) 'The Power to Police Effectively', in Benyon, J. and Bourn, C. (eds) *Police: Powers, Proprieties and Procedures*, Oxford: Pergamon Press, pp. 61–74.

PA Consulting Group (2001) *Diary of a Police Officer*, Police Research Series Paper 149, London: Home Office.

Palmer, S.H. (1988) *Police and Protest in England and Ireland, 1780–1950*, Cambridge: Cambridge University Press.

Panayi, P. (1996) *Racial Violence in Britain in the Nineteenth and Twentieth Centuries*, Leicester: Leicester University Press.

Paoline, E.A., Myers, S.M. and Worden, R.E. (2000) 'Police Culture, Individualism and Community Policing: Evidence from Two Police Departments', *Justice Quarterly*, 17(3): 575–605.

Phillips, C., Considine, M. and Lewis, R. (2000) *A Review of Audits and Strategies Produced by Crime and Disorder Partnerships in 1999*, London: Home Office.

Police Review (2001) 'President Delivers Race Relations Warning to BCU Commanders', February 16, 109(5609): 6.

Police Review (2002) 'Plan to Increase Ethnic Officers in Specialisms', 17 May, p. 13.

Praat, A.C. and Tuffin, K.F. (1996) 'Police Discourses of Homosexual Men in New Zealand', *Journal of Homosexuality*, 31(4): 57–73.

Prenzler, T. (2000) 'Civilian Oversight of the Police: a Test of Capture Theory', *British Journal of Criminology*, 40(4): 659–74.

Prenzler, T. (2005) 'Mapping the Australian Security Industry', *Security Journal*, 18(4): 51–64.

Punch, M. (1979) *Policing the Inner City: A Study of Amsterdam's Warmoesstraal*, London: Macmillan.

Putnam, R.D. (2000) *Bowling Alone: The Collapse and Revival of American Community*, New York: Simon and Schuster.

Ratcliffe, J. (2002) 'Damned if You Don't, Damned if You Do: Crime Mapping and its Implications in the Real World', *Policing and Society*, 12(3): 211–25.

Rawlings, P. (2002) *Policing: A Short History*, Cullompton: Willan Publishing.

Reiner, R. (1978) *The Blue-Coated Worker: A Sociological Study of Police Unionism*, Cambridge: Cambridge University Press.

Reiner, R. (2000) *The Politics of the Police*, 3rd edn, Oxford: Oxford University Press.

Reiner, R. (2003) 'Policing and the Media', in Newburn, T. (ed.) *Handbook of Policing*, Cullompton: Willan Publishing, pp. 259–81.

Reiss, A.J. (1971) *The Police and the Public*, New Haven, CT: Yale University Press.

Reith, C. (1948) *A Short History of the British Police*, Oxford: Oxford University Press.

Reuss Ianni, E. (1982) *Two Cultures of Policing: Street Cops and Management Cops*, New Brunswick, NJ: Transaction Publishers.

Reynolds, E. (1998) *Before the Bobbies: The Night Watch and Police Reform in Metropolitan London, 1720–1830*, London: Macmillan.

Roberg, R., Novak, K. and Cordner, G. (2005) *Police and Society*, 3rd edn, Los Angeles: Roxbury Publishing Company.

Robertson, A. (2005) 'Criminal Justice Policy Transfer to Post-Soviet States: Two Case Studies of Police Reform in Russia and Ukraine', *European Journal on Criminal Policy and Research*, 11: 1–28.

Robilliard, St J. and McEwan, J. (1986) *Police Powers and the Individual*, Oxford: Basil Blackwell.

Rosenbaum, D.P. (2006) 'The Limits of Hot Spots Policing', in Weisburd, D. and Braga, A. (eds) *Police Innovation: Contrasting Perspectives*, Cambridge: Cambridge University Press, pp. 245–63.

Rowe, M. (1998) *The Racialisation of Disorder in Twentieth Century Britain*, Aldershot: Ashgate.

Rowe, M. (2004) *Policing, Race and Racism*, Cullompton: Willan Publishing.

Rowe, M. (2007a) 'The Scarman Inquiry', in Newburn, T. and Neyroud, P. (eds) *Dictionary of Policing*, Cullompton: Willan Publishing.

Rowe, M. (2007b) 'Rendering Visible the Invisible: Police Discretion, Professionalism and Ethics', *Policing and Society*, 17(3): 279–94.

Rowe, M. (2007c) *Policing Beyond Macpherson*, Cullompton: Willan Publishing.

Russo, F. (2007) 'Who Should Read Your Mind?', *Time*, 29 January: 76–9.

Scarman, Lord (1981) *The Brixton Disorders*, London: HMSO.

Scraton, P. (1985) *The State of the Police*, London: Pluto.

Sharpe, J.A. (1984) *Crime in Early Modern England, 1550–1750*, London: Longman.

Shearing, C. and Johnston, L. (2003) *Governing Security: Explorations in Policing and Justice*, London: Routledge.

Shearing, C. and Stenning, P. (1983) 'Private Policing: Implications for Social Control', *Social Problems*, 30(5): 493–506.

Sheptycki, J. (2000) *Issues in Transnational Policing*, London: Routledge.

Silke, A. and Taylor, M. (2000) 'War Without End: Comparing IRA and Loyalist Vigilantism in Northern Ireland', *Howard Journal of Criminal Justice*, 39(2): 249–66.

Silver, A. (1967) 'The Demand for Order in Civil Society', in Bordua, J. (ed.) *The Police*, New York: Wiley, pp. 1–24.

Silverman, E.B. (2006) 'Compstat's Innovation', in Weisburd, D. and Braga, A. (eds) *Police Innovation: Contrasting Perspectives*, Cambridge: Cambridge University Press, pp. 267–83.

Simey, M. (1982) 'Police Authorities and Accountability: the Merseyside Experience', in Cowell, D., Jones, T. and Young, J. (eds) *Policing the Riots*, London: Junction Books, pp. 52–7.

Singh, G. (2000) 'The Concept and Context of Institutional Racism', in Marlow, A. and Loveday, B. (eds) *After Macpherson: Policing After the Stephen Lawrence Inquiry*, Lyme Regis: Russell House Publishing.

Skogan, W. (2006) 'The Promise of Community Policing', in Weisburd, D. and Braga, A. (eds) *Police Innovation: Contrasting Perspectives*, Cambridge: Cambridge University Press, pp. 27–43.

Smith, D.J. (1987) 'The Police and the Idea of the Community', in Wilmott, P. (ed.) *Policing and the Community*, London: Policy Studies Institute.

Smith, D.J. (1995) 'Race, Crime and Criminal Justice', in Maguire, M., Morgan, R. and Reiner, R. (eds) *The Oxford Handbook of Criminology*, Oxford: Oxford University Press, pp. 1041–118.

Smith, D.J. and Gray, J. (1983) *Police and People in London, vol. 4, The Police in Action*, London: Policy Studies Institute.

Solomos, J. (1999) 'Social Research and the Stephen Lawrence Inquiry', *Sociological Research Online*, 4(1).

Souhami, A. (2007) 'Understanding Institutional Racism', in Rowe, M. (ed.) *Policing Beyond Macpherson: Issues in Policing, Race, and Society*, Cullompton: Willan Publishing, pp. 66–87.

South, N. (1988) *Policing for Profit: The Private Security Sector*, London: Sage.

Sparks, R., Girling, E. and Loader, I. (2001) 'Fear and Everyday Urban Lives', *Urban Studies* 38(5–6): 885–98.

Stenning, P. (2000) 'Powers and Accountability of Private Police', *European Journal on Criminal Policy and Research*, 8: 325–52.

Stenning, P. and Shearing, C. (2005) 'Reforming Police: Opportunities, Drivers and Challenges', *Australian and New Zealand Journal of Criminology*, 38(2): 167–80.

Stenson, K. (2001) 'The New Politics of Crime Control', in Stenson, K. and Sullivan, R.K. (eds) *Crime, Risk and Justice: The Politics of Crime Control in Liberal Democracies*, Cullompton: Willan Publishing, pp. 15–28.

Stenson, K. (2002) 'Community Safety in Middle England', in Edwards, A. and Hughes, G. (eds) *Crime Control and Community*, Cullompton: Willan Publishing.

Stenson, K. and Waddington, P.A.J. (2007) 'Macpherson, Police Stops and Institutional Racism', in Rowe, M. (ed.) *Policing Beyond Macpherson: Issues in Policing, Race, and Society*, Cullompton: Willan Publishing, pp. 128–47.

Stephens, J.F. (1964) *A History of the Criminal Law of England*, New York: Burt Franklin.

Stone, V. and Pettigrew, N. (2000) *The Views of the Public on Stop and Searches*, Police Research Series Paper 129. London: Home Office.

Stonewall (2007) *Workplace Equality Index 2007: The Top 100 Employers for Gay People in Britain*, London: Stonewall.

Storch, R. (1975) 'The Plague of Blue Locusts: Police Reform and Popular Resistance in Northern England 1840–57', *International Review of Social History*, 20: 61–90.

Storch, R. (1976) 'The Policeman as Domestic Missionary: Urban Discipline and Popular Culture in Northern England, 1850–1880', *Journal of Social History*, 9: 481–509.

Styles, J. (1987) 'The Emergence of the Police: Explaining Police Reform in Eighteenth and Nineteenth Century England', *British Journal of Criminology*, 27(1): 15–22.

The Royal Borough of Kensington and Chelsea (2006) *Protocols for Disrupting Class A Drug Production, Use or Supply*, London: Royal Borough of Kensington and Chelsea.

Thompson, E.P. (1968) *The Making of the English Working Class*, Harmondsworth: Penguin.

Thurman, Q., Zhao, J. and Giacomazzi, A.L. (2001) *Community Policing in a Community Era: An Introduction and Exploration*, Los Angeles: Roxbury Publishing Company.

Tilley, N. (2003) 'Community Policing, Problem-Oriented Policing and Intelligence-Led Policing', in Newburn, T. (ed.) *Handbook of Policing*, Cullompton: Willan Publishing, pp. 311–39.

Trojanowicz, R. and Bucqueroux, B. (1990) *Community Policing: A Contemporary Perspective*, Cincinnati, OH: Anderson.

Trojanowicz, R.C. and Moore, M.H. (1988) *The Meaning of Community in Community Policing*, Michigan State University: National Center for Community Policing.

Van der Spuy, E. (2000) 'Foreign Donor Assistance and Policing Reform in South Africa', *Policing and Society*, 10: 342–66.

Waddington, P.A.J. (1982) '"Conservatism, Dogmatism, and Authoritarianism in British Police Officers": A Comment', *Sociology*, 16(4): 591–4.

Waddington, P.A.J. (1993) 'Dying in a Ditch: The Use of Police Powers in Public Order', *International Journal of Sociology*, 45(3): 335–53.

Waddington, P.A.J. (1994a) 'Coercion and Accommodation: Policing Public Order After the Public Order Act', *British Journal of Sociology*, 45(3): 367–85.

Waddington, P.A.J. (1994b) *Liberty and Order: Policing Public Order in a Capital City*, London: UCL Press.

Waddington, P.A.J. (1999) 'Police (Canteen) Sub-Culture: an Appreciation', *British Journal of Criminology*, 39(2): 287–309.

Waddington, P.A.J. (2005) 'HMIC Evangelists Preach Flawed Beliefs', *Police Review*, 113(5849): 16–17.

Waddington, P.A.J., Stenson, K. and Don, D. (2004) 'In Proportion: Race and Police Stop and Search, *British Journal of Criminology*, 44(6): 889–914.

Wakefield, A. (2004) *Selling Security: The Private Policing of Public Space*, Cullompton: Willan Publishing.

Wakefield, A. (2006) *The Value of Foot Patrol: A Review of the Literature*, London: Police Foundation.

Walklate, S. (1995) *Gender and Crime: An Introduction*, London: Prentice Hall.

Walklate, S. (1996) 'Community and Crime Prevention', in McLaughlin, E. and Muncie, J. (eds) *Controlling Crime*, London: Sage in Association with the Open University, pp. 293–331.

Walker, A., Kershaw, C. and Nicholas, S. (2006) *Crime in England and Wales, 2005/06*, Statistical Bulletin 12/06, London: Home Office.

Wall, D.S. (1998) *The Chief Constables of England and Wales: The Socio-Legal History of a Criminal Justice Elite*, Aldershot: Ashgate.

Weatheritt, M. (1987) 'Community Policing Now', in Wilmott, P. (ed.) *Policing and the Community*, London: Policy Studies Institute.

Weisburd, D. and Braga, A. (2006) 'Hot Spots Policing as a Model for Police Innovation', in Weisburd, D. and Braga, A. (eds) *Police Innovation: Contrasting Perspectives*, Cambridge: Cambridge University Press, pp. 225–44.

Westmarland, L. (2002) *Gender and Policing: Sex, Power and Police Culture*, Cullompton: Willan Publishing.

Whitfield, J. (2004) *Unhappy Dialogue: The Metropolitan Police and Black Londoners in Post-War Britain*, Cullompton: Willian Publishing.

Whitfield, J. (2007) 'The Historical Context: Policing and Black People in Post-War Britain', in Rowe, M. (ed.) *Policing Beyond Macpherson*, Cullompton: Willan Publishing.

Williams, M. (2006) *Virtually Criminal: Crime, Deviance, and Regulation Online*, New York: Routledge.

Williams, M. and Robinson, A. (2004) 'Problems and Prospects with Policing the Lesbian, Gay and Bisexual Community in Wales', *Policing and Society*, 14(3): 213–32.

Wilson, J.Q. (1968) *Varieties of Police Behaviour*, Cambridge, MA: Harvard University Press.

Wood, J. and Shearing, C. (2006) *Imagining Security*, Cullompton: Willan Publishing.

Young, J. (1999) *The Exclusive Society: Social Exclusion, Crime and Difference in Late Modernity*, London: Sage.

Zander, M. (2003) *The Police and Criminal Evidence Act 1984*, 4th edn, London: Sweet & Maxwell.

Zander, M. (2005) *Police and Criminal Evidence Act 1984*, 5th edn, London: Thomson/Sweet & Maxwell.

Zedner, L. (2006) 'Policing Before and After the Police: The Historical Antecedents of Contemporary Crime Control', *British Journal of Criminology*, 46: 78–96.

Index